Supporting Lifelong Learning
Volume 3

Making policy work

Edited by
**Richard Edwards, Nod Miller,
Nick Small and Alan Tait**

The Open
University

London and New York

First published 2002 by RoutledgeFalmer
11 New Fetter Lane, London EC4P 4EE

Simultaneously published in the USA and Canada
by RoutledgeFalmer
29 West 35th Street, New York, NY 10001

RoutledgeFalmer is an imprint of the Taylor & Francis Group

Typeset in Goudy by
Florence Production Ltd, Stoodleigh, Devon
Printed and bound in Great Britain by
St Edmundsbury Press, Bury St Edmunds, Suffolk

British Library Cataloguing in Publication Data
A catalogue record for this book is available from the
British Library

Library of Congress Cataloging in Publication Data
A catalog record for this book has been requested

ISBN 0–415–25930–4 (hbk)
ISBN 0–415–25931–2 (pbk)

Supporting Lifelong Learning
Volume 3

This book focuses on policy development in lifelong learning at local, regional, national and supranational levels. The international team of contributors explore and examine the policy context for lifelong learning, the policies themselves and their effects when implemented. In particular, they focus on the role of lifelong learning policy in relation to issues of economic competitiveness, technological change and social inclusion.

By providing a comparative international approach, this book encourages the reader to evaluate lifelong learning as a response to the globalizing of educational policy. It will appeal to postgraduate and doctorate level students with an interest in post-school education and training.

This book is one of three Readers prepared for the Open University MA Course: E845 *Supporting Lifelong Learning*. The three separate volumes provide an in-depth examination of lifelong learning from the perspectives of teaching and learning, organizing learning and policy making. They bring together for the first time theories from a diverse range of disciplines that are now central to our understanding of lifelong learning and provide a new and distinctive contribution to the field.

Richard Edwards is Professor of Education at the University of Stirling.

Nod Miller is Assistant Vice-Chancellor and Professor of Innovation Studies at the University of East London.

Nick Small is Staff Tutor in Education at The Open University in Nottingham.

Alan Tait is Sub Dean and Staff Tutor at The Open University Faculty of Education and Language Studies.

Supporting Lifelong Learning, Volume 3: Making policy work

The companion volumes in this series are:

Supporting Lifelong Learning, Volume 1: Perspectives on learning
Edited by Roger Harrison, Fiona Reeve, Ann Hanson and Julia Clarke

Supporting Lifelong Learning, Volume 2: Organizing learning
Edited by Fiona Reeve, Marion Cartwright and Richard Edwards

All of these Readers are part of a course: *Supporting Lifelong Learning* (E845), that is itself part of the Open University Masters Programme in Education.

The Open University Masters Programme in Education
The Open University Masters Programme in Education is now firmly established as the most popular postgraduate degree for education professionals in Europe, with over 3,000 students registering each year. The Masters Programme in Education is designed particularly for those with experience of teaching, the advisory service, educational administration or allied fields.

Structure of the Masters Programme in Education
The Masters Programme is a modular degree, and students are, therefore, free to select from the programme which best fits in with their interests and professional goals. Specialist lines in management, applied linguistics and lifelong learning are also available. Study within the Open University's Advanced Diploma can also be counted towards a Masters Degree, and successful study within the Masters Programme entitles students to apply for entry into the Open University Doctorate in Education Programme.

OU-Supported Open Learning
The Masters Programme in Education provides great flexibility. Students study at their own pace, in their own time, anywhere in the European Union. They receive specially prepared study materials, supported by tutorials, thus offering the chance to work with other students.

The Doctorate in Education
The Doctorate in Education is a part-time doctoral degree, combining taught courses, research methods and a dissertation designed to meet the needs of professionals in education and related areas who are seeking to extend and deepen their knowledge and understanding of contemporary educational issues. The Doctorate in Education builds upon successful study within the Open University Masters Programme in Education.

How to apply
If you would like to register for this programme, or simply find out more information about available courses, please write for the *Professional Development in Education* prospectus to the Call Centre, PO Box 724, The Open University, Walton Hall, Milton Keynes, MK7 6ZW, UK (Telephone 0 (0 44) 1908 653231). Details can also be viewed on our web page http://www.open.ac.uk

Contents

Illustrations

Figures

Tables

Acknowledgements

We are indebted to the following for allowing us to make use of copyright material:

Chapter 1: Tuijnman, A. (1999) 'Research agenda for lifelong learning: a report by the Task Force of the International Academy of Education', in A. Tuijnman and T. Schuller (eds) *Lifelong Learning Policy and Research: Proceedings of an International Symposium*, pp. 1–22. London: Portland Press. Reproduced by permission of Portland Press Ltd.

Chapter 2: Alheit, P. (1999) 'On a contradictory way to the "learning society": a critical approach', in *Studies in the Education of Adults*, 31: 1, pp. 66–83.
Reproduced by permisssion of NIACE.

Chapter 3: Livingstone, D.W. (1999) 'Lifelong learning and underemployment in the knowledge society: a North American perspective', in *Comparative Education*, 135: 2, pp. 163–186.
Reproduced by permission of Taylor & Francis Ltd, 11 New Fetter Lane, London EC4P 4EE.

Chapter 4: Schuller, T. and Field, J. (1998) ''Social capital, human capital and the learning society', in *International Journal of Lifelong Education* 17: 4, pp. 226–235.
Reproduced by permission of Taylor & Francis Ltd.

Chapter 5: Darmon, I., Frade, C. and Hadjivassiliou, K. (1998) 'The comparative dimension in continuous vocational training: a preliminary framework' in F. Coffield (ed.) *Why's the Beer Always Stronger Up North?* Bristol: The Policy Press.
Reproduced by permission of The Policy Press.

Chapter 6: Green, F., James, D., Ashton, D. and Sung, J. (1999) 'Post-school education and training policy in developmental states: the case of Taiwan and South Korea', in *Journal of Educational Policy*, 14: 3, pp. 301–315.
Reproduced by permission of Taylor & Francis Ltd.

Chapter 7: Griffin, C. (1999) 'Lifelong learning and welfare reform', in *International Journal of Lifelong Education*, 18: 6, pp. 431–452.
Reproduced by permission of Taylor & Francis Ltd.

Chapter 8: Kenway, J. (1999) 'Change of address? Educating economics in vocational education and training', in *Journal of Education and Work*, 12: 2, pp. 157–178.
Reproduced by permission of Taylor & Francis Ltd.

Chapter 9: Coffield, F. (1999) 'Breaking the consensus: lifelong learning as social control', in *British Educational Research Journal*, 25: 4, pp. 479–499.
Reproduced by permission of Taylor & Francis Ltd.

Chapter 10: Field, J. (2000) 'Governing the ungovernable: why lifelong learning policies promise so much yet deliver so little', in *Educational Management and Administration*, 28: 3, pp. 249–261.
Reprinted by permission of Sage Publications Ltd © British Educational Management and Administration Society (BEMAS) 2000.

While the publishers have made every effort to contact copyright holders of the material used in this volume, they would be grateful to hear from any they were unable to contact.

Introduction
Making policy work in lifelong learning

*Richard Edwards, Nod Miller, Nick Small
and Alan Tait*

Lifelong learning has become a significant topic of policy and academic debate in the last ten years. Many national governments have moved to develop policies to support notions of lifelong learning, encouraged and supported by international organizations such as the Organization for Economic Co-operation and Development (OECD) and the European Union (EU). In relation to a range of economic and social challenges, lifelong learning is increasingly posited, at least in part, as a solution. If people are given the opportunities to engage in lifelong learning and become lifelong learners, so it is said, the challenges they face in the coming century may be ameliorated if not overcome altogether.

The contemporary interest in lifelong learning should not cloud recognition that in earlier periods there have been similar eruptions of policy interest in lifelong learning. In the 1970s, notions of lifelong education and recurrent education were promoted by organizations such as the United Nations Educational, Scientific, and Cultural Organization (UNESCO) and OECD. For countries emerging from colonization, lifelong education was conceived as a fundamental human right and part of the strategy for economic modernization and development. Recurrent education was based on a more straightforwardly economistic rationale aimed at supporting the development of capitalist economies. However, while these notions were promulgated internationally, they had little impact on most national policy making. It is only since the 1990s that lifelong learning has become a significant part of policy development – and the shift in discourse is significant, as Colin Griffin argues in his chapter. With the development of contemporary lifelong learning discourse has come the development of a greater body of work concerned with lifelong learning policies. The collection provided here is an attempt to give a flavour of the breadth and depth of such work, drawing on a range of literature from around the globe that addresses some of the policy issues in lifelong learning.

The Introduction was written especially for this volume.

We have chosen to call this text *Making policy work* because of the different meanings the phrase can carry. *Making* policy work could provide us with descriptions of the processes through which policy is developed, consulted over, placed into legislation and implemented. Here the focus is on the process of policy making rather than its substantial content. The institutional and societal interactions and dynamics through which policies are developed and enacted provide a focus for analysis. Such analysis may draw upon a range of theoretical positions – such as Weberian notions of bureaucratic rationalization, Marxian capitalist state theory, feminist critiques of patriarchy, post-colonial critiques of institutional racism – to examine how policy is made. Fundamental to this is the relationship between the state, employers, trade unions and other interest groups, like non-governmental organizations and voluntary bodies, which is both part of the policy-making process and can be an outcome of policy itself. As the chapters by Isabelle Darmon and colleagues and Frances Green and colleagues argue respectively, different approaches to policy making result both from particular histories and contexts and result in differing policy outcomes, even where the goals of policy – providing more opportunities for people to continue to learn – may be similar.

A second sense in which we can discuss making policy work emphasizes the *work* that policy does and that it is intended to do. Policies are put in place to address certain issues and achieve certain goals. In the case of life-long learning, the educational goals may be to widen and increase participation in post-school education and training. However, the educational goals may not be the end point, as the rationales for much lifelong learning policy address the multiple goals of increasing economic productivity and competitiveness, developing social inclusion and cohesion, and enabling personal development. Thus there may be multiple goals to be achieved through policy, and potential gaps between what is intended and what is achieved. It is sometimes suggested that there is a gap between policy rhetoric and reality. However, this is too simplistic, as the attempt to persuade us that it offers the best way forward is fundamental to the rhetorical work of policy. This underpins some of the discursive approaches to policy analysis – examining the discursive work of policy – that have become influential, drawing upon post-structuralist theoretical approaches.

In relation to this sense of making policy work, while the processes through which policy is developed are fundamental, the study of policy tends to focus more on that which it seeks to address, its content and its effects. To be effective policies need to be based on adequate understanding of the issues to be addressed. The identification of the issues and how they are identified helps to shape the policy responses. Thus, for instance, if female participation in certain forms of learning is identified at least in part as resulting from inadequate provision of childcare facilities, policies and funding to support such provision may be put forward as a response to this situation. How well the issues addressed are understood is therefore crucial to policy development.

Governments want to act and to be seen to act effectively, but as well as being circumscribed by the context in which they work they are also bounded by the information and evidence available to them. This illustrates the importance of research to policy making.

For example, the issues that are often put forward as a basis for lifelong learning in policy texts are lack of productivity and competitiveness in the economy and social exclusion. The development of individual skills and qualifications through lifelong learning are seen as avenues through which these can be addressed. Yet the evidence base for this is not as robust as it might appear. As Albert Tuijnman argues in his elaboration of a research agenda for lifelong learning, much detailed research needs to be done in a range of areas to help inform policy and practice. An example of such a detailed piece of work is provided by David Livingstone, who, drawing on statistical analysis in North America, argues that far from there being a shortage of skills and qualifications, employers are demanding more from the workforce regardless of what is required to do the job. He argues that life-long learning can result in systematic underemployment. Similarly, Peter Alheit, drawing on research in Germany, suggests that society consists of a range of different milieux and that without a detailed understanding of them, broad-based policies to support lifelong learning will have highly differen-tial effects. Thus the chapters in this selection raise questions about the adequacy of our understanding of the issues to be addressed in lifelong learning policy.

The examination of the content and effects of policy can take different forms. Evaluation studies form one strand of such analysis, often with a view to establishing how policy could work better. For example, the introduction of accreditation for certain forms of learning that were previously non-accredited may affect the profile of participation, as those who do not wish to be assessed develop alternative non-formal learning. If the policy goal is to enable wider participation, then support for more informal and community-based learning may be a way of making policy work better. More critical evaluations of the capacity of policy to work and of the work it does may emphasize its ideological effect and the forms of exploitation, oppres-sion and exclusion that policy either fails to address or else reproduces. This is what Jane Kenway emphasizes in her analysis of Australian vocational education and training policy and its focus on the economic rather than social and personal rationales for education. The emphasis on the individual's increasing responsibility for her or his own learning and life course, it can be argued, marginalizes the structural factors – employment, housing, health – that determine people's life opportunities.

There can also be examinations of the assumptions underpinning policy and the limitation thus placed on the work it does and the effects it has.

For instance, a policy that assumes the economic model of human capital theory, which places emphasis on skills and qualifications for economic competitiveness, may not only exclude the other factors that might contribute to the latter – such as capital investment, or transport – but may also offer a limited view of the role of educational and training. This is a point made in the chapters by Frank Coffield and by Tom Schuller and John Field. The latter also explore the notion of social capital as a means of helping to explain patterns of participation in lifelong learning. Social capital emphasizes informal relations of trust and can be seen to provide a rationale for community-based policies to support social inclusion and cohesion as opposed to the emphasis on individual skills in human capital theory. In examining such theories it can be tempting to favour one over the other, but each might have a role to play in providing underpinning rationales for certain approaches in lifelong learning policy.

There is another sense of making policy work to which we have already referred in the previous paragraphs. This is the work of policy analysis and the academic study of policy. There is no single way in which to engage in the study of policy. As in any other academic arena, there are competing views on how best to engage in policy analysis, drawing upon the many traditions in the social sciences and elsewhere. While there has been extensive debate about the work of policy analysis in relation to initial education, less has been discussed in relation to lifelong learning. Much policy analysis of lifelong learning does not therefore explicitly identify its own methodological or value positions. This does not help our understanding of the work lifelong learning policy does nor of the effects it has.

In the essays we have collected here we witness multiple ways in which policy is made to work in lifelong learning. In most, more emphasis is placed on the content of policy – an engagement with its assumptions and effects – rather than on the detailed processes through which policies are developed. Where the latter are discussed, it tends to be in the broad sense of differing relations between the state, employers, trade unions and other social partners and their implications for policy. In particular, the question of the role of markets and regulation in the development of lifelong learning is emphasized as well as the positioning of the individual as responsible in some ways for her or his life courses.

Within this text, there is also a range of approaches to policy analysis. For instance, David Livingstone draws on quantitative studies of the employment opportunities and the qualifications and skills demanded of the labour force to support his argument that lifelong learning is not a response to the need for greater skills, but is rather producing forms of underemployment. A qualitative approach is provided by Frank Coffield, who draws on evidence from a research programme on The Learning Society to suggest that lifelong learning policy in the UK rests on inadequate assumptions and is therefore incapable of having the effects intended. While many governments are influenced by the notion of evidence-based or evidence-informed policy, Coffield suggests that this is insufficiently the case in the UK and that the effects of lifelong learning policy will be quite different to those intended.

More fundamentally, Colin Griffin argues that in focusing on lifelong learning rather than on the provision of education and training, governments are abandoning *policies*, which focus on structures of provision, and adopting *strategies*, which aim to shift to a culture of learning by empowering individuals. In this sense, lifelong learning policies are as much about reconfiguring the relationship between the state, civil society, families and individuals as they are about providing opportunities for lifelong learning. This point is also made in the analysis by John Field.

A text that is concerned with making policy work in lifelong learning must also be concerned with the work it does itself. 'Making policy work' is the subtitle of this text, which is volume three of *Supporting Lifelong Learning*. In the title, there may be an implicit view of the inherent benefits of lifelong learning and the need to ensure that policies are effective in providing opportunities for them to be developed. However, the chapters we have selected suggest a different story. Policy work is multiple, contested and complex. There is no linearity in its assumptions, intentions or effects. There are different approaches to how lifelong learning should be developed, how it is being developed, the nature of the problems it is addressing, the extent to which it contributes to overcoming such problems, and what the significance of it all is. There is no single recipe for lifelong learning and, in certain forms, it may not even be desirable or beneficial. This text suggests critical support of lifelong learning policy. We may also want to be oppositional in relation to certain policies, as lifelong learning can be a stick with which to beat people as much as it can be an opportunity for them. We hope through this volume to enable policy to work better, but not in an easy or straightforward way. That is the role of the academic study of policy and the work we have attempted in our selection here. As readers, you will do your own work upon this text and in the process do policy work of your own.

Chapter 1

Themes and questions for a research agenda on lifelong learning

Albert Tuijnman

Introduction

At a meeting held in Brussels in November 1996, the International Academy of Education appointed a Task Force to identify gaps in the knowledge base on lifelong learning. This was because Academy members were concerned about the apparently growing gap between important policy statements about the implementation of lifelong learning on the one hand and the knowledge base required for evaluating educational developments on the other. In examining the issues, the Task Force was to take a broad view of what constitutes lifelong learning in a modern society, ranging from learning in early childhood through to learning in retirement, and occurring in many different environments. The aims and objectives to be accomplished were as follows:

- to analyse the shifting *meanings of concepts*, such as lifelong education and lifelong learning;
- to identify and map the central *problems besetting the implementation* of lifelong-learning policies and practices, especially in advanced countries;
- to propose *questions and priorities* for educational research relevant to lifelong-learning objectives, particularly adult education and informal learning in the workplace.

This report comprises two parts. The first deals with concepts and theories of lifelong learning. The evolution of concepts such as recurrent education and lifelong learning is briefly discussed, and some areas where further conceptual work is needed are identified. Questions posed to educational research are offered in the second part. These questions concern both the specific sectors of provision, such as early childhood education, lower

This is an edited version of a chapter previously published as 'Research agenda for lifelong learning: a report by the Task Force of the International Academy of Education', in A. Tuijnman and T. Schuller (eds) (1999), *Lifelong Learning Policy and Research: Proceedings of an International Symposium*, London: Portland Press.

secondary schooling or adult education, and major cross-cutting themes, which are relevant to all sectors. Examples are professional roles of teachers in lifelong learning, student selection, streaming and differentiation, pre-career preparation, management and governance, economics and educational finance, monitoring and evaluation, and the assessment and recognition of knowledge and competence.

The context

Opinion polls show that education ranks high among the priorities and concerns expressed by the general public in many countries. Questions are raised not only about the quality and content of school education or fair access to affordable higher education, but also about the supply and quality of learning opportunities for adults.

Statements attaching high and growing expectations to the concepts of 'lifelong education' and 'lifelong learning' abound. Prominent examples are the report prepared by the International Commission for Education in the 21st Century, which was chaired by Jacques Delors (Delors et al., 1996), the white papers by the Commission of the European Union (1994 and 1995), and the background report on Lifelong Learning for All, which was prepared for the 1996 meeting of the Education Committee at ministerial level (OECD, 1996). Indeed, policy makers and observers – especially in the economically advanced countries – appear convinced about the 'necessary utopia' of creating an all-encompassing 'learning society' (Jacques Delors in (Delors et al., 1996)).

In Europe, North America and increasingly in the rest of the world, policy makers are endorsing the concept of lifelong learning and pursuing its implementation. Lifelong approaches to learning are being justified on grounds of the realization, now widespread, that countries, communities and businesses will continue to manage a fundamental adjustment in the forces and factors of production, brought about by a shift from an industrial to a 'knowledge-based' economy. But lifelong learning is also being promoted for non-economic reasons, on the grounds that education forms the basis for a rational, enlightened and democratic society.

There can be no denying that vast social, cultural and economic changes have been building up for a long time, propelled by 'global' developments in technology, trade and financial services, manufacturing and agriculture. These developments interact with other factors, such as aging populations, migration and urbanization, and emerging new values and attitudes to family, work and leisure. The new situation brings new opportunities but also dilemmas.

According to the OECD Jobs Study (OECD, 1994), policy makers would have to deal with uncertainty about the future by strengthening the capacity of labour markets, employers and individuals to adjust to change. Flexibility arguably depends on many factors – macroeconomic, structural, cultural and social – but human knowledge and skills are singled out as being among the most important (see OECD, 1998). Whereas change can open up new opportunities for highly educated and skilled individuals, this is not the case for poorly educated people and those who lack the necessary skills, either because of a lack of formal schooling, or because of the depreciation of knowledge and skills once acquired. Lifelong learning, then, is being considered a means for raising the skills of workers: making already well-trained people even more flexible and productive, while upgrading the skills of the poorly trained who otherwise would probably face unstable jobs, low wages or unemployment (see Commission of the European Union, 1997).

Thus lifelong-learning policies and practices, as currently conceived, are assigned their meaning in a situation characterized by uncertainty, change and anticipated further structural adjustment. Approaches go far beyond providing a second or third chance for at-risk adults. The concept of lifelong learning, as advocated by agencies such as the Commission of the European Union, United Nations Educational, Scientific, and Cultural Organization (UNESCO) and the Organization for Economic Co-operation and Development (OECD), embraces social and individual development of all kinds. The settings for learning are 'lifelong' and 'life-wide'. Viewed in this context, the research community is faced with the momentous task of conceptualizing what lifelong learning is and what it is not, and clarifying the options for making it a reality for all people regardless of age, previous educational experience, employment status or income.

As can be inferred from the large number of policy statements and advisory reports in the mid-1990s produced by and for governments in countries all over the world, there is no dearth of ideas about what lifelong learning means and what policies should be pursued to make it a reality. But behind the commonplace rhetoric there are many unanswered questions about the goals, shapes, means and ends of a so-called 'learning society'.

- What would such a society look like, and in what ways would it differ from today's society? How useful is a lifelong-learning approach, and what criteria should be used to assess progress, or possibly failure? Will more education really be beneficial in shaping people's life courses, in reinforcing rational action, or in fostering culture and human values? Do strategies for lifelong learning indeed contain the ingredients of a 'miracle cure' for economies in transition, or are such strategies currently being over-sold to policy makers and the general public? If so, can one expect there to be a harmful backlash any time soon?

Statements about lifelong learning tend to be formulated in 'positive' terms. From an educational and social science perspective, what appears to be lacking is a theoretical foundation and critical, scholarly reflection based on concrete empirical evidence. Scholars should go beyond common ideas about desirability and anticipated benefits and investigate the possible negative impacts of lifelong learning.

Considerations for agenda setting

Setting priorities for educational research is indeed an ambitious and delicate task. A 'let many flowers bloom' approach to research planning has many advantages. Nevertheless, there is a realization that certain questions require more urgent attention than others, while resources are arguably always limited. Considering priorities is therefore a potentially useful tool in shaping a strategic research agenda.

A number of developments influence the orientation and identification of priorities for educational research in this area. Major circumstances that will have to be taken into account are as follows.

Augmented demand for policy-relevant knowledge

The apparent emphasis on lifelong-learning goals and objectives in current policy has implications for the information needs of governments and policy makers. Examples are increased demand for information about the *outcomes of adult education* and evaluation studies of the success or failure of particular innovations in workplace learning.

Broadened clientele for information

In a lifelong approach to learning, in which increased weight is given to decision making by many partners and at all levels, the knowledge base must necessarily be multilevel and widely accessible. The information needs not only of policy makers but of all other stakeholders – such as the learners themselves, children and their parents, teachers, administrators and employers – should be considered and accommodated.

Balancing the relations between fields of study relevant to education

Many observers agree that the current knowledge base on education is fragmented, insufficiently synthesized and poorly accessible – especially if the understanding of what constitutes 'knowledge' is subject to change as a result of the proclaimed move to 'learning societies'. Its various elements are also heavily biased in their coverage towards mainstream schooling, and pay relatively little attention to adult learning. Some researchers have expressed concern about this imbalance in coverage. Others have pointed to the uneasy relationship of education with other disciplines in the human and social sciences.

Further strengthening of the international and comparative dimension

Educational research is still tied to predominantly national, regional and local conditions, and tends to be rather provincial in its orientation. Countries have different policy agendas, reflecting their particular concerns. But in an increasingly interdependent world, the knowledge base for lifelong learning can no longer be informed solely by information gathered at a national or provincial level. Insights derived from international and comparative studies are increasingly needed. The dearth of comparative information about the incidence and duration of participation in adult education and training in various countries is a special concern.

Increased investment in educational research and development

Educational research is weakly developed in certain important domains; for example, information on life skills and competencies, performance standards in adult education, and the cumulative effects of adult education and training on life career. This situation results from underfunding and insufficient attentiveness to the long-term needs of the research field, which include the continued development of theory, research methodology and longitudinal databases. Educational research and development will need to be sustained at a critical level, above evaluation and other studies that are intended to produce conclusions of immediate relevance to decision making.

Concepts and theories

Concepts and theories of lifelong learning have evolved since the 1960s. The first major publications appeared towards the end of that decade, and these set out an encompassing view of learning across the entire lifespan. Yet today many researchers still equate lifelong learning with adult education, defined as organized educational processes whereby persons regarded as adults by the society to which they belong engage in systematic and sustained learning activities. Other researchers consider not only organized activities but also non-formal, self-directed and experiential forms of adult learning. For yet another group, lifelong learning is not confined to adults, but includes the full range of learning extending over the life course of men and women, from birth to death.

Various concepts and theories of lifelong learning are considered below. The discussion serves to highlight the conceptual problems arising from a broad and inclusive definition of lifelong learning. Many conceptual, theoretical and methodological issues arise in an attempt to reorient educational research in a lifelong-learning perspective. A major problem is encountered because there is no agreed common understanding of what lifelong learning means. Definitions vary not only over time but also between regions, countries and according to various contexts and fields of study. Addressing these problems requires an interdisciplinary and multilevel framework. Some examples are offered of areas where interdisciplinary work could usefully be undertaken, without, however, attempting to present a representative picture of all the disciplines that could be involved in a research agenda for lifelong learning.

From recurrent education to lifelong learning

The lifelong-learning concepts advocated today have grown out of the 'lifelong education', 'permanent education' and 'recurrent education' plans proposed in key documents several decades ago (Faure *et al.*, 1972; Husén, 1968 and 1986; OECD, 1973). Many of the principles espoused still apply today, even though both the contexts and the concepts themselves have changed in certain ways (e.g. see Tuijnman, 1994; Hasan, 1996).

Recurrent education launched by the OECD in the early 1970s, for example, emphasized the correspondence and interaction between formal education and work, and implied some instances of interruption in the process of *lifelong education*. It also considered that educational opportunities should be spread out over the entire life course, in alternation with other activities such as work and leisure, and as an alternative to the lengthening of formal schooling early in life. In contrast, today's notions of *lifelong learning* pay less regard to the role of formal institutions and more to non-formal and informal learning in a variety of settings – at home, at work and in the community. Further, full retention in broad-based secondary education until at least 17 or 18, and even the further expansion of tertiary education, are no longer considered problematic in certain countries. Achieving a full cycle of secondary education for all has in the economically more advanced countries become one of the cornerstones of policy strategies.

A major contextual difference concerns the role of government. Partly because it emphasized formal education, the recurrent education strategy assigned a large role for government in organizing, managing and financing the system. The past years have seen a partial retreat from this principle, and partnership and shared responsibility have become the norm. This can be seen, for example, in the policy emphasis currently placed on the strengthening of continuing vocational training and, especially, on on-the-job training in enterprises, rather than expanding formal adult education in institutions fully or partly financed from the public budget. The notion that work ought to be alternated on sporadic basis with formal education has been replaced by strategies to promote learning while working and working while learning. Reliance on the responsibilities of employers and individual learners is reflected in countries' reluctance to implement arrangements for paid study leave. Concomitantly with the rising emphasis on accountability and choice, the concept of 'social demand', which was central in the recurrent education philosophy, appears to have been replaced with 'individual demand' as a guide to the provision of adult education and training. This serves to illustrate that concepts of lifelong education and learning are not static but evolve with time, that they vary according to context, and that they are given meaning according to political, economic, social and cultural factors.

Current policy statements on lifelong learning released by international organizations are similar in certain respects. Lifelong learning generally defines a broad set of beliefs, aims and strategies around the central tenet that learning opportunities available over the whole lifespan and accessible on a widespread basis should be key attributes of modern societies. Lifelong learning is not in the strict sense an empirical concept but rather a normative and value-laden one. It is based on the beliefs that everyone is able to learn, that all must become motivated to learn, and should be actively encouraged to do so throughout the lifespan, whether this occurs in formal institutions of education and training or informally, at home, at work or in the wider community (OECD, 1996).

Dilemmas for research

This understanding of lifelong learning is pervasive because it is not restricted to learning that is somehow intentional and structured, or that takes place in specific and/or formal settings. For researchers this poses many conceptual problems because it is not possible to draw a clear boundary between what would be considered learning activities and other experiential and behavioural activities. Further, because the concept is not tied to any specifically institutional context, it would require researchers to take a holistic perspective. They would have to consider the whole range of educational provision from pre-schooling, through all stages of education at primary, secondary and tertiary levels, to continuing vocational training in educational and labour-market institutions, informal learning on the job, and self-directed and co-operative learning at large in society.

Lifelong-learning concepts are thus characterized by a strain of 'anarchy' – developments are difficult to observe, and the relationships never straightforward. For example, a trend towards deinstitutionalization can be observed in both education and work; various developments with impacts on people's life patterns and styles occur simultaneously. This state of anarchy has certain virtues, but tensions arise because social systems tend to require and impose a certain order. A vast and inclusive concept of lifelong learning holds certain appeal to policy makers, in part because it can serve to obscure attempts to define clearly what educational goals should be pursued and who should be responsible for which specific provisions and actions. For educational researchers, however, this all-embracing approach holds much less appeal, not least because the concept evades clear definition and hence is not directly amenable to measurement or evaluation. Examples of questions posed are as follows.

- What can educational research, being moderately strong in observing the current scene, do to help understand fluid and dynamic change or an emerging future 'utopia of learning'?
- How can research, being strong in putting the spotlight on selected aspects of a phenomenon, provide evidence and analyses concerning the complex settings associated with a lifelong-learning society?
- How can research handle the many normative implications of lifelong learning?
- How can research address the multilevel nature and organization of lifelong learning 'as a lifestyle'?
- How can research cope with the long-term effects implied by a lifelong approach, amidst evidence of concomitant and rapid social, cultural and economic change?
- How can research cope with the phenomena of inarticulate and relatively 'soft' demand, rather vague views of learning needs, heterogeneous and dispersed institutional settings for learning and a generally 'fuzzy' delineation between adult learning and other social and cultural activities?

Theoretical and disciplinary perspectives

In identifying problems, exploring answers and elucidating options, educational researchers will need much imagination as well as a varied toolbox. The questions cannot properly be handled in the narrow disciplinary perspective traditionally associated with schools and formal schooling. An *interdisciplinary* effort is called for that extends beyond even adult education. Further, an agenda for research should reflect the multilevel nature of the many cross-cutting issues that are present. In pursuing such interdisciplinary and multilevel work, researchers will need to apply various scientific methods, ranging from conceptual-analytic, qualitative to quantitative methods. Many of the cross-cutting themes presented in a subsequent section are likely to require interpretative rather than explanatory research methods.

Lifelong learning could be seen as presenting an inclusive framework for the organization of educational research, bridging research on the learning of very young children with that of young adults and senior citizens (lifelong) and spanning several dimensions of living experiences distributed in time and space (life-wide). Such an inclusive framework would have implications for structuring educational research and its relationships with other fields of study. Some examples of the variety of research perspectives that will need to be brought to bear on lifelong learning are offered below.

First of all, there would be an obvious need to strengthen the *collaboration* among specialists and researchers working in various fields denoted with terms such as *pedagogy, andragogy* and *didactics*. Scholars and practitioners have long argued the case that adult education differs in fundamental ways from formal schooling. It is recognized that there are some major differences between the aims, means and ends of adult education and those of the school. Yet the main distinctive characteristic of adult education, it is often argued, lies not so much in its instrumentalist nature as in its epistemological orientation, which refers to both humanist and critical notions of knowledge, and which involve concepts such as self-direction, facilitation and emancipation.

Of importance in a lifelong-learning perspective, however, is neither a distinct epistemology of adult learning nor, indeed, the kind of institutional or educational pathway the individual has followed, but rather what he or she has acquired during the 'learning trip', regardless of the means used. Educational practice, as carried out by teachers and learners, and regardless of whether it involves children or adults, is influenced by an amalgamation of previous experience and theoretical insights gained from a wide range of education fields and related disciplines. Research on formal schooling and research on adult education both contribute to the development and unity of a larger domain of study concerned with lifelong learning, which is informed also by knowledge contributed by other behavioural, social science and humanities disciplines.

- What are the implications of a lifelong-learning approach for unity in educational research, and how can the field be better structured so as to reinforce the linkages with other major disciplines?

A lifelong approach is said to reinforce the importance of learning early in life to ensure that all children and youth are well equipped to acquire a general and broad knowledge base. Young adults also should acquire intermediate-level skills that provide a relevant and high-quality groundwork for active and continued participation in the worlds of work and learning beyond schooling. A better understanding of the curriculum for foundation and subsequent learning is needed. *Curriculum studies* should therefore receive more and continued attention.

- Is a broad-based content, with a stress on developing understanding and relevance to later learning, preferable and more effective than narrow content? What contents should be selected? How should the selected contents be structured and assessed?

A point noted previously is that policy strategies for promoting and implementing lifelong learning are necessarily long term and have their roots in educational developments going back far in history. This immediately suggests the importance of *historical studies* on ideas relevant to lifelong learning. The time dimension that is inherent in notions of lifelong learning as a moving target suggests, moreover, the need for *prospective and futures-oriented studies*. Such studies could employ a variety of methods, both qualitative and quantitative.

- In what ways, and why, does the concept of lifelong learning advocated today differ from those previously promoted? Does a lifelong approach to learning have merits when viewed over the longer term?

Another distinguishing feature of the lifelong-learning approach advocated today is that it is supposed to establish and pursue '*partnerships*' and 'straddle the interests' of many participants. This will require policy makers and researchers to re-examine what the goals for education and training should be, and to articulate the balance between them relative to the needs of the many stakeholders in the education field, including individuals, families, employers and communities. Lifelong learning is understood to require the co-operation of these stakeholders, including teachers, but this is easier said than done, given the diverse interests that are at play. At a minimum this suggests the need for a *political science* perspective on concepts of lifelong learning. The co-operation of experts in *business administration and management* would also be invaluable.

- What are the goals and objectives a lifelong-learning strategy is supposed to serve? What are the different criteria to be used in assessing the outcomes of lifelong learning? Are there goal conflicts and what are the trade-offs among them? What are the different constituencies for lifelong learning, and what are their respective expectations, roles and responsibilities?

Lifelong learning ideas are often focused on personal development: by focusing on and exploiting the active-learning potential of the individual, the concept places the individual at the centre stage. Careful attention therefore has to be devoted to questions such as how human beings develop over the lifespan, how learning influences such development, and how and why adults learn. Much is already known, but many questions remain open. Studies in *human development*, *cognitive psychology* and *instructional psychology* have a large contribution to make to the common knowledge base concerned with lifelong learning.

- How do adults learn? What are the elements of learning as a lifestyle?

Because of the emphasis on lifelong learning *for all*, the framework clearly invites *sociological studies* of distribution effects, equity and disparities, and the various barriers to learning. Specific studies on selected variables such as urban/rural location, social status and gender, and their associations with lifelong learning, are also needed.

- What are the characteristics of adult learners? How is adult learning distributed in the general population and to what extent and why are there differences between men and women? If there are large differences, why? What are the socio-economic determinants of adult learning for men and women? What is the relative weight of the work environment compared with factors such as home background and schooling in determining adult education participation? To what extent can adult education offer a way out of early life-course determination, and how does it benefit women in mid-life?

By seeking to improve the conditions for and efficiency of investment in human-resource development and skills formation as a means of improving flexibility, raising productivity and promoting economic growth and job creation, a lifelong-learning framework begs fundamental questions of *macroeconomists* and *labour economists*.

- How can human capital investment be treated in national accounting as well as in the accounts of public and private employers? What are the advantages and disadvantages of doing so?

Questions are increasingly asked about the appropriateness of applying what are seen as essentially 'industrial' models to the organization of schools and institutions for adult education in the information age. Plant and physical settings are important, in that they influence the quality and effectiveness of education in a number of ways. Lifelong learning implies a new agenda for studies of the *architecture* of learning environments.

- What might be the characteristics and organizational options for community learning centres conducive to lifelong learning?

In conclusion, there appears to be a discrepancy between the seemingly high consensus regarding the changes requiring lifelong learning on the one hand, and the actual slow pace of change of the immediate conditions for lifelong learning on the other. The educational system is, by its very nature of *responding* to socio-economic changes and not directly inducing them, conservative.

- To what extent is there really an expert consensus and evidence on the economic, social and cultural conditions requiring a shift in policies in favour of a lifelong-learning approach? How can one overcome the simplistic ways of inferring educational needs on the basis of analyses of the employment system? What evidence exists to show that the labour market cannot easily adapt to a non-reforming educational system? What do we really know about the individuals' perceptions of and willingness to share the values underlying the concept of the learning society, let alone the likelihood of their partaking in it voluntarily?

Sectoral and 'cross-cutting' themes

Major sectoral as well as 'cross-cutting' themes and questions for a research agenda are presented here. These themes relate to all sectors of provisions for lifelong learning.

Motivation and readiness to learn

Ability and motivation to learn are established rather early in life. Equipping individuals with the skills and the motivation to learn on a continuing basis implies a holistic, life-cycle view in which an early start is crucial for the cognitive, social, emotive and physical development of children. The importance of early education experiences for later readiness to learn appears to be a well-established fact in the research literature. But readiness to learn is a factor also in later life – lack of motivation on the part of adults to continue learning in more 'formal' environments may have to do with poverty, irrelevance and even lack of educational supply.

- What are the factors influencing the willingness of people to engage in learning throughout life? What are the important elements of 'readiness to learn'? How can these elements be assessed, and what kind of experimental studies or sample surveys would be needed to establish or refute value-added progress in cumulative learning?

Teachers and teaching

Changes in the goals for education in response to larger social and economic developments are assumed to have wide-ranging implications for educators and members of the teaching profession. For example, the realization of a lifelong approach to learning for all is believed to be possible only with a teaching force that is itself committed to maximizing its own learning opportunities.

- What are the demands a shift toward a lifelong-learning strategy is likely to make on the teaching staff? What evidence exists to show that a new model of the lifelong-learning teacher is emerging? if so, what are its characteristics? What impact will the concept of lifelong learning have on pre-, in- and on-service teacher training? What measures might be needed to assist teachers to evaluate their own learning performance effectively?

Learning environments

Good learning environments are those that offer positive experience to learners – places where learners like to be. In the literature there is much support for theories of 'active' and 'self-directed' learning, with students 'constructing' their own learning experience and knowledge bases. In such a scenario teachers are believed to become 'guides' and 'facilitators' of learning: they no longer hold a near-monopoly on a repository of content and teaching methods.

- To what extent is it correct, in a lifelong-learning approach, to emphasize that teachers should act not as instructors but as the facilitators of individual progress in learning? What is the empirical basis for the constructivist approach in school and adult learning? Is this approach currently being oversold? In what respects can a teacher serve as a role model during the various stages of learning throughout life?

Learning technologies

New information and communication technologies can open up new opportunities for 'individualizing' instruction and for students to control their own learning activities. Multimedia can generate greater student interest, and open up windows to the outside world, for example through the use of networks. The individualization of teaching made possible through the new information and communication technologies has consequences for teaching methods and assessment practices.

- What can be the role of new information and communication technologies in creating positive learning environments that enable all students to acquire a selected knowledge base? Does an increase in computer-based activities imply a reduction of time spent learning exercises by rote and an increase in time spent on learning and practising metacognitive skills?
- What can be the role of new information technologies, especially on-line self-assessment packages, in improving the validity and reliability of large-scale assessment of cross-curricular competencies? What is known about how to link individual assessment with individualized learning plans and programmed instruction?
- In what respects and to what extent can teachers be 'replaced' by communication technologies?

Student differentiation and pre-career preparation

Some researchers contend that the best preparation for lifelong learning, including informal learning at the workplace, is a broad and general education early on in a formal school setting, with vocational preparation deferred until later. It has been said that the skills constituting the core of general education, because of their wide applicability, provide the best vocational education at an early stage of formal schooling. But others emphasize that general education, as a preparation for lifelong learning, also needs to include some work experience for all students. As a result, traditional distinctions between general and pre-career vocational education are becoming increasingly blurred in some countries, whereas in others there remains a wide divide between the two and the esteem in which each is held.

- What knowledge and skills acquired at one stage or in one setting can provide a good basis for subsequent learning at other stages and in other settings? To what extent should general and vocational programmes be integrated or remain separate tracks? At what age level should separation occur? Is the distinction between initial education and further vocational education becoming too blurred as a consequence of a more protracted transition pathway from education to employment?

Higher education and lifelong learning

Increasing participation rates in higher education in many countries can be taken as indicators of rising expectations. Demand continues to rise, influenced in part by opportunities opened up by the information society, by sustained increases in the standard of living over long periods of time, and by the frequent changes of skills and competencies demanded at work. Another aspect of this is that learning opportunities stimulate the desire to take advantage of further opportunities.

- What are the limits to the growth of universities in learning societies? What proportion of the population can be expected to profit from university teaching? Can an upper limit with respect to enrolment be identified?

Currently, most systematic information regarding the relationship between higher education and lifelong learning is available on the following three topics: university extension activities; open and distance learning; and continuing professional training. The quantity and relevance of the research agenda in this domain would be expected to improve substantially if it were not so strongly preoccupied with the already existing forms of involvement of higher-education institutions in the teaching of adult learners and in providing continuing professional education. Rather, further research in this domain should focus on the systematic transformation from the currently prevailing approach of relatively clearly denoting the distinction between initial and continuing education, to the much more fluid and continuous approach relevant to lifelong-learning policies.

- What are the possible roles that universities can play in lifelong learning? How do globalization and free-market orientations affect the university sector as an integral part of a lifelong-learning society? How does lifelong learning as a response to 'mass' higher education differ from lifelong learning as a response to a less expanded, more selective, system of initial education – in terms of the intellectual capacities and learning abilities required, the prior learning achievements to be built on, the values and attitudes shared in common by the learners, and the job or career requirements involved?
- Should continuing professional training develop as a separate track in traditional higher education or should it be an integral part of the university system? How can universities respond better to the individual learning needs of a heterogeneous student body, including older adults and, especially, how can university studies be made more compatible with the learning demands of working adults?

Demand-and-supply issues

At the threshold of the twenty-first century, engagement in organized forms of adult education has grown to a stage where more than half of the entire adult population of some economically developed countries is active over the course of a given calendar year. The 'silent explosion' of the demand for and supply of adult-learning opportunities results both from economic and labour-market changes and from a series of 'quiet' transformations in the conditions of people's non-working lives (see Bélanger and Tuijnman, 1997).

- What is the nature, extent and distribution of the demand for and supply of adult education? What factors influence demand and supply? What are the effects of the aging of the labour force on the need for lifelong learning? What evidence is there to support the view that the absence of effective learning opportunities, or lack of access to them, contributes to unemployment, low earnings and social exclusion? How can inequalities in access and participation in adult education be reduced? How can 'at-risk' individuals be best served? What incentives increase the learning potential of low-skill workers?
- What empirical evidence is there about the sweeping changes in the employment system that are relevant to lifelong learning? What are the effects of certification and standardization of workplace learning on the demand and supply of learning opportunities for adults? What patterns of adult education do the world of work and related life conditions really

induce, what offerings do educational institutions really stimulate, and what offerings are the learners themselves inclined to pursue? Do, as a result of these factors, regular stages of adult education emerge? Or does adult education remain casuistic and dramatically unevenly distributed? Is there any evidence that adult education might become an optional choice model of rational life restructuring?

- What are the lifelong-learning demands of women, or of senior citizens? What are the learning needs of the already well educated and those employed in professional occupations? Is current supply adequate to meet their specific needs and interests? If not, should it be?

Institutional aspects and linkages

Lifelong learning, as is evident from what has been said above, implies a very large agenda for research on adult education. The growing importance of adult education in a framework for lifelong learning raises many issues about the institutional relationships between the formal education sector catering for young people and the more diffuse, heterogeneous provisions of continuing education for adults.

- There are competing hypotheses advanced concerning the 'typical' character of adult-education institutions. Are they adaptive, flexible and responding to the needs of various adult learners? Are they 'amateurish', poorly managed institutions, employing badly trained and occasional staff, and using trial-and-error programmes? What institutional characteristics are actually prevailing? What are the impacts of the institutional styles and conditions of the educational provisions on offer on access and the motivation of potential adult learners, on substance, and on the modes of teaching and learning? To what extent are those who obtained a privileged formal education early in life taking advantage of learning opportunities compared with the less privileged?
- In which respects does the relatively open nature of lifelong-learning policies reduce or increase social and economic disparities between those with a good initial, formal education and those who lost out on their educational formation early on in life? Are there specific patterns of social exclusion that might be endemic to a system of lifelong learning? What distribution of knowledge and skills across the adult population do the changes in the employment system and the political system encourage and reinforce with the use of incentives?

Informal learning in the workplace

Informal learning in the workplace constitutes a large and increasing part of provisions for lifelong learning. Factors impinging on this development are the increase in job-turnover rates and the insecurity associated with flexible work contracts and the new forms of organizing employment in core and peripheral contingent labour markets. The building of knowledge networks and the changing nature of work in learning organizations are additional factors.

- How do work-time patterns relate to different learning pathways? What settings of work organization raise barriers and obstacles to adult education and informal learning in the workplace, and what practices can be used to overcome such inhibiting factors?
- Does informal learning at work improve the adjustment capacity of economic factors and, if so, in what ways and to what extent? What is the role of workplace learning in contributing to flexible labour markets, for example by facilitating the progression from one job to another? What might be the drawbacks, for example in terms of social mobility or new segregation, in the workplace? How can a system of lifelong learning be aligned with arrangements for unemployment insurance? What incentives encourage the adoption of work organization methods that facilitate the use of skills in the workplace? What are the relationships between on-the-job training and the internal organization of work within firms?

Management and planning

Approaches to lifelong learning emphasize partnerships and a greater sharing of responsibilities for the content, organization and funding of education and training systems. This raises a number of implications for the role of governments and other stakeholders. Education has in many countries long been a legitimate and central domain of government policy. But the degree of state involvement in education is not static, but shaped by factors such as internationalization, the deregulation of services and monopolies, renewed emphasis on cost control and increased attention paid to learning outcomes.

- Can the application of lifelong-learning principles assist governments in playing a more strategic role in the governance and management of education and training systems? If so, how? What are the trade-offs and what are the advantages? Does government cease to be a major actor in the lifelong-learning society. Who stands to lose?

A key feature of the response to date has been a redefinition of the role of governments as part of a general trend in which responsibilities for education and training have been redistributed. Often referred to as decentralization, the trend is perhaps better described as a convergence towards a distribution of responsibilities in which the outcomes to be achieved are more widely specified and assessed. In the meantime, the decisions about the means used to achieve them are left more to the education and training establishments, communities and the individual learners.

- How does the role of the government as a steering, supporting, control- ling, assessing and service-providing agency of education change in the process of progressively implementing policies for lifelong learning? To what extent can any changes observed be attributed to specific policy options, to national educational traditions, to universal needs inherent in the logic of a learning society, or to specific technological, economic or cultural contexts?
- What balance is to be struck between central legislation and directives and local discretion or individual choice; and what should be the balance between direct regulation and steering indirectly by means of incentives? What are the necessary conditions for effective implementation of the government's role in new approaches to governance and management? To what extent is the actual scope for the exercise of responsibility limited or enhanced through regulation and financing incentives? Are the new approaches to management and governance sufficiently connected to teaching and learning? How can learners, teachers and education and training establishments be encouraged to become more active and take ini- tiative?

Issues in economics

Acceptance of a coherent strategy of lifelong learning for all immediately begs difficult questions about the investment risks and costs, the returns, and the implications for financing strategies. As the strategic roles of govern- ments and their partners in managing education and training provision are being reviewed as a consequence of the move towards lifelong learning, tradi- tional approaches to the financing of education and training are also being called into question. In a lifelong-learning framework, more actors, as a rule in the private sector, become involved, agendas will be broadened and 'quasi- markets' for learning established.

Three sets of questions need to be addressed. First is the question of mobiliz- ing additional resources, since the implementation of lifelong learning for all will most likely require more money. This raises the issue of short-term costs.

- What are the cost and priority implications of reorienting systems toward a lifelong-learning approach? What are the trends in the development over time of the costs of formal education and training provision? What evidence is there for achieving economies of scale in formal education and training systems? How can differences between countries in the development of costs be explained, and what are the relationships between aggregate costs and indicators of educational outcomes?

Second is the question of how lifelong learning can be made affordable for all of the partners. This is about financing strategies. A careful analysis needs to be undertaken of devices for financing lifelong learning, each of which would have different effects in terms of encouraging a pattern of lifelong learning, leveraging resources from the partners and promoting cost-effectiveness. These include, for example, direct government funding, educational entitlements, student vouchers, the franchise model, learning accounts, auctioning (where institutions bid for funded students), parafiscal funds (all employers, private and public alike, would be subject to a training levy), single-employer financing (although this restricts training so that it becomes largely vocation-specific) and self-financing through tuition fees.

- What are the sources of revenue used for educational spending? What does the research say about the advantages and disadvantages of student choice? Are there systematic differences between low- and high-cost countries in the sources of revenue and the distribution of spending by levels of education? Is the current allocation and distribution of funds and other resources by levels and sectors efficient and effective in a lifelong-learning perspective? What alternative options are there for the financing of learning opportunities over the entire lifespan?

The third question is how, within each level and sector of provision, equity and efficiency may be improved through a better understanding of the rates of return and wider social benefits accruing to lifelong learning. In the perspective of shared responsibility for governance, management and financing, information about who benefits from education, training and self-directed learning, in what respects, and how much, is pertinent to thinking about who may be asked to contribute how much to foot the bill. The question of how the costs should be distributed and shared cannot be posed independently of the questions of who benefits, in what ways, and how much. However, determining how the benefits of education are distributed in relation to the amounts invested by government, employers, learners and other actors has proved to be difficult. Patterns in rates of return to different forms of learning and to different groups of learners offer, at present, an inadequate basis for making decisions about cost sharing. This is because the estimates fail to account fully for other factors not so easy to grasp, and which give rise to earnings differences, such as cognitive ability, 'learning-to-learn' skills and perseverance. Further, the rate-of-return estimates do not take into account certain externalities that tend to be, on balance, positive – by some estimates, as much as double the monetary returns. Better knowledge about the rates of return to education and training is therefore a high priority.

- What is the evidence about the benefits, both economic and non-monetary, that accrue to investments in education and training for individuals, firms, governments and society at large, by level of education and across time? Will social and private rates of return to tertiary and upper-secondary education decline with expanding participation?

Evaluation and monitoring

As countries adopt a lifelong approach to learning, there will be a need to reconsider current approaches to *evaluation* and *monitoring*. This applies not only to system-internal aspects of evaluation but also to the relationships between education and training systems on the one hand, and the 'external' worlds of work and culture, family and community life, and the social dynamics of human security, justice and democracy on the other hand. In a lifelong-learning philosophy, opportunities to learn outside the formal system are to be placed on an equal footing with those occurring within. An important condition for this is that such learning is properly evaluated.

*   Why have standard setting and monitoring been brought to the fore of attention in a number of countries in recent years? How should standards be set and monitored? What new approaches to evaluation and monitoring are needed in a lifelong-learning perspective? What value-added-performance indicators can be constructed to highlight the institutions and approaches that best promote the success of a range of students?

Assessment and certification

Some aspects of individual pathways can be measured usefully and certified in terms of established standards of achievement and recognized qualifications. They imply that continuing learning not only enhances the freedom and adaptability of learners but also leads to a potentially useful accumulation of knowledge and skills. Recognition of skills and competencies can result either from a structured learning process, or from a competency-based approach focusing only on outcomes. Recognizing and certifying the prerequisite and acquired knowledge and competencies of individuals are among the most challenging tasks for institutions, public agencies and employers.

Lifelong learning implies that qualifications increasingly need to become transferable or portable from one work situation to another, or from an academic to a professional position and vice versa. Assessment processes will need to reflect learning progress over time, and the individualization of learning geared to employment, career development and personal fulfilment. But the procedures for skill accreditation and assessment of prior learning are currently still underdeveloped. The accreditation system is at a loss if it has to assess at one and the same time both academic knowledge and work experience, since one lies in the formal, and the other in the non-formal, domain. Standards in formal education tend to lie within the purview of the education minister or an authorized public body, whereas in non-formal learning they are often defined, implicitly or explicitly, by enterprises, professional bodies and the like, or set personally by self-motivated learners.

- Which labour-force skills are the most important? Can core competencies be identified and, if so, how can these be measured and assessed in an operational manner? What might be the implications for the recognition, transfer and portability of skills in the labour market? To what extent are core-foundation skills reflected in the qualifications traditionally awarded by educational institutions? What is known not just about upskilling, but also about the depreciation of skills?
- How adequate are the measures of the stock of human capital currently available? Does it matter that they rely on static proxy measures of educational qualifications conferred by the formal education system? What would more dynamic and flow-oriented measures of human capital stock look like?

Conclusions

There is no single, ideally structured, system of lifelong learning that suits all countries and types of economy. Accordingly, there can be no uniform implementation strategy that all countries can follow. Instead, practices will need to build upon specific national and cultural heritages, and policies should be modified to suit particular conditions and needs. Even though the scope and content of strategies for lifelong learning may well be unique to the specific circumstances of countries, certain questions are pertinent to all, whether economically developed or developing (Husén, 1997).

In drafting the report, the Task Force had to strike a balance between the need to avoid being encyclopaedic and the need to avoid a too-narrow perspective. The result is a somewhat eclectic set of issues and questions for educational research that emerges from an analysis of the aims and objectives of various lifelong-learning strategies currently pursued by governments in many countries. A further issue concerns the identification of research priorities. Generally members considered that it would be impossible to propose a detailed ranking of priorities. In spite of this, exceptional priority was given to the need to improve the quantitative database on the outcomes of learning in all settings, formal as well as non-formal. Another overriding priority was the need to initiate longitudinal research studies in the field of adult education and training, with an emphasis on both contextual and process variables.

The Task Force generally has preferred to avoid assigning specific priorities to questions for educational research. This is in line with the observations made previously, namely that lifelong-learning concepts are fluid and that interpretation is to a large extent context-specific. Overarching general issues concern the clarification of the meanings of lifelong-learning concepts. For employers, women and many other groups in society, the recognition of the plurality of values that foster a learning society, and an understanding of the 'hidden curriculum' of lifelong-learning approaches and programmes, are important.

Specifically with respect to adult-education research, the Task Force offers the following five recommendations.

- Studies on 'integrative' adult learning. The field of adult education is highly heterogeneous and segmented. A priority for research is to illuminate how existing programmes and learning options can be better aligned and used in combination to produce the best possible outcomes for adult learners with varying interests and needs. The purpose of mapping the field is to produce, using clear rubrics and classifications, a comprehensive inventory of the mix of provisions and opportunities, particularly for adult learners, currently available: a picture that is lacking at present. In addition, studies could usefully shed light on the specifications for an idealized system of lifelong-learning opportunities. This orientation would examine carefully the *contexts* and settings in which lifelong-learning programmes can be optimal.
- Studies on skills and competencies. Applicable in a wide repertoire of situations: terms such as metacognitive skills, multiple intelligences, key or start qualifications, essential, foundational or necessary skills and competencies are used with increased frequency. What evidence is there to suggest that there are indeed a limited number of key skills and competencies, and to what extent are they similar or do they differ between countries or vary by level of economic and social development? What are these key competencies, and how can they be measured and assessed? These questions are at the forefront of the debate today. This is an area where further conceptual and analytic work is greatly needed.
- Research on outcomes. In the field of adult education the quantitative knowledge base on learning outcomes is especially deficient. Studies are needed that investigate the participation of adults in learning activities in relation both to contextual and background variables and information on results and outcomes. Contextual information is especially important for studies examining the learning pathways and outcomes relevant to specific population groups, such as women, highly skilled professionals, immigrants or educationally disadvantaged adults.
- Longitudinal investigations. Because the time dimension is inherent in lifelong learning, there is a clear need to map learning across the individual life course and investigate the cumulative age-, cohort- and period-related effects of learning over time. This calls for the extension of already ongoing longitudinal surveys of children and youth into

adulthood, as well as the launch of new follow-up surveys of representative samples of adults. Life-course biographical research – the study of individual learning trajectories – has an important contribution to make because human development and learning pathways seldom follow a straightforward linear progression. In addition, this suggests the need for studies on family and intergenerational learning.

* Comparative studies. There has been much progress in recent years in the development of internationally comparative statistics and indicators of education systems. Besides the lack of comprehensive information on outcomes, the main gap in the current information base concerns comparative data on adult education and training and more informal learning. The comparative study of inclusions and exclusions in adult education using quantitative statistics and indicators is a high priority. As for indicators, trend data will become increasingly important.

In conclusion, it is hoped that this chapter will provide a basis for further discussions about the questions and priorities for educational research with a lifelong-learning perspective. Such discussion will occur within the research community. There will also have to be dialogue with policy makers and the sponsors of research. Clearly, as this agenda hopes to illustrate, the research field is virtually inexhaustible, and it needs sustained support over many years. Long-term commitments on the part of both the academic community and the sponsors of research will be forthcoming only if the effort is meaningfully focused and staged. But where is one to start? Continued discussion on the questions and priorities for educational research in the perspective of lifelong learning would benefit all communities concerned.

References

Bélanger, P. and Tuijnman, A. (eds) (1997) New Patterns of Adult Learning: A Six-country Comparative Study, Oxford, Pergamon Press.

Commission of the European Union (1994) Growth, Competitiveness and Employment: The Challenges and Ways Forward in the 21st Century, Luxembourg, Office for Official Publications.

Commission of the European Union (1995) Teaching and Learning: Towards the Learning Society, Luxembourg, Office for Official Publications.

Commission of the European Union (1997) Accomplishing Europe through Education and Training, Luxembourg, Office for Official Publications.

Delors, J. et al. (1996) Learning: The Treasure Within, Paris, UNESCO.

Faure, E., Herrera, F., Kaddoura, A.R., Lopes, H., Retrovsky, A.V., Rahnema, M. and Ward, F.C. (1972) Learning to Be: The World of Education Today and Tomorrow, Paris, UNESCO.

Hasan, A. (1996) Lifelong learning, in The International Encyclopedia of Adult Education and Training, 2nd edn (A.C. Tuijnman, ed.), pp. 33–41, Oxford, Pergamon Press.

Husén, T. (1968) School in a changing and industrialized society. *Educational Leadership* **25**, 524–530.

Husén, T. (1986) *The Learning Society Revisited*, Oxford, Pergamon Press.

Husén, T. (1997) An agenda for the education of world citizens. *Prospects* **27**, 201–205.

OECD (1973) *Recurrent Education: A Strategy for Lifelong Learning*, Paris, OECD.

OECD (1994) *The OECD Jobs Study: Evidence and Explanations*, Paris, OECD.

OECD (1996) *Lifelong Learning for All*, Paris, OECD.

OECD (1998) *Human Capital Investment: An International Comparison*, Paris, OECD.

Tuijnman, A.C. (1994) Recurrent Education, in *The International Encyclopedia of Education*, 2nd edn (T. Husén and T.N. Postlethwaite, eds), Oxford, Pergamon Press.

Chapter 2

On a contradictory way to the 'learning society'

A critical approach

Peter Alheit

Introduction

The current discussion of lifelong learning makes it convincingly clear to us that we live in a 'learning society'. At the same time, it also conveys the irritating impression that we attach very different notions to this label. Is it new knowledge that turns modern societies into *cognitive societies* and forces each of us to be a lifelong learner? Is it the breathtaking speed and nature of social transformation processes, with all their inestimable risks, that threaten us and coerce us to take part in incessant learning? Or is it ultimately our own life 'programme' that has changed – the biographical constructions that 'reflexive modernity' compels us to adopt, to borrow that almost populist label coined by Beck (1992) and Giddens (1990)?

We can obviously sense the changes in modernised modernity with some precision. We experience that macro-sociological transformations are occurring. We also notice that micro-sociality is affected, too. What we are missing, it would seem, is a 'concept' that renders these changes transparent for our understanding. The *learning society* seems to be nothing more than an auxiliary construct – an aid.

As early as 1995, Richard Edwards pointed out that the reason why the label *learning society* has acquired so much acceptance is that its conceptual clarity is extremely limited and that very different notions can hide behind it. In a brief analysis of the international debate (see Edwards, 1995), he identifies three dominant types of *learning society*:

Type 1: The concept of a *free, democratic education society*, which offers all its members the same opportunities to use formal education facilities (which therefore must be expanded accordingly). This concept has been developed mainly by liberal, urban educators in western welfare states in the 1960s and 1970s.

This is an edited version of an article published in *Studies in the Education of Adults* 31, 1 (1999): 66–82.

Type 2: The concept of a *free education market* where various education
         institutions offer competing learning arrangements aimed at
         improving people's (vocational) training and raising their level of
         qualification, and at increasing the economy's competitive strength.
         This concept emerged during the years of economic uncertainty
         from the mid-1970s and has been propagated primarily by (conser-
         vative) governments and industrial associations.
Type 3: The 'postmodern' concept of *open learning networks*, which are able
         to foster a wide range of skills and abilities. This concept foresees
         learners using those networks creatively on a 'self-directed' basis
         just to satisfy their learning needs according to their own notions.

Edwards noted rather realistically that current practice is dominated by
the economic concept of a learning market based on the principle of competition. As a result, the 'equal opportunity gap' between social strata is growing
disproportionately, and the goal of achieving a broader mobilisation of yet
undeveloped skills and abilities remains unmet. In practice, the egalitarian,
democratic ideal of expanding educational institutions and opening them to
everyone has, undoubtedly, a smaller basis in a society for self-directed
learning than in a society that functions with an underlying structure of
entitlement and qualification.

Richard Edwards, however, believes (and in this respect he accords not
only with the position of other European experts, as in Günther Dohmen's
noteworthy expertise (1996), but also with the crucial statements in the
prominent *Delors Report*), that neither the further expansion of the formal
education system nor a radical commercialisation of educational provision
are a solution. Instead, future development must lead to overlapping local,
regional, national and global learning networks that people who are interested in learning can use autonomously to examine the structured diversity
of the modern world in an open learning environment.

Attractive though this option may sound, it could suffer from analytical
weaknesses. The following thoughts are a cautious attempt to fill this 'analytical gap' and to illustrate by means of a developed conceptual framework
what characterises a *learning society* of the future and what research issues
are raised on the way to this goal. My thesis is that learning societies are
not characterised (or at least not exclusively) by changes at the social macro-
level, i.e. the level of social system, nor by the fact that micro-sociality –
the individual, biographic activity of social actors – is undergoing change.
Instead, I am convinced that we must focus much more social scientific attention on the *meso-level*, on institutional and non-institutional *learning
environments*, and that the perspectives of the learning society are determined at this level.

However, I consider it essential that macro-social changes are at least
referred to. I do this in the first section, in which I try to provide evidence

for a kind of 'postmodernisation' of society. My theoretical references are less the well-known diagnoses of our age produced by Anthony Giddens (1990) or Ulrich Beck (1992), which I am sceptical about as far as their empirical basis is concerned, but rather some studies in the tradition of Bourdieu (1979), particularly since I was myself involved in a major empirical social structure study that drew heavily on Bourdieu's theory.

In the second section, I shall define the micro-social changes with greater precision and attempt to substantiate the thesis of a 'biographisation of the social'. This idea derives similarly from many years of empirical research.

In the third section, I focus on the redefinition of the 'meso-level' to which I have already referred. Its special nature is due to much more than its range. There is no doubt that it operates below the state or the market, but above the action targets of individual actors. Its special nature consists in a change that affects institutions, enterprises and non-institutionalised publics alike, a change that could be termed the 'informalisation trend'. Drawing loosely on Antonio Gramsci (1977) and Jürgen Habermas (1962), I should like to outline the perspectives of such informalisation trends more precisely, and render them useful for the concept of the learning society.

Finally, in the fourth section, I want to summarise the insights obtained, in the form of three theses that may be read as future research foci for adult education research (from my highly subjective viewpoint, of course).

The macro-social challenge: 'postmodernisation' of society

If there is one issue that has lent wings to adult education research in the post-war period, it is the question of the 'non-public' of organised adult education, as Filippo de Sanctis (1988), the Italian adult education theorist, used to call it; the analytical search for those members of society who keep away – either deliberately or through lack of information – from the adult education programmes publicly on offer.

The fact that this question has managed to occupy research interest in a number of countries since the late 1950s, including Scandinavia, Great Britain, Germany and France, was due to a specific hegemonial constellation that no longer arose in the decades that followed, namely a somewhat unusual alliance between social-democratic reformism and capital's drive to modernise both itself and society (see Friedeburg, 1994). What one side envisaged as an emancipatory opportunity for personal growth, especially for the working classes, was seen by the other side as the benefits of having the wide-ranging skills within the workforce that were considered essential if Europe was to remain competitive against the USA on the world market. This joint initiative produced ideas like 'second chance education' from Scandinavia to Austria, from the 'Open University' in Britain to the '150 hours' project in Italy.

The impulse generated by these reforms did indeed change the respective societies of northern and central Europe. In my own country (my comments are based on figures for West Germany prior to unification), the percentage of working-class children who go on to study at universities has more than quadrupled since the early 1950s, from just 4 per cent to almost 18 per cent (see Vester *et al.*, 1992). The proportion of women in higher education – certainly another indicator of reform – virtually tripled over the same period from 14 per cent to 39 per cent (ibid.).

In Scandinavia we are witnessing developments that are sometimes even more radical than this, or, for example in Great Britain or France, more gentle. The tendency is clearly apparent. Educational reforms are *opening* the social space in European societies and mobilising and modernising social structures (see Figure 2.1). Adult education plays a crucial role in this process, frequently acting as a catalyst for educational processes that lead into the institutions of higher education.

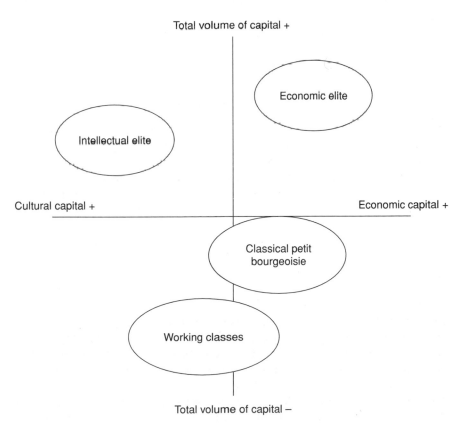

Figure 2.1 A simplified version of Bourdieu's social space.

No major theory in Europe has explained this process more succinctly than Pierre Bourdieu's (1979, in particular). But none has been so ruthless in taking the wraps off the ambivalence inherent in this development. Reading Bourdieu helps us to understand what the educational reforms have actually brought about. His concept of '*symbolic capital*' (Bourdieu, 1983) has rendered the complexity of social change more transparent. Once we realise that no man or woman is situated in the social space purely according to his or her economic capital assets, then education can be assigned the value and significance it actually has as a factor in social change. This is because we possess different kinds of 'capital' besides the economic, namely *cultural* and *social* capital, the total volume of which ultimately assigns us to our place in society.

In a well-known television interview, Bourdieu used the metaphor of a casino. We gamble not only with the 'black chips' that represent our economic capital. We also use the 'blue chips' symbolising our cultural capital, our exams and titles, what we know about people, about our minds and bodies, about art and society. The 'red chips' are perhaps the social capital we possess, our 'connections', the social access to resources that not everyone has. Taken together, all these different sorts of chips form our 'capital'.

I am introducing this rather simple 'exercise' in order to awaken our senses to the kind of changes that the educational reforms of the last 30 years have brought about in Europe. Adult education played a key role here, not just because it brought about upward educational mobility, but also because parents were encouraged to envisage educational pathways for their children that were out of bounds to themselves and their own parents. This effected a shift in placements within the social space – from lower right to centre left (Figure 2.2).

Working-class children could suddenly become teachers or social workers, technical employees or medical technologists. Sons and daughters from the petty bourgeoisie could rise to become university professors. The feeling of being able to change society through education seemed to be substantiated by the facts. In many European societies in that period – we are referring to the 1960s and 1970s – there was a special kind of euphoria that 'anything is possible' (Friedeburg, 1994). New perspectives appeared to be opening up without difficulty.

The intoxication of this reformist euphoria did not survive the cohorts that profited directly from its impacts. Bourdieu's theoretical framework is useful here, too, for understanding where the surprising ambivalences lay. Those who are granted the opportunity to acquire educational titles that their parents could not even dream of experience two disturbing things:

- Academic titles shed value in proportion to the extent they are acquired by these people and others like them. The supply of 'blue chips', if you like, has swollen artificially as a result of government policy. Therefore,

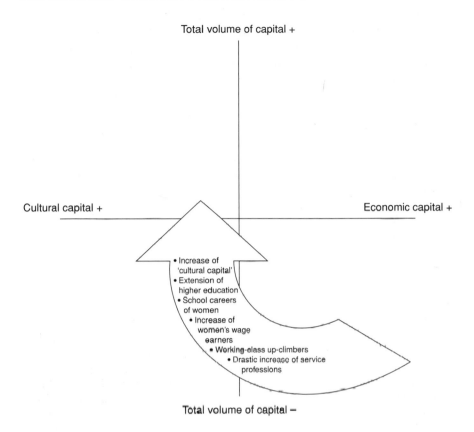

Total volume of capital +

Cultural capital +

Economic capital +

- Increase of 'cultural capital'
- Extension of higher education
- School careers of women
- Increase of women's wage earners
- Working-class up-climbers
- Drastic increase of service professions

Total volume of capital −

Figure 2.2 The opening of the social space.

their 'market value' has fallen sharply. The social prestige of teachers or even university professors – traditionally very high in all European societies after World War II – has shrunk considerably: a classical example of *inflation* (Alheit, 1993, 1994).

- Acquiring the title has by no means provided an 'entry ticket' to the 'better society'. Many of the upwardly mobile notice that they have left behind the milieu they stem from, but are not at all at home in their new social surroundings. They are made to feel, or they notice intuitively, that a title does not guarantee the *habitus* that was classically associated with it. In many cases, those who have climbed the ladder feel socially out of place. They come to realise that distinction is something beyond mere titles.

The successor cohorts – Bourdieu calls them 'the bamboozled generation' – are harder hit. They might have the chance to acquire recognised titles, but the jobs to go with them no longer exist. The labour market closes precisely at that locus where the social space had opened a decade before: in the 'human services' and particularly in the educational field. Many university departments, in the humanities and social sciences at least, discharge their graduates into the ranks of the unemployed (Alheit, 1995).

Adult education is doubly afflicted by this trend. First, entry into the labour market is generally made more difficult for people with academic qualifications. The long process of scientisation and professionalisation is obviously slowed down. Second, openings in public service are increasingly scarce due to budgetary constraints. Academic careers have been replaced by 'social loopings' (Alheit, 1995), and educational reforms have degenerated into orgies of public spending cuts. Equality of opportunity in society has not improved in the slightest (Alheit, 1993). Even if specific 'cleavages' have shifted position, class society is by no means eradicated.

However, 'class society' has actually acquired a new function. Classes have ceased to be milieux that convey social morals and which give people a home in society. Social origins have more or less degenerated into a mere resource for the coerced creation of new biographical perspectives – temporary and fluctuating identities (Alheit, 1994).

This indicates a kind of 'postmodernisation' of society. Classical modernity's recognition of societal inequalities and its essential aim of eradicating these through 'enlightenment' is covered over and obscured by an untrammelled process of differentiation. This is manifested by, at least, two new and symptomatic constellations that are worth analysing and which could prove of major importance for the future development of European adult education research:

- a kind of *pluralisation* of class society, involving some surprising effects; and
- the tendency of *knowledge diffusion* in the so-called 'cognitive society'.

The pluralisation of class society

It is no chauvinism on my part if I cite my home society in order to illustrate this symptom. The reason I do this is, as I mentioned before, that I was involved in a larger analysis of social structure in the former state of West Germany that tried to embark on new methodological pathways, so for that reason I am well acquainted with the German context. However, I am also convinced that the key findings of this study hold true not just for Germany, but are general symptoms of social modernisation within the majority of modern European societies.

What is astonishing first of all is the observation that the main strata of West German society – the upper, middle and lower strata – have not undergone any dramatic shift over the last 70 years or so. A *distinctive* and relatively unchanged upper-class *habitus* is evident for about 20 per cent of the population who possess a deeply rooted conviction of being predestined, unlike the 'masses', for social leadership roles. Of the population, 50 to 60 per cent display the middle-class *habitus*, the *pretentious* ambition of 'being somebody' and to actually achieve this end through hard work. The worker *habitus* is followed by 20 to 30 per cent, a mentality that adapts and conforms to what is *necessary and constrained*, within which framework the available opportunities to enjoy life and conviviality with others are indeed lived out and actually realised (see Vester *et al.*, 1993; Alheit *et al.*, 1994).

This 'conservatism' of social structure contradicts the fact that the inner coherence of the various strata has clearly relaxed. *Milieux* with their own internal life have developed from the old class fractions. The traditional class boundaries, which run vertical, are joined by horizontal 'cleavages' that are perhaps even more effective at creating distances between social groups. Differentiation occurs via *modernisation processes* that are difficult to link to the conventions of the classical strata. The dimension of 'self-realisation' is one element that lends these processes a certain dynamic, in contrast to established traditions. Modernised milieux are on the rise, whereas traditional milieux are shrinking. In other words, social integration and systemic integration are drifting further and further apart. Attachment to specific social positions is losing the aspect of 'estates' that Max Weber (1964) sees capitalist societies as still possessing (see Beck, 1992). The feeling of belonging is no longer derived from the attributes 'income', 'title', 'rank' and 'prestige' alone, nor, as a matter of course, from class experience in the 'moral economy'. Particular lifestyles, gender- and generation-related experiences can substitute for them and indeed become temporarily predominant (see Kreckel, 1992) – undoubtedly a sort of '*postmodernisation*' of society.

The apparently stable social status that someone possesses is defined reflexively to an increasing extent. In itself, it does not guarantee any rights to a particular place or to integration in a (post)modern society. The significance of education – even where its effects are contradictory or indeed inflationary – has heightened sensitivity to the right to *self-realisation* and has led to a cultural focus and an orientation to consumption even where financial resources are tight. Nevertheless, this substantiates the basic importance of adult education and certainly qualifies all-too-pessimistic perspectives.

Knowledge diffusion

The gradual change from class society to the 'lifestyle' or 'event society' (Schulze, 1992) has also altered social knowledge. Knowledge is no longer a secure fundus, or a resource comprising a clear hierarchy of meanings, but rather a phenomenon that is dependent on its contexts. If we look at the latest picture from the ongoing analysis of milieux in Germany, the impression is created of a confused landscape of mentalities that, each for itself,

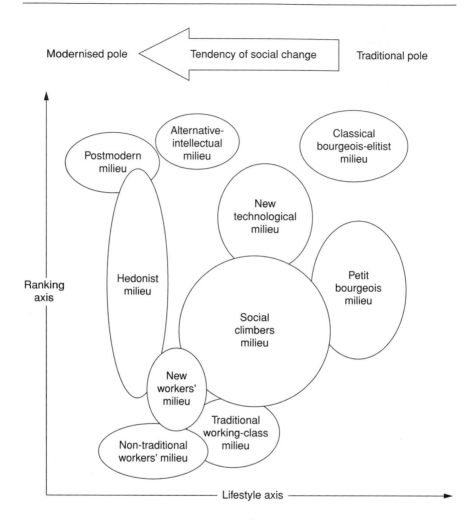

Figure 2.3 Map of milieux in the contemporary German society.

have both inclusive and exclusive impacts simultaneously. The classical 'us down here and them up there' metaphor used with effect by the labour movement to mobilise its constituents has long become obsolete as a description of one's location in the social fabric. Mutually excluding milieux have come into being both 'down here' and 'up there'. Social inequality possesses not only a 'ranking bias', but also a 'lifestyle dynamic' (see Figure 2.3).

The hedonism of the young generation conflicts with the conservatism of old people, regardless of whether the young in question are higher or lower in the social rankings. Women's lifeworlds compete with male views of reality, with women professors and secretaries demanding their rights. The 'contextuality' of knowledge is becoming a fashionable phrase, with opinions being generated in 'discourses' hermetically sealed off from each other, such that any shared understanding between the diverse social worlds would seem to arise more by chance than anything else. Lyotard's (1979) prediction that we have lost the 'meta-narratives' of modernity has been subsequently corroborated, it would seem.

What this also means is that the euphemistic notion of the *cognitive society* fails at its own scientistic roots to make real sense. In late modernity, scientific knowledge itself has lost its function as a source of orientation (Beck, 1996; Alheit, 1994). The sceptical realisation that science must waive any final value judgements because it is no longer capable of providing the truth is something we owe to Max Weber. We now know that even Weber's trust in the correctness of scientific *methods* is no longer tenable for us. The decision as to what is 'scientifically' correct depends not on inner-scientific consensus, but on the specific contexts in which such knowledge is applied. Scientific arguments are advanced not only by the champions but also by the opponents of nuclear power. Both sides lay claim to the scientific seriousness of their positions. The 'struggle between demystified gods' that Weber believed scientists should keep away from has been waging *within* the scientific community itself. The fashionable distinction between fundamental and applied research appears as a futile attempt to preserve the 'purity' of scientific enterprise. Such attempts fail because 'pure' research is infected by the same virus as 'applied research'. A major proportion of scientific activity takes place far away from the 'freedom and isolation' of academic institutions, in the research laboratories of the military-industrial complex. One can also calculate the time it takes for allegedly non-purposive knowledge to be boiled down to the possible applications (Alheit, 1994: 146ff.).

The diffusion of knowledge becomes apparent to all through the dramatic spread of information technologies in the second half of the twentieth century. For individuals, the media worlds they generate form a kind of 'second-grade reality' that is starting to make the boundaries to social reality increasingly blurred. Reality TV and computer games, the Internet and cyberspace have a tendency to cause extreme losses of reality and to obliterate the experiential world of social agents. In the picture puzzle of a gradual, insidious virtualisation of perception, the *cognitive society* is threatened by the 'agony of the real', as predicated by Jean Baudrillard (1983) almost 20 years ago.

Knowledge appears to have become something arbitrary, and its distribution is a matter of chance to an astonishing degree. If the ability to use the new media varies dramatically with age, if young computer virtuosi can easily hack their way into the host computers of banks, multinationals or even the Pentagon, the result may be an endearing type of anarchy. However, it also means that the dependability or reliability of knowledge in the modern age is undermined. Here, too, postmodern fragmentation seems to be the consequence.

Does this signify the 'deconstruction of the subject', as Derrida claims – in other words the final dissolution of modernity that originated in Descartes' *cogito ergo sum* equation? Is the *learning society* losing its classical protagonist, the learning individual? I take a very sceptical view here as well, for empirical reasons, and thus come to my second train of thought.

The micro-social challenge: 'biographisation' of the social

There is no doubt whatsoever that the conditions in which social subjects act – their biographical action environments – have undergone drastic change, particularly in the opening corridor of the social space I have already described. Elsewhere (Alheit, 1996), I have provided a detailed analysis of three crucial symptoms related to the change in biographical action environments, namely:

• an erosion of traditional lifeworlds;
• a breakdown of classical milieux; and
• a disappearing of 'normal' life course scripts.

One of the surprising results of this analysis is the recognition that reactions on the individual level are obviously less dramatic than we would expect. The path from systemic diffusions to a dramatic crisis of biographical action is a long one. Even the step from challenging experiences to new patterns of biographical construction seems to be more complicated than contemporary sociologists suppose. The reason for this is the theoretically highly interesting observation that the reaction to the collapse of environments is not necessarily a 'panic' reaction, but can include the rebuilding of action environments. In other words, the interdependency of action and action environments is not unilinear, but double-poled. Biographical activities may be transitional in nature. They reconstruct collapsing environments at a new level.

In many years of biographical research with social groups exposed to risk – young unemployed persons, women after divorce, teachers without work, migrants, epileptics and MS patients, homosexuals and young computer freaks – we were able to identify certain strategies with which these people successfully combat the symptoms of erosion and breakdown referred to above. We found three highly interesting biographical coping patterns that I should like to outline in brief:

• the pattern of biographical *'networking'*;
• the pattern of biographical *'patchworking'*; and
• the strategy of biographical *'designing'*.

Networkers are biographical engineers who react in a particularly sensitive way to the erosion of their former lifeworld. The disintegration of the family system and the immediate social nexus is processed actively at the biographical level. The result is not necessarily the neurotic attempt to cure everything, but more often the unpretentious effort to find a replacement. For example, we can observe many women after a divorce who preserve the intergenerational kinship networks of the 'old' family, and not merely for the sake of their children. We see that they construct completely new networks and that they fix 'matrilinear' relationships in the generational sequence of both their own and other families. This leads to new traditions, new obligations and new certainties (Hagestad, 1989).

We have also discovered that innovative lifeworld networks can develop within the new social movements. Examples here are various communitarian projects, children's initiatives, or building and shopping co-operatives (Effinger, 1990). But here, too, women dominate the activities. Networkers are female. This fact must be clearly stated in the face of changing male identity. The erosion of lifeworlds is treated in a biographically active form by women.

Patchworkers invent biographical constructions against the threatening consequences of social differentiation and the loss of social integration in a traditional milieux. Their strategy commonly consists in organising milieu-switching as a kind of biographical sequencing. We find examples of this particularly among upwardly mobile males who, unwillingly, progress from one qualification pathway to another without ever testing out the 'market value' of the various certificates acquired (Alheit, 1995). This leads to moratorium cycles at progressively higher levels, where 'the sky's the limit'. Those strategies probably owe their biographical attractiveness to the fact that such passages are not 'individualised', but are traversed in new peer groups, so that loss of solidarity can be compensated by new patterns of social integration that are, of course, less binding in nature.

However, there are also the typical female patchworkers. At a first glance, these are 'hoppers' between employment and family phases in biography. If we observe this group more closely, we also see how they gradually detach themselves from their background milieux and how they frequently achieve quite astonishing leaps in qualification level (Schlüter, 1993). But again, the way they go is no 'career', the experiences they make in various passages are 'in relation'. It could almost seem as if patchworking is an alternative integration strategy for coping with the breakdown of social backgrounds involved in upward social mobility – ambivalent as it is for both men and women. How this process affects biography is completely open, both socially and individually.

The third and final type, namely designers, are biographical engineers for whom the openness of social space has become the design principle for their biography. They have established the greatest distance from the 'normal' life-course scripts and utilise the free space provided by the 'artificiality' inherent in the biographies of upwardly mobile. They are no longer 'narrators', but collage artists. Designers stage and aestheticise their own biography: the relationship to their parents, brothers and sisters, their hetero- and homosexual passions, their sophisticated preferences (Scheuermann, 1994). Designers are hedonists. They utilise their biographies as a stage.

We find this group in the most recent milieux of Western societies, among homosexuals, ravers and computer freaks. It is difficult to establish at first whether such self-stylisations represent a mere transitional phase, part of a temporary lifestyle as it were, or whether they conceal new and increasingly independent patterns for the biographical processing of reality.

What is striking, however, is that a cautious separation of concrete biographical actions from their action environments is apparent in the very presentation of these three types of construction. The basic assumptions of classical socialisation theories, namely that social expectations can be linked to individual needs, are thrown into question. System integration and social integration drift apart. There is also increasing evidence to suggest that it is the individuals themselves who have to create their own action environments on their own terms first of all.

What we are dealing with in the case of the coping patterns described in the foregoing are not just simple reactions to macro-social changes, *outputs* that occur in predictable ways in response to social *inputs*, but also in a certain sense '*intakes*', with forms of coping that are primarily determined not by the social impulse, but by an extant logic of biographical experience (Alheit, 1997; Alheit and Dausien, 1999). Just as Maturana's organisms respond to 'perturbations' in their environment according to their own *inner* logic, as opposed to the laws of that external environment, so, too, do modern biographies process social change according to the 'logic' of amassed self-referential experience, not the patterns generated by systemic functionalities (see Maturana and Varela, 1988).

There are, of course, historical dimensions to this observation. The individual in traditional societies was still an integral part of society as a totality, and biographical reality was not yet a distinct phenomenon alongside the individual's social reality. These spheres diverge in modernity, are unable to combine without generating problems, and may indeed come into a precarious conflict with each other in late modernity. The discoveries of symbolic interactionism, the highly interesting reconstructions of the 'society within us' (see Mead, 1934), provide indications in this respect. If such insight into the 'sociality' of the biographic is one of the central discoveries of 'classical' modernity in industrial society, then perhaps the '*biographicity*' *of the social* is a major discovery of the second, 'reflexive' modernity.

However, this does not imply in any way that there is no longer any relationship between the individual and society, that arbitrariness is supplanting the understanding and shaping of our social future. What it does mean, however, is that a risk-laden gap is opening up between the human-centred shaping of the total and the autonomous self-realisation of the individual. The postmodernisation of society and the biographisation of the social are contradictory learning processes at first that do not automatically end in a utopian *learning society*.

The opportunities provided at the 'meso-level': civil public spheres as new learning environments

I will admit at once, of course, that these insights are by no means absolutely new for educationalists. In a certain sense they belong to the everyday business of the well-informed adult educator. We find statements of a similar bent in the *Delors Report* (Delors, 1996), for example. Its 'banner', *Learning: The Treasure Within*, could well be understood as a tribute to the 'networkers', 'patchworkers' and 'designers' I have been talking about. 'The idea of *lifelong learning*', writes John Field (1998: 1) in a recent paper,

> draws attention not to education or training – traditional domains of policy makers – but to learning, which is undertaken by individuals and organisations without much involvement by the state. A policy approach based on learning will be radically different from one based on education and training.

The stimulating and pioneering study by Paul Fordham *et al.* (1979) provides excellent insights into the socio-political importance of informal learning. The peculiar euphoria attached to the Assessment of Prior (Experiential) Learning concept (AP(E)L) is another indication of this. Members of the 'fan club' for informal learning range from management consultants to alternative adult education initiatives. Sensitisation to an *informalisation* of the entire education domain is thus an indisputable phenomenon.

Yet here, too, the devil is in the nuts and bolts. The APEL debate is an instructive case in this respect. The problem is not the 'discovery' and 'acceptance' of informal learning, but rather its *evaluation*. This presupposes more precise notions about the extent to which informal learning can be operationalised. Quite obviously, it is not enough for emphatic educationalists to emphasise the benefit or usefulness of informal learning, perhaps with reference to Polanyi's concept of 'tacit knowledge'. The British example shows us how crucial it is that self-reflexive objectivations of one's own learning experiences be made *visible* in some sense. This 'accounting to oneself' must then be subjected to certain assessments – namely an evaluation concept with a strong political bias.

So far, all power has been in the hands of those on the receiving end of informal learning. They have the capacity to determine which informal prerequisites are useful and which are not. In the process, the newly discovered forms of learning run the risk of being instrumentalised and exploited. A more precise analysis, particularly of the vocational training system, shows that although this selective power is *legalised* as a rule, it is by no means *legitimised*. In the German system of vocational training, for example, it is never disclosed why or how a particular form of entitlement to participate in segments of the labour market, and the abundance of regulated training procedures that this generally involves, is related to subsequent processes of work, utilisation and learning. The precondition for integrating informal learning processes, however, would be that companies or continuing education institutions that link entry to specific evidence of entitlement reveal and justify their particular requirements. Only then are applicants given the chance to adapt their learning profiles to the perspectives of those on the 'customer' side, and to integrate any potentially important informal skills in a meaningful way. As long as the vocational training system merely regulates, while in essence lacking any legitimation, there is a risk of uncontrolled exploitation.

What we are obviously facing here is the political core of the *learning society* debate. Major projects fired by a certain theoretical understanding of society (as in the 1960s and 1970s) are not the central issue here, but rather the realisation that informal learning in modern societies can unfold its quality only if the intermediary locations for learning (companies, organisations and educational institutions) change in parallel, if genuinely new learning environments and new learning publics come into being. A generally accepted informalisation of learning cannot be achieved without democratisation.

Now there are indeed some highly developed concepts that attribute outstanding significance to this rather self-willed intermediary level. Gramsci's (1977) idea of a *società civile*, a civil society, provides impulses in this respect that are just as important as Habermas's (1962) concept of *Öffentlichkeit*, or 'public sphere'. Both sets of proposals are based on communicative processes of consensus-building that are neither state-regulated nor economically instrumentalised. Another factor common to both is that they do not isolate the intermediary level within civil society, but relate instead to real social conflicts and debates. Gramsci speaks – from a more militant stance than Habermas – of 'wars of position' for cultural and political hegemonies, while Habermas uses the terms 'deliberative politics', the capacity of civil associations to achieve their ends with arguments.

In 1997, Neil S. Smelser, the influential American sociologist, gave a series of lectures on the state of the art in current sociology while he was the incumbent of the Georg Simmel guest professorship at the Humboldt University in Berlin. One of the key points he made was a prediction that 'if we do not keep our eye on the meso level, we are likely to be ignoring the most important features of the society of the coming decades'. Smelser uses the term 'meso level' to refer to the self-same intermediary processes in social life, juxtaposed between the macro- and micro-levels, in which Gramsci and Habermas are also interested. They are 'the heart and soul of civil society'.

Adult education in virtually all Western societies has its origins in this sphere. Over the last hundred years, however, it has increasingly become either a vehicle for implementing state control, or indeed a market instrument. The diffusion and postmodernisation of macro-level structures and the surprising growth in the importance of the micro-level are now generating an opportunity to root adult education in civil society. There are already some highly interesting examples of this.

In the process by which titles have become devalued, especially those in the 'human services' and educational sectors, more and more university graduates in Europe are compelled to define new fields of professional practice *themselves*. After graduation, they gather experience in initiatives, non-profit-making associations and the like. More and more work on a freelance or self-employed basis. Some set up staff-managed associations organised along quasi-co-operative lines. In Austria, Germany, Denmark or the Netherlands, for example, these co-operatively structured organisations have developed into an important segment of the labour market and a terrain on which social science and teacher-training graduates can gain practical experience (see Körber and Effinger, 1995; Körber, 1998).

A professional action sphere gradually ensues between private households and informal communities, on the one hand, and the public spheres of the market and the state, with their formal organisations of companies and public administration, on the other. New organisations of this kind may be conducted like public institutions or private-sector enterprises, but they do not perform any state functions, nor do they have a definite commercial purpose (Alheit, 1994).

The protagonists of these new, *intermediary* forms of work perform their person-related services in the educational, social and health-care fields with such success because they mostly operate outwardly as 'staged communities'. The traditional primary communities, such as family, neighbourhood and organic milieux, are partly supplemented and partly substituted by them. Such tasks can no longer be performed *en passant* within the complex framework of housework and family work, through voluntary commitment or sporadic unpaid labour, as used to be the case.

How symptomatic and crucial this development could be is shown by the fact that traditional institutions such as schools, evening schools, theatres or broadcasting companies are also starting to take on intermediary functions (Körber and Effinger, 1995). The relationship between 'producers' and 'consumers' of the respective services is 'de-hierarchised' in the process. The user of such services is viewed less and less as a client, in the original sense of *ward*, i.e. as a dependent and unknowing pupil, a recipient of aid, a person affected or in need of care, and instead as an autonomous and knowing *customer*, who is also actively involved in the production of the service in his or her capacity as co-producer.

What we are already seeing here are elements of the 'New Way' with which adult education could reach its public, and the public change itself as part of a civil *Öffentlichkeit*. An interesting aspect here is that a model is developing in response to scarcity, and not as an artificial academic construct.

It is true, of course, these are still rather marginal phenomena at present, and that the informalisation of the classical meso-level institutions, the actual organisations, enterprises and associations, is still in its infancy. Yet the thesis I am propounding is that it is precisely here that the tasks and the opportunities of the *learning society* lie; in a civil bargaining process, it is essential to fill and shape the important space between systemic macro-structures and the biographical micro-world, two spheres that are drifting further and further apart. This involves not only risks of systemic monopolisation, but also and without doubt interesting perspectives for a new civil public sphere.

I would like to conclude by summarising my analytical observations in the form of three theses that I consider to be research desiderata for adult education in the years to come.

Outlook: three theses

Thesis 1   The idea of the *learning society* is not a concept divorced from the political, bus represents a programme for civil publics that have to be further developed and newly shaped in institutions and enterprises, urban districts and associations, in trade unions and co-operatives. It bears a greater affinity to traditions like the 'study circles' in Sweden or the '*associazionismo*' in Italy than to the discourse in the USA on self-directed learning. The crucial legitimation for a *learning society* in this sense derives from the collapse of systemic integration and social integration in the advanced societies of Western Europe and North America, and in the transitional societies of Central and Eastern Europe. How to fill this gap is thus an empirical research issue as well. The notion of *popular adult education* suggests the beginnings of an empirical focus on similar issues. The debate on the significance of *social capital* in social learning processes, initiated by Tom Schuller (1998) in particular, would be another interesting research variant.

Thesis 2   We are observing a paradigm shift away from the concepts of education and training towards the concept of *learning*, in other words from a 'system-controlled' to a 'learner-controlled' notion of education and training. This has impacts on adult education in everyday practice. We must abandon classical 'pathways' in education and hermetic qualification cycles, and invent more flexible, more informal ways of learning. To achieve this, we first need in-depth research on the educational biographies of the most diverse target groups, on their very specific constructional achievements in the face of social change (Alheit and Dausien, 1996). Second, we need a more precise concept for the 'modularisation' of useful qualification assets. The qualifications of learners are increasingly constituted as a kind of 'patchwork' or 'mosaic'. It must therefore be possible to acquire parts of this patchwork in very different ways and in very different phases of biography (Alheit et al., 1998). There is a lack of research here on the 'matching' of informal skills and formalised expectations on the part of institutions and enterprises regarding the 'elementarisation' of social learning.

Thesis 3   It has never been more apparent than nowadays that neither syllabi nor didactic expertise provide a guarantee for participant-oriented education. Instead, autonomous development on the part of the learning subject is enabled by *learning environments*. And learning environments include economic and social structures. We are familiar with the latent middle-class bias of informal learning settings. We know that 'learning companies' or 'learning organisations' (Jones and Hendry, 1994) do not adopt a more open and inviting attitude vis-à-vis educationally excluded groups, but a more defensive stance instead. We therefore need the courage to pursue educational alternatives in this area as well. Debate on a *civil sector* (Alheit, 1997, 1998) or a *'civilian's society'* (Beck, 1996) are starting points at best. In order to test them out, the learning society needs discourses and controversial debate, real utopias and 'future workshops'. What it needs above all are agents drawn from both the scientific community *and* everyday life. Both are equally important.

References

Alheit, P. (1993) 'Die Ambivalenz von Bildung in modernen Gesellschaften: Strukturprinzip kumulativer Ungleichheit oder Potential biographischer Handlungsautonomie?', *Pädagogische Rundschau*, 47, 1, 53–67.

Alheit, P. (1994) *Zivile Kultur. Verlust und Wiederaneignung der Moderne*, Frankfurt, New York.

Alheit, P. (1995) ' "Patchworkers": Biographical Constructions and Professional Attitudes – Study Motivations of Adult Education Students', in Peter Alheit *et al.* (eds), *The Biographical Approach in European Adult Education*, Wien: Edition Volkschochschule.

Alheit, P. (1996) 'Changing Basic Rules of Biographical Construction: Modern Biographies at the end of the 20th Century', in Ansgar Weymann and Walter R. Heinz (eds), *Society and Biography. Interrelationships Between Social Structure, Institutions and the Life Course*, Weinheim.

Alheit, P. (1997) 'Individuelle Modernisierung' – Zur Logik biographischer Konstruktion in modernisierten modernen Gesellschaften, in Stefan Hradil (ed.), *Differenz und Integration. Die Zukunft moderner Gesellschaften*. Verhandlungen des 28. Kongresses für Soziologie 1996 in Dresden, Frankfurt, New York.

Alheit, P. (1998) 'Two Challenges to a Modern Concept of Lifelong Learning', in P. Alheit and E. Kammler (eds), *Lifelong Learning and its Impact on Social and Regional Development*, Bremen.

Alheit, P. and Dausien, B. (1996) Bildung als 'biographische Konstruktion'? Nichtintendierte Lernprozesse in der organisierten Erwachsenenbildung, *Report*, 37, 33–45.

Alheit, P. and Dausien, B. (1999) Die biographische Konstruktion der Wirklichkeit Überlegungen zur Biographizität des Sozialen, in Erika M. Hoerning (ed.), *Biographische Sozialisation*, Stuttgart.

Alheit, P. *et al.* (1994) *Die Kehrseite der 'Erlebnisgesellschaft'. Eine explorative Studie.* 2. erweiterte und überarbeitete Auflage, Bremen.

Alheit, P. *et al.* (eds) (1998) *'Assessment of Prior Experiential Learning (APEL)', Eine Dokumentation*, Bremen.

Baudrillard, J. (1983) *Die Agonie des Realen*, Berlin.

Beck, U. (1992) *Risk Society*, London.

Beck, U. (1996) 'Kapitalismus ohne Arbeit', *Der Spiegel* 20/1996, 140–146.

Bourdieu, P. (1979) *La distinction. Critique sociale du jugement*, Paris.

Bourdieu, P. (1983) Ökonomisches Kapital, kulturelles Kapital, soziales Kapital, in Reinhard Kreckel (ed.), *Soziale Ungleichheiten*, Göttingen, 183–198.

Delors, J. (1996) *Learning: the treasure within*, Paris, UNESCO.

Dohmen, G. (1996) *Das lebenslange Lernen. Leitlinien einer modernen Bildungspolitik*, Bonn.

Edwards, R. (1995) 'Behind the Banner. Whither the Learner Society?' in *Adults Learning*, 187–189.

Effinger, H. (1990) *Individualisierung und neue Formen der Kooperation*, Wiesbaden.

Field, J. (1998) Informal and Social Learning (unpublished paper, DfEE/ESRC Research Seminar on Lifelong Learning, Sheffield, 8 July).

Fordham, P., Poulton, G. and Randle, L. (1979) *Learning Networks in Adult Education: Non-formal Education on a Housing Estate*, London.

Friedeburg, L. v. (1994) 'Bildung zwischen Aufklärung und Anpassung', in Peter Alheit *et al.* (eds), *Von der Arbeitsgesellschaft zur Bildungsgesellschaft? Perspektiven von Arbeit und Bildung im Prozeß europäischen Wandels*, Bremen.

Giddens, A. (1990) *Consequences of Modernity*, Oxford.

Gramsci, A. (1977) *Quaderni del carcere*. Edizione dell'Istituto Gramsci. A cura di V. Gerratana, Vol. 4, Torino.

Habermas, J. (1962) *Strukturwandel der Öffentlichkeit. Untersuchungen zu einer Kategorie der bürgerlichen Gesellschaft*, Neuwied, Berlin.

Hagestad, G. (1989) 'Social Perspectives on the Life Course', paper to be published in R. Binstock and L. George (eds), *Handbook of Aging and the Social Sciences* (3rd edn), New York: Academic Press.

Jones, A.M. and Hendry, C. (1994) 'The Learning Organization: Adult Learning and Organizational Transformation', *British Journal of Management*, 5, 153–162.

Körber, K. (1998) 'From Social Movement to Professionalisation – New tasks and New Institutions Between Market, State and Communities', in Peter Alheit and Eva Kammler (eds), *Lifelong Learning and its Impact on Social and Regional Development*, Bremen.

Körber, K. and Effinger, H. (1995) 'Zur Professionalisierung von personenbezogenen Dienstleistungen in intermediären Organisationen', *Grundlagen der Weiterbildung*, 6, 347–352.

Kreckel, R. (1992) *Politische Soziologie sozialer Ungleichheit*, Frankfurt, New York.

Lyotard, F. (1979) *La condition postmoderne. Rapport sur le savoir*, Paris.

Maturana, H.R. and Varela, F.J. (1988) *Der Baum der Erkenntnis*, Bern, München.

Mead, G.H. (1934) *Mind, Self and Society*, Chicago.

Sanctis, F. de (1988) *Verso un duemila educativo*, Torino.

Scheuermann, A. (1994) Homosexualität als biographische Konstruktion. Eine Studie über Sexualitätsbiographien, Diss. Phil. Bremen (unpublished manuscript).

Schlüter, A. (ed.) (1993) *Bildungsmobilität. Studien zur Individualisierung von Arbeitertöchtern in der Moderne*, Weinheim.

Schuller, T. (1998) 'Human and social capital. Variations Within a Learning Society', in Peter Alheit and Eva Kammler (eds), *Lifelong Learning and its Impact on Social and Regional Development*, Bremen.

Schulze, G. (1992) *Die Erlebnisgesellschaft. Kultursoziologie der Gegenwart*, Frankfurt, New York.

Vester, M. *et al.* (1992) Neue soziale Millieux und pluralisierte Klassengesellschaft. Endberichte des Forschungsprojekts 'Der Wandel der Sozialstruktur und die Entstehung neuer gesellschaftlich-politischer Milieus' (unpublished paper), Hanover.

Vester, M. *et al.* (1993) *Soziale Milieux im gesellschaftlichen Strukturwandel. Zwischen Integration und Ausgrenzung*, Köln.

Weber, M. (1964) *Wirtschaft und Gesellschaft*, Tübingen.

Chapter 3

Lifelong learning and underemployment in the knowledge society

A North American perspective

D.W. Livingstone

Introduction

Since the 1970s there has been a quantum leap in advocacy for 'lifelong learning' in most advanced capitalist societies. The increasingly pervasive general assumption is that people will have to intensify their learning efforts in order to keep up with the rapidly growing knowledge requirements of a new 'knowledge economy'. This chapter will argue to the contrary that we are already living in a 'knowledge society' in which the collective learning achievements of adults far outpace the requirements of the economy as paid work is currently organized. The knowledge society dwarfs the knowledge economy. Lifelong learning is alive and well. It is the relative withering of good jobs with decent pay that is the central problem creating the education–jobs gap. Unprecedented levels of adult learning coexist with burgeoning underemployment of this knowledge in the workplace. The major focus of this chapter will be on documenting the extent of adult learning and underemployment with particular attention to Canada and the USA. But first it may be useful to try to unpack some of the multiple meanings attributed to 'lifelong learning'.

Dimensions of lifelong learning

All human beings are continually engaged in social learning. We are born more helpless than most other species and then constantly socialized by ever more complex and sophisticated communications with other humans throughout our lives. By adulthood, we are likely to engage in a multitude of individually or collectively initiated learning activities in different contexts and with distinct orientations.

Three general sorts of adult learning practices are commonly distinguished in terms of the context in which they occur: formal education or schooling;

This is an edited version of an article published in *Comparative Education* 135, 2 (1999): 163–186.

informal learning; and non-formal, continuing or further education (see Selman and Dampier, 1991; and Percy, 1997). *Formal education* has been defined as full-time study within state-certified school systems. *Informal learning* refers to all those individual and collective learning activities that we do beyond the authority or requirements of any educational institution. Any deliberate effort to gain new understanding, knowledge or skill to which we devote a discernible amount of time and recognize as such may be considered to be an informal learning project. *Continuing education* is all other organized educational activities, including further courses or training programmes offered by any social institution. It is such organized continuing educational programmes offered mainly to adults on a part-time basis by diverse authorities that have been the primary focus in most recent academic and policy discussions about 'lifelong learning' and 'permanent education culture'.

But these learning contexts overlap and interact. While a lock-step march from the end of schooling into the permanent workforce used to be common, we now see multiple transitions between full-time school and full-time work, and frequent combining of part-time paid work with part-time schooling. Informal learners can base their learning without a formal instructor on the same curricular materials as formal schooling or continuing education programmes. In spite of the preoccupation in most recent discussions on the growth or need for growth of continuing education, most adult learning, as we shall see, remains informal. Informal learning is the usually hidden part of the adult learning 'iceberg' that supports and animates these more visible parts (see Knowles, 1970; and Brookfield, 1981).

The growth of the knowledge society: pyramids and icebergs of learning

The cumulative body of human knowledge has grown greatly as we have created new means of collecting raw data, converted the data into useful information and organized information into diverse bodies of knowledge (Machlup, 1962, 1978–80, 1980; Porat, 1977). By virtually every measure on every dimension of learning, *people are now spending more time acquiring knowledge than ever before in the history of our continually learning species.* We will document the recent expansion briefly in terms of schooling, continuing education and informal learning.

The continuing growth of schooling

The rate of participation in formal schooling has grown almost continuously throughout the past century. In the USA, from a tiny minority participating in high school in the early years of the century, the majority of youths were graduating from high school by the end of the 1930s' depression. The high

Table 3.1 Formal educational attainments, employed USA labour force, 1972–94

Attainments	1972 (%)	1976 (%)	1980 (%)	1986 (%)	1990 (%)	1994 (%)
<High school	32	25	18	15	12	10
High school diploma	52	52	58	56	56	54
College certificate	2	3	4	5	7	7
Bachelor degree	10	15	17	17	17	20
Graduate degree	5	6	7	7	9	10

Source: Davis and Smith (1994).

school enrolment ratio continued to climb to near universality in the 1990s. Although 'stopping out' has become greater since the early 1970s, over two-thirds of each age group are now graduating from high school with their cohort and over 90 per cent graduate eventually (Sandia Laboratories, 1993). Between 1900 and 1980, the participation rate in college doubled every 20 years, with majority participation of the eligible age group being reached by the early 1970s. During the past generation, the formal educational attainment profile of the employed American labour force has changed very substantially, as Table 3.1 suggests. Clearly, the portion of the labour force without a high school diploma has been reduced to a small minority during this period, while the percentage who have post-secondary credentials has doubled, to about a third of the labour force.

A comparable Canadian profile of recent changes in the formal educational attainment level of the active labour force appears in Table 3.2. This table documents changes between 1978 and 1996 in the formal attainments of the labour force in Canada's industrial heartland of Ontario, on the basis of biennial population surveys (Livingstone *et al.*, 1997). During this period, the aggregate educational attainments of the Ontario workforce have also increased very significantly. In 1978, high school drop-outs made up nearly half the labour force. By 1996, only about a quarter had less than a high school diploma, while there had been very substantial gains in the proportions completing high school, college and university programmes. Particularly in the light of the very rapid development of the community college programme in Canada since the late 1960s, more workers now have some kind of post-secondary credential than have only a high school diploma.

While the American and Canadian labour forces remain the most highly schooled in the world, similar trends have occurred in other OECD countries, with high school diplomas rapidly becoming commonplace and substantial growth in the proportions with post-secondary credentials (OECD, 1994). Virtually everywhere, the labour force has quickly continued to become more highly schooled.

Table 3.2 Formal educational attainments, employed Ontario labour force, 1978–96

Attainments	1978 (%)	1980 (%)	1982 (%)	1984 (%)	1986 (%)	1988 (%)	1990 (%)	1992 (%)	1994 (%)	1996 (%)
<High school	47	42	40	36	33	33	27	26	25	24
High school diploma	29	32	33	34	36	36	38	38	39	36
College certificate	12	12	13	15	16	15	17	18	18	21
University degree	12	13	13	14	15	15	17	18	19	19

Source: OISE Survey of Educational Issues Data Archive.

The further education boom

Since the 1960s, largely voluntary adult participation in further education courses on a part-time basis, or non-formal education, has generally increased even more quickly than formal school enrolments in most OECD countries. In North America, adult participation has grown from very small numbers. According to the best available estimates, summarized in Table 3.3, the American annual participation of people over the age 17 years in further education courses went from minuscule levels to over 10 per cent by the early 1980s, and then tripled again by 1995. Similarly, only 4 per cent of Canadian adults were enrolled in continuing education courses in 1960, but the participation rate grew to 20 per cent by the early 1980s and to about a third by the mid-1990s. According to a Canadian national survey in 1989, over a quarter of employed workers had plans to begin a major educational programme during the next 5 years (Lowe, 1992: 58–59), while a 1986 Ontario survey found that about half of all adults intended to take at least a single *course* in the foreseeable future (Livingstone et al., 1995: 6–7).

A more detailed analysis of recent trends in adult education participation in Ontario (Livingstone, 1998) indicates that these increases have occurred across virtually all social groups. Between 1986 and 1992, participation rates of the total adult Ontario population almost doubled from 20 per cent to 36 per cent. Significant increases were found in all age groups and at all levels of formal educational attainment, especially among younger adults and high school drop-outs. Young employed high school drop-outs tripled their participation rates. Enthusiasm for further education is also indicated by the fact that public support for increased government funding of adult literacy and retaining programmes has consistently been even stronger than for the formal school system (Livingstone et al., 1989, 1991, 1993, 1995).

Many European countries, particularly Scandinavia, have much longer traditions of active participation in and state support for adult recurrent education courses than the USA and Canada. Sweden has probably been

Table 3.3 Annual adult education course participation rates, USA and Canada, 17+
population, 1960–95

	1960 (%)	1981–83 (%)	1991 (%)	1995 (%)
USA	<5	13	32	40
Canada	4	20	28	38

Sources: Devereaux (1985); Merriam and Caffarella (1991); Selman and Dampier (1991); Statistics Canada (1995, 1996); US Department of Education (1996).

the world leader in promoting more flexible ways of combining education with work and leisure throughout the adult life course. Consequently, adult education participation rates there lead the world. As Tuijnman observes, on the basis of a unique longitudinal study: 'the past three decades have witnessed a nearly exponential growth in the extent to which people in Sweden have taken part in programs of adult recurrent education' (Tuijnman, 1989: 59). By the end of the 1980s, about half the adult Swedish population was participating annually in further education courses (Tuijnman, 1989: 60). Comparable figures for Germany were around 40 per cent (German Ministry of Education, 1993). British adult education participation rates appear to be somewhat lower, but have also been increasing substantially since 1980 (Sargent, 1991). Nearly all European governments have recently been expanding provision for adult education and facilitating participation, especially in vocational retraining courses (OECD, 1991; Tuijnman, 1992). In Japan as well there has been a recent proliferation of lifelong learning centres where people of all ages can study any subject; the best estimates suggest that over 30 per cent of the adult population are now participating in such courses annually (Japanese Ministry of Education, 1994; Masatoshi et al., 1994). A permanent education culture is rapidly becoming a reality in all of these countries.

Adult job training programmes

Comparing adult job training programmes across countries is very difficult, both because of differences in the forms of provision and the lack of surveys using similar criteria (OECD, 1991). Very few comparable surveys are even available within most countries to assess trends in employee participation in training courses over time. But there are strong indications that workplace-based training programmes have generally been growing and broadening their functions since at least around 1980. Three roughly comparable American surveys suggest fairly rapid growth. In 1983 only about a quarter of American employees had received any training courses since being hired (OECD, 1991: 147). By 1991, well over half had participated in a training course within the last 2 years (Knoke and Kalleberg, 1995), and by 1993 over 70 per cent of employers claimed to be providing some type of formal job training programme to their employees (US Department of Labor, 1994). A number of the most comparable and inclusive Canadian surveys suggest that annual participation in employer-sponsored training programmes has increased from around 5 per cent in the mid-1960s to between 10 and 15 per cent in the next two decades and to over 20 per cent in the mid-1990s (Betcherman et al., 1997, p. 4). Other Canadian studies also indicate that there has been an acceleration of the number of workers taking various training courses since the 1980s (Crompton, 1992: 30–38; Bennett, 1994: 22–25). In Europe as well, as Tuijnman (1992: 677) summarizes, 'the overall picture is one of expansion in continuing vocational education, especially job training'. In Japan, over two-thirds of all employees have received some off-the-job training since joining their current enterprise and many new institutions have recently been developed to provide such training (OECD, 1991: 149; Makino, 1996).

Employers are spending increasing amounts to fund employee training programmes. In the USA, rapid expansion is suggested by recent growth rates of over 10 per cent per year in the expenditures on direct training by organizations with over 100 employees (cited in Marschall, 1990). Canadian firms have been spending about half as much on training employees as American firms (Crompton, 1992; Bennett, 1994). In Japanese firms, training budgets have consistently grown faster than wages, generally over 10 per cent per year (Dore and Sako, 1989: 80). Many European governments have traditionally spent more on training programmes than North American and Japanese regimes (OECD, 1989). But it should be noted here that there is no simple correlation between employer expenditures on training courses and employee participation in them. In the first place, few firms have kept accurate records of even their direct training expenditures, and there is no international standard as to what counts as a direct cost (OECD, 1991: 145). Japanese data, for example, are relatively minimal estimates, excluding the wages of those engaged in training courses. It appears that Japanese workers themselves spend about six times as much as their employers do on their workplace-related training (Dore and Sako, 1989: 143), whereas North American employers have been paying for about two-thirds of their employees' work-related courses (Betcherman, 1992). Nevertheless, the best available international comparisons suggest that Japanese employers spend from two to five times as much on employee training as North American employers do.

By any measure, North American employers appear to be underinvesting in long-term employee training programmes relative to employers in most other OECD countries (see Betcherman, 1992; and Bishop, 1992). While the incidence of employer-sponsored training for legislated health and safety provisions, specific job-related computer skills and encouraging employee teamwork have certainly increased (Betcherman *et al.*, 1997), there remains little short-term incentive for North American employers to invest in broader-based and longer-term training programmes when skill surpluses abound and both current and prospective employees are already making extraordinary efforts to get further education on their own.

The most immediate consequence of the distinctive North American combination of very high formal educational attainments, rapidly increased popular demand for adult education and employers' relative reluctance to pay for more ongoing training programmes is the greater growth of general certification and general interest courses than substantial job training programmes, as has been the case in Ontario adult education programmes since the mid-1980s (Livingstone *et al.*, 1993: 26–27). In the longer term, this trend portends a North American labour force that is even more highly educated, but without some of the specific technical vocational skills that may be immediately required to do some specific jobs.

The informal learning iceberg

Informal learning is much more difficult to distinguish and measure than participation in formal schooling or continuing adult participation in institution-based education programmes. Whether such learning is initiated incidentally or by premeditation, and whether it occurs in individual or collective contexts, the critical point is that this knowledge has been acquired through our own voluntary efforts (see Garrick, 1996). The empirical research studies initiated by Allen Tough in the late 1960s document that *most* adults are regularly involved in deliberate, self-directed learning projects beyond school and training programmes. As Tough summarized the central finding from a wide array of studies in the 1970s:

> The typical learner conducts five quite distinct learning projects in one year. He or she learns five distinct areas of knowledge and skill. The person spends an average of 100 hours per learning effort – a total of 500 hours per year.
>
> (1978: 252)

The few roughly comparable sample surveys conducted in the USA and Canada since the early 1970s on the general frequency of informal learning are summarized in Table 3.4. The findings suggest that, in spite of the substantial expansion of participation in formal and non-formal education, North American adults generally have continued to spend much greater and perhaps increasing amounts of time on informal learning projects (see also Candy, 1993). Certainly the proliferation of information technologies and exponential increases in the production of information have created

Table 3.4 Estimated average frequency of informal learning activities, USA and Canada, 1975–96

Survey	No. of projects	Hours/ project	Total hours	% informal learners
Hiemstra (1976) [N = 256; Nebraskans over 55 years]	3.3	98	325	84
Penland (1977) [N = 1,501; American national adult population]	3.3	155	514	76
Tough (1978) [estimate based on 1970s case studies]	5	100	500	N/A
Lecan and Sisco (1981) [N = 93; rural Vermont school drop-outs]	4	106	425	98
Livingstone et al. (1997) [N = 1,000; Ontario adult population]	N/A	N/A	600+	86

massively greater opportunities for informal learning beyond their own direct experience by people in all works of life in recent years. Institutional education programmes and courses are indeed, as Tough (1979) originally suggested, the tip of the adult learning iceberg.

Informal learning on the job

A recent international study of skill formation at work concluded that:

> Learning-by-doing, while the most prevalent kind of work learning, is also the most invisible and the least documented. Visibility increases where skill formation is the product of a mixture of on-the-job and off-the-job training or of off-the-job training alone. There has been a relative paucity of empirical work on skill formation which is work-led rather than training-led.
>
> (OECD, 1993: 30)

Several recent American and Canadian national surveys have found that over 70 per cent of the job training received by employees is informal (Ekos Research Associates, 1993; US Department of Labor, 1996). The most recent in-depth American study of over 1,000 workers in seven companies across seven states (Center for Workforce Development, 1998) again finds this 70 per cent figure and concludes that:

Informal learning was widespread and served to fulfill most learning needs. In general, we noted that informal learning was highly relevant to employee needs and involved knowledge and skills that were attainable and immediately applicable ... Workers constantly learn and develop while executing their day-to-day job responsibilities, acquiring a broad range of knowledge and skills.

(1998: 1)

The cumulative evidence clearly demonstrates that the populations of the USA and Canada have achieved unprecedented levels of formal credentials and these levels have continued to increase rapidly. It is not inevitable, however, that these trends will continue. Participation at lower levels of schooling has reached universality. The proportions of young people enrolling in universities and colleges could decline if the tuition costs continue to increase and the benefits decrease. But the popular demand for knowledge *per se* shows few signs of declining and even now is not centred in the pyramids of formal schooling and further education courses for most adults. As the evidence further documents, the levels of informal practical knowledge attained in the workplace and in everyday life by even the least formally educated people have been both very extensive and generally unrecognized or discounted in public debate and job hiring policies. The pyramids of schooling continue to be supported by massive icebergs of informal learning in most spheres of life in our increasingly knowledgeable society. The icebergs are at least as deep as the pyramids are high. However, as we will see in the next section, getting decent work even with extensive formal educational credentials is quite another matter for growing numbers of people.

Underemployment and the myth of the 'knowledge economy'

The emergence of a 'post-industrial' workplace dominated by highly educated information service workers has been heralded since the early 1960s (see especially Bell, 1973). The theories of post-industrialism have promoted the belief that the prevalence of information processing over material handling in the mode of production would necessitate skill upgrading and greater creativity and critical thinking of workers. In short, post-industrial/knowledge economy theories generally assume or assert that *workers increasingly require more skill, become more involved in planning their own work, and increasingly constitute a professional class.* As I have documented in detail elsewhere (Livingstone, 1998), the image of contemporary society inherent in post-industrial/knowledge economy and human capital theories has proven to be illusory. While an aggregate upgrading of the technical skills needed for job performance is gradually occurring, our collective acquisition of work-related knowledge and credentials is far outpacing this incremental shift. Such underemployment is scarcely recognized in post-industrial and human capital theories, beyond the 'frictional adjustment' that is regarded as natural in market economies.

'Underemployment' denotes the wasted ability of the eligible workforce, including both job holders and those without paid employment. Six basic dimensions of underemployment have been identified (see Livingstone, 1998). These dimensions are: (1) the talent use gap; (2) structural unemployment; (3) involuntary reduced employment; (4) the credential gap; (5) the performance gap; and (6) subjective underemployment. All six of these dimensions now appear to represent very substantial chronic problems.

The talent use gap between those from socially disadvantaged origins and more affluent families, as indicated by the attainment of university degrees, has remained very wide throughout most of the past century of unprecedented expansion of formal schooling. Estimates of the extent of underemployment of initial talent are bound to be speculative because of the array of mediating factors that intervene between time of first school enrolment and entry into the labour market. But conservative estimates suggest that less than half the people from lower-class and some visible minority racial backgrounds who have the capability actually complete university. There are persistent systemic barriers that deny equal educational opportunity to these people on ascriptive grounds and result in underusing the learning talents of millions of people, at least 10–20 per cent of the adult US and Canadian populations in these terms (Curtis et al., 1992).

Structural unemployment refers to a persistent gap between the excess number of job seekers and the scarce number of available jobs. OECD (1994) studies of official unemployment rates have found that:

> Unemployment of 35 million, some 8.5 per cent of the OECD labour force, represents an enormous waste of human resources, reflects an important amount of inefficiency in economic systems, and causes a disturbing degree of social distress.
>
> (1994: 9)

But in all countries the official unemployment rates seriously underestimate the actual numbers of people who want full-time jobs. Researchers operating in the 'subemployment' tradition have estimated that underemployment in the USA ranged from 20–30 per cent of the available labour supply between 1969 and 1992 (Clogg, 1979; Sheak, 1994). These estimates include mainly official unemployment rates, discouraged workers and involuntary reduced employment (i.e. those who want full-time jobs but can only obtain part-time ones). Subemployment rates for Canada may be somewhat less accurate but are likely to be even higher given official Canadian unemployment rates (see Carrick, 1996).

The underemployment of those people who actually have jobs in less easily documented. I will examine two of these dimensions in more detail: the *credential gap* between educational attainments and established job entry requirements (Diamond and Bedrosian, 1970); and the *performance gap* between job holders' educational attainments and the actual task requirements of their occupations (Berg, 1970; Collins, 1979).

The credential gap

How closely matched are the educational attainments of job holders with the credentials required for entry into their current jobs? We hear frequent claims of 'credential inflation'. But there have been very few large-scale empirical studies of employers' actual entry requirements. Collins (1979: 5–7) reviewed the findings of the few prior American surveys based on employers' own reports. We have conducted a more recent series of Ontario surveys between 1982 and 1996 based on employees' reports of current entry requirements for their own jobs (see Livingstone *et al.*, 1997). Holzer (1996) has carried out 1992–94 surveys of employers in four American cities (Atlanta, Boston, Detroit and Los Angeles).

While these surveys deal with quite different populations, they do permit several basic trend inferences. First, while formal schooling was of little significance even for the professions through the mid-nineteenth century, by the 1930s post-secondary credentials had become an important criterion for entry into most professions; by the 1960s this requirement had become almost universal. With the post World War II expansion of the school system, post-secondary credentials also began to be commonly required for managerial posts, and by the 1980s a college degree had become a standard entry requirement. A high school diploma also became a common entry condition for clerical work after World War I; since then, entry requirements have increased fairly steadily, so that now nearly half the clerical jobs have post-secondary entry requirements, typically a community college certificate. The most dramatic recent increases in entry requirements have been among manual workers. In the 1930s hardly any manual labour jobs required a high school diploma. By the early 1980s, the majority of skilled manual jobs required a diploma for entry, and about a quarter called for some post-secondary certification. Since the early 1980s, there has been a very rapid increase in the use of high school graduation as a screen for entry into most unskilled manual jobs. Holzer's (1996: 54–57) recent surveys of the array of possible hiring criteria and activities finds that about three-quarters of all non-college jobs now use high school diplomas as an initial screen. Even to push a broom in a steel mill, you now need to have a diploma (see Livingstone, 1996). The 'credential society' has definitely arrived.

Since the late 1960s, the employment of large numbers of post-secondary graduates in jobs that only require lower educational entry credentials has been widely documented, especially in North America (Shelley, 1992; Holzer and Vroman, 1993: 81, 112; Livingstone, 1994). Their plight has become a regular feature in our newspapers (e.g. Theobald, 1997: C1). Several different measures of attainment–entry requirement mismatches have been used. Using a measure of surplus education based on differences between *years* of schooling attained and self-reported years of schooling required for job entry, Duncan and Hoffman (1978) found that over 40 per cent of American workers had 'surplus education' for their jobs in 1976. Subsequent studies have relied on more conservative estimates of mismatches based on *credentials attained* and *credentials required* rather than years of schooling. Canadian surveys suggest that around 20 per cent of the entire employed workforce and larger proportions of younger, more highly educated workers are 'overqualified' or underemployed in this sense of having a higher credential than their job requires for entry, and that another 20 per cent or so are underqualified (McDowell, 1991). Credential underemployment surely became greater with the explosion of post-secondary schooling in the 1960s, but have attainment–entry credential mismatches increased further among the employed workforce since then?

The best available data source to assess recent trends in the relationship between employees' educational attainments and the job entry requirements established by their employers is probably the 1982–96 biennial series of eight general population surveys we have conducted in Ontario (Livingstone *et al.*, 1997). These measures are based on respondents' self-reports of both their formal educational attainments and the current job entry credential requirements of their employers. During this period, aggregate educational credential attainments have increased significantly, with a reduction of high school drop-outs from around 40 per cent to about a quarter of the work-force, and roughly equal gains in the proportions who have completed high school, college or university programmes. Educational entry requirements have similarly increased, with an even sharper reduction in jobs that do not require a diploma, from over 40 per cent to less than a quarter of all jobs; most of this reduction occurred during the 1980s. The proportion of jobs requiring a high school diploma increased rapidly during the 1980s, from 26 to 45 per cent. During the 1990s, post-secondary credentials have increasingly been used as a screening criterion for job entry. Overall, it appears that job entry requirements have been increasing in fairly close correspondence with the increasing educational attainments of the labour force.

Further analysis (Livingstone, 1998) documents that substantial mismatches persist and there has been little significant general change in the proportions of credentially underemployed, matched and underqualified employees during this 14-year period in Ontario. At least half the workforce has consistently held educational credentials that match the entry requirements for their jobs. Around 20 per cent of the labour force has been underemployed. Slightly more have usually been underqualified. If employers increase entry requirements, it follows that many of those who are already performing the job with lower credentials will instantly become

underqualified in these terms. But a major recent change in entry requirements has been experienced by working-class employees. Among all industrial workers, the proportion of jobs with no diploma requirement has dropped
from over 60 per cent to about a third since 1982, while for all service workers the drop has been from over 50 per cent to around a quarter. But these
drastic aggregate increases in entry requirements for working-class jobs are
only reflected in marginal increases in the underqualification of the working
class, and are hardly noticeable for the labour force as a whole, because of corresponding increases in educational attainments. The recent rapid increases
in employers' job entry requirements have kept credential underemployment
levels fairly stable, and ensured that around a quarter of a workforce that has
increasingly become one of the most highly educated in the world remains
credentially underqualified for their jobs.

The performance gap

To what extent do employees have the levels of skill and knowledge actually needed to perform their jobs? The most commonly used indicator of
job skill levels for the USA and Canada has been the general educational
development (GED) scale, which provides estimates of required levels of
reasoning, mathematics, and language skills. The estimation of technical
skill requirements has been carried out primarily by government job analysts
and published in occasional dictionaries of occupational titles. The basic
pattern of findings about the extent of and recent changes in the performance gap is based on the best available data sources on the employed labour
forces for the USA and Canada (see Livingstone, 1998: 78–85) and the most
plausible GED-educational attainment equivalencies by Berg (1970).

The general trends are similar for both countries. The extent of performance underemployment appears to have increased during the current
generation. According to this measure, there was a gradual increase from
46 per cent to over 60 per cent of the employed American labour force being
underemployed between 1972 and 1990; the comparable figures for Ontario
suggest an increase from 44 per cent underemployment to just under 60 per
cent between 1980 and 1996, a slightly shorter but more recent period.
According to these equivalences, performance underemployment has now
become a majority condition for the North American labour force.

Age differences in the performance gap are quite pronounced, with nearly
two-thirds of workers between 18 and 24 years being underemployed
compared with one-third of those over 50 years. People with higher educational attainments are also more likely to be underemployed, but even
high school drop-outs frequently still have more education than their jobs
actually need. In conjunction with increasing performance underemployment trends these age and education differences suggest that the educational

attainments of the employed labour force recently have been increasing more quickly than the actual performance requirements of most jobs.

Other studies, not based on GED measures, have found that since the early 1970s almost a third of the employed North American workforce have had work-related skills that they could use in their jobs but have not been permitted to do so; this actual underuse appears to have grown to include over 40 per cent of the entire workforce in the 1990s.

In spite of much rhetoric about skill deficiencies of the current workforce, there is little evidence of any general and persistent technical skill deficit among employed workers. A recent survey by the National Center on the Educational Quality of the Workforce (1995) has found that American employers consider over 80 per cent of their employees to be fully technically proficient in their current jobs, and that most employers are more concerned with prospective employees' attitudes than their industry-based skills or prior school performance. The basic point is that the performance gap between high educational attainments and lower actual technical job skill requirements in North America is extensive and increasing on all available measures.

Subjective underemployment may have been slowly increasing during the past 25 years as several objective dimensions of underemployment have become more obvious. But in the most recent attitude surveys only 20–40 per cent of the entire workforce still express these sentiments about such aspects as perceived overqualification, untapped skills and entitlement to a better job (Livingstone, 1998). Consciousness of underemployment has not coalesced into a coherent viewpoint, at least not yet, perhaps partly because of the continuing public invisibility of both the credential gap and the performance gap.

The massive scale of underemployment

Since the USA and Canada have the most expanded systems of advanced formal schooling in the world, it is likely that the general extent of underemployment in most other advanced industrial countries is somewhat lower. But the available data on subemployment measures (i.e. official unemployment, discouraged workers, involuntary reduced employment) suggest that extensive underemployment on most dimensions probably exists in OECD countries.

An overall estimate of the extent of underemployment cannot simply be additive. In the USA and Canada, *objective* underemployment would affect well over 100 per cent of the workforce! However, it is safe to say that over half the potential American and Canadian adult workforces have experienced some of the overlapping dimensions of objective underemployment, and that significantly less have a coherent sense of their underemployment.

The massive scale of the underuse of knowledge and skills in current industrial market economies that is revealed by this analysis may still be difficult for most analysts to accept and may well appear incredible to the general reader – in spite of the fact that estimates of similar magnitude have been made by reputable scholars for over a generation now. But this assessment is based on merely applying the array of conventional measures of underemployment to the array of available databases.

Some critics will undoubtedly be able to find empirical grounds for lower estimates on specific dimensions of underemployment in particular times and places. Others have already suggested discarding underemployment as a social problem because underemployed college graduates have not become massively disaffected politically; and, furthermore, with continued post-secondary educational expansion, the marginal economic utility of more education is diminishing and seen to be leading to widespread acceptance of credential inflation (Smith, 1986). The relatively stable and limited nature of job entitlement beliefs in a context of increasing subemployment and performance underemployment over the past decade lends some support to the political aspect of this argument. But there is little credible aggregate-level evidence for declining capacity among college students. Objective underemployment, as estimated by various measures, continues to increase. The growing wastage of knowledge and skills in our workplaces should not be dismissed or relativized just because the highly schooled have not taken to the barricades. Rather than presumptively trivializing the problem, interested researchers should be looking more closely at the actual experiences of those currently living in the education–jobs gap.

Underemployment and lifelong learning

In-depth studies with people in various types of underemployment (see Livingstone, 1998) find that the underemployed typically continue to see themselves as active agents who aspire to transcend these conditions. The choices that are most frequently referred to are the pursuit of more work-related knowledge, either in terms of further schooling and continuing education courses or through their own informal learning.

Underemployment and continuing education

It was often suggested in the early studies in the underemployment tradition that workers might tend to become disenchanted both with further work-related learning and established society in general (e.g. O'Toole, 1975). But more recent empirical studies have found that the underemployed have been at least as likely as other employees to be planning further education. On the basis of a 1989 Canadian national survey, Lowe (1992: 58–59) concludes that:

Ironically, many individuals possessing higher credentials than required for their particular job believed that they must obtain even more education to compete effectively for a better job.

According to the 1989 Canadian national survey, further education plans were most common in sales and service jobs where people were most likely to feel overqualified (Lowe, 1992: 53–59). Further analysis of Ontario survey data indicates that the underemployed have been slightly more likely than others to have such plans, but that the majority of those who were underqualified also expect to take further courses. Only among the tiny numbers of workers who were highly underqualified on performance criteria and had only elementary schooling was there little expressed interest in further education courses in the mid-1980s (Livingstone et al., 1987).

General Ontario surveys between 1986 and 1996 have found no significant differences in *actual* participation rates between credentially underemployed, matched and underqualified workers (e.g. Livingstone, 1993). The credential gap has little effect on participation in further education courses. Those whose educational qualifications exceed the actual performance requirements of their jobs are also just as likely as those with matched statuses to participate in further education courses. However, the officially unemployed have increased their participation rates in further education programmes quite dramatically over the past decade, from relatively low rates of less than 10 per cent in the mid-1980s to around a third in the 1990s, as high a frequency as any other social group.

For the underemployed, the equation between more education and better jobs is far from certain in light of the underuse of education in their present jobs. But the apparent necessity to respond to this uncertainty by pursuing yet more formal education also remains largely unquestioned. Among the underqualified, there is a virtually unanimous equation between further educational credentials and either a better job or a fuller life. So, in spite of their common experience of a superficial connection between their formal educational attainments and the requirements of their current or recent jobs, both underqualified school drop-outs and underemployed university graduates continue to believe and act as if more education is the personal solution to living in the education–jobs gap. There are undoubtedly many motives associated with the popular demand for and engagement in adult education. But whether the major motivation is seen to be competition for scarce jobs, the desire to be an effective consumer or citizen, assertion of the democratic right to equal educational opportunity, a more generic quest for knowledge to cope with uncertain times, or even the joy of learning, there is now an almost universal general perception that more education is a fundamental imperative for adults in contemporary society.

Underemployment and informal learning

The empirical research on self-directed learning has demonstrated that informal learning outside organized courses is more extensive than course-based learning among adults. However, this research has paid virtually no attention to the informal learning practices of the underemployed (see Candy, 1933; and Adams et al., 1997). Our 1996 survey of the general adult population of Ontario (Livingstone et al., 1997) asked all respondents to estimate the amount of time they typically devoted to informal learning activities outside organized coursework. We have analysed these estimates by underemployment statuses.

Analyses of the incidence of informal learning by the credential gap have found no significant differences in either the amount of work-related or general interest learning between the underemployed, the matched and the underqualified. Regardless of one's credential gap status, the amount of informal learning people engage in appears to be very similar. Relations between the *performance gap* and informal learning activities are a bit different. Those who are moderately underqualified on performance criteria average more time in work-related informal learning than anybody else, about 400 hours a year. This may reflect their greater need to upgrade their skills for adequate job performance. But the small number who are highly underqualified for their jobs tend to spend less time in both work-related and general interest informal learning activities than any other group; this pattern is very similar to their participation in adult education courses. This group only represents about 5 per cent of the labour force and includes mainly people who are older with very little schooling; they typically have very limited income and very limited time for informal learning beyond their low-wage jobs. But even these people with little schooling and little discretionary time estimate that they devote an average of over 400 hours a year to informal learning.

Our in-depth follow-up studies with underemployed and underqualified people in Ontario (Livingstone, 1998) have confirmed that both underemployed university/college graduates and underqualified non-college workers spend at least as much time on informal work-related learning as people whose credentials match their jobs. They also spend much more time in informal learning projects than they do in organized course-based learning, generally about *ten times as much time*. Neither underemployment nor under-qualification serves to shrink the iceberg of informal learning.

As in prior studies that have compared patterns of informal learning across social groupings, variations in learning time *within* the underemployed college and underqualified non-college groups are much greater than the differences between them. In particular, there is no systemic difference between the credentially underemployed or underqualified and the rest of the workforce in their work-related continuing learning capacities and interests. Regardless of their work status and in spite of various institutional and material barriers, most people living in the education–jobs gap continue to engage in quite substantial informal learning activities.

In terms of the more specific content of their learning activities, both underemployed college graduates and underqualified non-college respondents participate in a wide array of work-related courses. School upgrading courses are most common among the credentially underqualified, while the underemployed are frequently involved in courses to develop additional vocational skills such as business administration. But the most common course participation in both groups now is in computer training.

Some of the flavour of the kinds of informal learning that underemployed and underqualified people engage in around their paid workplaces is conveyed by our in-depth respondents' comments:

> Our products are constantly changing. We're reading blueprints, drafting all kinds of new things. I learn something new almost every day. We're learning all the time, but it's not job retraining.
>
> (Underemployed middle-aged male industrial worker with a community college certificate)

> Once you get into a job, you realize how you start to learn more about business and what goes on. Formal education only has a minor role in the picture. There's a lot more learning to do once you finish school. You learn everyday at work.
>
> (Underemployed middle-aged female service worker with a university degree)

> Much of my learning in the last year has been in response to the downsizing of our whole plant. They're reorganizing the entire work structure, giving us more accountability. We have to learn new concepts of team participation. But I've also been taking the time to read up about my rights and options if the next lay-off hits me.
>
> (Underqualified middle-aged male factory worker with some high schooling)

> I've spent a lot of time in internal cross-training, with someone else to cover a different job. We always do lots of on-the-job training with new techniques. And I've spent a fair amount of time in learning new computer programs.
>
> (Underqualified young male technician with a high school diploma)

The irreversible popular demand for knowledge

Overall, the surveys and follow-up interviews indicate that there is increasing general popular demand for more adult education courses and few significant differences between matched and mismatched employees in their increased general participation rates in organized adult education courses. The Ontario population survey of informal learning activities and the follow-up interviews with credentially mismatched employees demonstrate that there are also no major differences between underemployed and underqualified employees in the total amount of time they now devote to work-related learning activities. It appears that these mismatched employees are spending more time in informal learning than adult learners generally were in the 1970s, an average of over 600 hours per year compared with the earlier general average of about 500 hours. The condition of underemployment has evidently not discouraged people from continuing both their work-related and general learning activities. As for the small numbers of workers who are objectively underqualified in GED terms – most of whom deny they are actually underqualified for their jobs – the evidence suggests that most of them are devoting at least as much effort to continuing work-related learning activities as matched and underemployed workers. The learning efforts of both the underemployed and the underqualified are much more extensive than the dominant rhetoric about the pressing need for more education would suggest.

It is fairly clear that one of the most common current responses to underemployment is to seek more education and training. This mindset is as common among underemployed university and college graduates as it is among underqualified school drop-outs. These people live with a deep-seated recognition of the arbitrariness of the formal educational credential requirements set for the jobs they have had. They understand, more intimately than those living within the current comfort of job requirements matched to their educational attainments, that employers are upping the ante for job entry and that the link between job performance requirements and educational attainments is being loosened in an 'employer's market'.

Those living in the education–jobs gap give no serious indication of giving up on the faith that more education should get them a better job. Indeed, their current situation seems to have provoked in many at least a quiet sense of desperation that somehow they must continue to get more and still more education, training or knowledge in order to achieve any economic security. Such increasingly common learning efforts among the unemployed and underemployed underline just how wide the gulf between the knowledge base of the general population and the limited knowledge required in most jobs has become.

The conviction of these marginalized people that our current economic system can produce the jobs to which they continue to feel at least ambiguously entitled has definitely been shaken severely. But, in the absence of any economic alternative that seems practical, most of those living on both sides of the education–jobs gap are actively engaged in trying to revise rather than reject this conviction. As in the 1930s, the waste of human potential is immense and gut-wrenching. Just as during the 'dirty thirties', the economic polarization between the haves and have-nots has also increased greatly. The difference is that the promise and pursuit of further education are now playing a much larger role than make-work programmes in preoccupying the swelling number of outcasts and misfits of the labour market.

Concluding remarks

The shortage of adequate paid work is a far more profound problem than most political leaders are yet prepared to admit publicly. The real scope of under-employment continues to be underestimated because so much of it beyond official unemployment counts remains hidden in the underground economy, the household and prisons, among discouraged and involuntary part-time workers, and in the largely invisible credential and performance gaps. Most political leaders persist in focusing on enhancing a 'training culture' as the primary policy response, when a continual learning culture is already thriving across the current and potential workforce. In collaboration with corporate business leaders, elected politicians continue to promote partnership programmes to try to ensure that specific groups of potential workers obtain better employability skills (see Farrar and Connolly, 1991; Spangenburg, 1995; and Taylor, 1996). Indeed, the focus on education and training solutions has continued to mount, to the level of colleges now offering warranties that include taking back their graduates from unhappy employers for retraining (Lewington, 1994). Many educational reforms may be admirable in themselves. But they remain utterly incapable of resolving the problem of underemployment. Basically, most political leaders continue to be preoccupied with shuffling education and training deckchairs on increasingly computerized workshops while the sea of underemployment mounts.

If underemployment of people's knowledge and skills in the legal labour market economy of advanced capitalist societies is as extensive as the prior analyses suggest, recommendations that stress a growing need for lifelong learning miss the point. Our primary emphasis should rather be on reorganizing work to enable more people to apply in legitimate and sustainable ways the knowledge and skills they already possess. As I have argued in detail elsewhere (Livingstone, 1998), we need to:

1   understand more fully the full array of past, present and possible future forms of work;
2   recognize that unpaid household and community work and informal learning can aid in bridging the gap between paid work and organized schooling and lead to a sustainable knowledge society;

3   explore further the reduction of underemployment in basic economic alternatives to the currently dominant 'shareholder capitalism', namely 'stakeholder capitalism' and 'economic democracy'; and

4   appreciate the existing popular support for these alternatives, especially features of economic democracy (i.e. socialized markets; worker self-management; reduced standard workweeks; green work) that can serve to close the education–jobs gap. Without *active popular support for economic alternatives related to more democratic visions of work organization,* little substantial reduction in current levels of underemployment is likely in the near future.

Some of the underemployed people we have interviewed who are most critical of capitalism's economic imperatives express explicit hopes that interactive educational and workplace reforms will lead to a more human-centred system:

> We need a society which puts human beings first, not money. The education system needs to be more geared to practicalities. Whatever you learn you should be able to apply to your job. Learning on the job should also be recognized as learning experience by educational institutions. It works both ways. There should be an ongoing process of on-the-job and in-school learning. Education–job gaps are bound to happen, because the economy is changing and types of qualifications don't match, because institutions of learning have different timetables and don't react so fast to the market . . . There needs to be more co-ordinated planning among governments, schools/colleges and business. But businesses are not taking that initiative at all . . . The people who control things need a massive dose of education to bring them down to the human level as opposed to a preoccupation with money.
>
> (Underemployed middle aged female service worker with a university degree)

Overall, there is serious public support for democratizing measures such as co-operative forms of ownership, workplace participation, shorter workweeks and gender equity in unpaid labour. People in general are giving these progressive economic alternatives more serious consideration than the writings of professional economists. The elements of viable solutions to the education–jobs gap exist in the tacit foreknowledge (Polanyi, 1983) of the general public.

Will the popular support among both the fully employed and the growing ranks of the underemployed for progressive economic reforms, such as genuine workplace democratization and a reduced normal workweek, be taken up effectively in local, national and international initiatives by progressive political movements such as the advocates of the new economics and political ecology? Or can vested economic and political power hierarchies continue to promote the 'more education as secular salvation' solution in conjunction with individual internalization of the blame for underemployment, fear for unemployment and a sense that there is really no economic alternative? The massive systemic extent of underemployment in all of its aspects must be widely recognized and the false claims for a 'knowledge economy' full of 'high performance', 'learning organizations' must be directly confronted. Otherwise, the wastage of much of our work-related education and training, along with the relative withering of our collection opportunities to use this knowledge in any future workplaces, is likely to continue to grow.

References

Adams, M. *et al.* (1997) *Preliminary Bibliography of the Research Network for New Approaches to Lifelong Learning (NALL)* (Toronto, Centre for the Study of Education and Work, Ontario Institute for the Study of Education at the University of Toronto).

Bell, D. (1973) *The Coming of Post-industrial Society* (New York, Basic Books).

Bennett, K. (1994) Recent information on training, *Perspectives on Labour and Income*, 6, pp. 5–11.

Berg, I. (1970) *Education and Jobs: the great training robbery* (New York, Praeger).

Betcherman, G. (1992) Are Canadian firms underinvesting in training?, *Canadian Business Economics*, 1, 25–33.

Betcherman, G., Leckie, N. and McMullen, K. (1997) *Developing Skills in the Canadian Workplace: the results of the Ekos workplace training survey* (Ottawa, Canadian Policy Research Networks).

Bishop, J. (1992) *The French Mandate to Spend on Training: a model for the United States* (Cornell Center on the Educational Quality of the Workforce, Cornell University).

Brookfield, S. (1981) The adult education learning iceberg, *Adult Education (UK)*, 54, pp. 110–118.

Candy, P. (1993) *Self-direction for Lifelong Learning: a comprehensive guide to theory and practice* (San Francisco, Jossey-Bass).

Carrick, R. (1996) Jobless rate understated, bank reports, *The Toronto Star*, 10 May, p. E3.

Center for Workforce Development (1998) *The Teaching Firm: where productive work and learning converge* (Newton, MA, Education Development Center).

Clogg, C. (1979) *Measuring Underemployment: demographic indicators for the United States* (New York, Academic Press).

Collins, R. (1979) *The Credential Society* (New York, Academic Press).

Crompton, S. (1992) Studying on the job, *Perspectives on Labour and Income*, 4, pp. 30–38.

Curtis, B., Livingstone, D.W. and Smaller, H. (1992) *Stacking the Deck: the streaming of working class kids in Ontario schools* (Toronto, Our Schools/Our Selves Educational Foundation).

Davis, J.A. and Smith, T.W. (1994) *General Social Surveys 1972–1994* (Chicago, National Opinion Research Center).

Devereaux, M. (1985) *One in Every Five: a survey of adult education in Canada* (Ottawa, Statistics Canada and Education Support Section, Secretary of State).

Diamond, D. and Bedrosion, H. (1970) *Hiring Standards and Performance*. US Department of Labor, Manpower Research Monograph No. 18 (Washington, US Government Printing Office).

Dore, R. and Sako, M. (1989) *How the Japanese Learn to Work* (London, Routledge).

Duncan, G.J. and Hoffman, S. (1978) The economic value of surplus education, in: G. Duncan and J. Morgan (eds) *Five Thousand American Families – patterns of economic progress*, Vol. 6 (Michigan, ISR Survey Research Centre, Institute for Social Research).

Ekos Research Associates (1993) *Reskilling Society (Phase I): industrial perspectives. The national survey of employers on training and development issues* (Hull, Que., Human Resources Development Canada).

Farrar, E. and Connolly, C. (1991) Improving middle schools in Boston: a report on Boston compact and school district initiatives, *Educational Policy*, 5, pp. 4–28.

Garrick, J. (1996) Informal learning: some underlying philosophies, *Canadian Journal for the Study of Adult Education*, 10, 21–46.

German Ministry of Education (1993) *Berichtssystem Weiterbildung 1991* (Bonn, Helmut Kuwan).

Heimstra, R. (1976) *Lifelong Learning* (Lincoln, Professional Educators Publications).

Holzer, H.J. (1996) *What Employers Want: job prospects for less-educated workers* (New York, Russell Sage Foundation).

Holzer, H.J. and Vroman, W. (1993) Mismatches and the urban labor market, in: G.E. Peterson and W. Vroman (eds) *Urban Labor Markets and Job Opportunity*, pp. 81–112 (Washington, DC, The Urban Institute Press).

Japanese Ministry of Education (1994) *Educational Policy in Japan 1994* (Tokyo, Ministry of Education).

Knoke, D. and Kalleberg, A. (1995) Job training in U.S. organizations, *American Sociological Review*, 59, pp. 537–546.

Knowles, M. (1970) *The Modern Practice of Adult Education: andragogy versus pedagogy* (Chicago, Follett).

Leean, C. and Sisco, B. (1981) *Learning Projects and Self-planned Learning Efforts among Undereducated Adults in Rural Vermont* (Washington, DC, National Institute of Education).

Lewington, J. (1994) Nova Scotia plans to offer warranties on grads, *The Globe and Mail*, 3 February, p. A1.

Livingstone, D.W. (1993) Working at Stelco: 're-tayloring' production relations in the eighties, in: J. Corman *et al.* (eds) *Recasting Steel Labour: the Stelco story*, pp. 13–53 (Halifax, Fernwood Publishing).

Livingstone, D.W. (1994) Searching for missing links: neo-Marxist theories of education, in: L. Erwin and D. MacLennan (eds) *Canadian Sociology of Education*, pp. 55–82 (Toronto, Copp Clark Longman).

Livingstone, D.W. (1996) *Steel Work: Recasting the Core Workforce at Hilton Works*, 1981–96. Final Report of the Work-place Change Section of the Steelworker Families Project (Toronto, Department of Sociology and Equity Studies in Education).

Livingstone, D.W. (1998) *The Education–Jobs Gap: underemployment or economic democracy* (Boulder, Westview Press).

Livingstone, D.W., Hart, D. and Davie, L. (1987) *Public Attitudes Toward Education in Ontario, 1986: Sixth OISE Survey* (Toronto, OISE Press).

Livingstone, D.W., Hart, D. and Davie, L. (1989) *Public Attitudes Toward Education in Ontario, 1988: Seventh OISE Survey* (Toronto, OISE Press).

Livingstone, D.W., Hart, D. and Davie, L. (1991) *Public Attitudes Toward Education in Ontario, 1990: Eighth OISE Survey* (Toronto, OISE Press).

Livingstone, D.W., Hart, D. and Davie, L. (1993) *Public Attitudes Toward Education in Ontario, 1992: Ninth OISE Survey* (Toronto, OISE Press).

Livingstone, D.W., Hart, D. and Davie, L. (1995) *Public Attitudes Toward Education in Ontario, 1994: Tenth OISE Survey* (Toronto, OISE Press).

Livingstone, D.W., Hart, D. and Davie, L. (1997) *Public Attitudes Toward Education in Ontario, 1996: The Eleventh OISE/UT Survey* (Toronto, University of Toronto Press).

Lowe, G. (1992) *Human Resource Challenges of Education, Computers and Retirement* (Ottawa, Statistics Canada).

Makino, A. (1996) The theoretical problem of recent educational reform in Japan: the collapse of the framework. Unpublished paper (Nagoya University).

Machlup, F. (1962) *The Production and Distribution of Knowledge in the United States* (Princeton, Princeton University Press).

Machlup, F. (1978–80) *Information through the Printed Word: the dissemination of scholarly, scientific and intellectual knowledge*, 4 Volumes (New York, Praeger).

Machlup, F. (1980) *Knowledge, Its Creation, Distribution and Economic Significance* (Princeton, Princeton University Press).

Marschall, D. (1990) *Upgrading America's Workforce through Participation and Structured Work-based Learning*. UCLP Research Report (Washington, DC, Human Resources Development Institute).

Masatoshi, N., Koji, K. and Hiroshi, S. (eds) (1994) *The State of Continuing Education in Japan* (Tokyo, Research Institute of Educational Systems, Nyhon University).

McDowell, R. (1991) *The Flow of Graduates from Higher Education and Their Entry into Working Life* (Ottawa, Research and Information on Education Directorate, Secretary of State).

Merriam, S. and Caffarella, R.M. (1991) *Learning in Adulthood: a comparative guide* (San Francisco, Jossey-Bass).

National Center on the Educational Quality of the Workforce (1995) *First Findings from the EQW National Employer Survey* (Philadelphia, National Center on the Educational Quality of the Workforce).

OECD (1989) *Educational Attainment and the Labour Force Employment Outlook* (Paris, Organisation for Economic Co-operation and Development).

OECD (1991) Enterprise-related training, *OECD Employment Outlook* (Paris, Organisation for Economic Co-operation and Development).

OECD (1993) *Industry Training in Australia, Sweden and the United States* (Paris, Organisation for Economic Co-operation and Development).

OECD (1994) *The OECD Job Study: facts, analysis, strategies* (Paris, Organisation for Economic Co-operation and Development).

OISE (Ontario Institute for Studies in Education) Survey of Educational Issues Data Archive. See the project website – http:edv.oise.utoronto.ca/OISE-Survey

O'Toole, J. (1975) The reserve army of the underemployed: I – The world of work, and II – The role of education, *Change*, May/June, pp. 26–33, 60–63.

Penland, P. (1977) *Self-planned Learning in America* (Pittsburgh, University of Pittsburgh).

Percy, K. (1997) On formal, non-formal lifelong learning: reconceptualizing the boundaries for research, theory and practice, in: P. Armstrong, N. Miller and M. Zukas (eds) *Crossing Borders, Breaking Boundaries: research in the education of adults*, pp. 380–384 (London, SCUTREA).

Polanyi, M. (1983) *The Tacit Dimension* (Gloucester, Peter Smith).

Porat, M.U. (1977) *The Information Economy* (Washington, DC, US Department of Commerce, Office of Telecommunications).

Sandia Laboratories (1993) Perspectives on education in America, *Journal of Educational Research*, 86, pp. 259–310.

Sargent, N. (1991) *Learning and 'Leisure': a study of adult participation in learning and its policy implications* (Leicester, National Institute of Adult Continuing Education).

Selman, G. and Dampier, P. (1991) *The Foundation of Adult Education in Canada* (Toronto, Thompson Educational Publishing).

Sheak, R. (1994) The chronic jobs' problem in the United States: no end in sight, *Free Inquiry in Creative Sociology*, 22, pp. 23–32.

Shelley, K.J. (1992) The future of jobs for college graduates, *Monthly Labor Review*, July, pp. 13–21.

Smith, H. (1986) Overeducation and underemployment: an agnostic view, *Sociology of Education*, 50, April, pp. 85–99.

Spangenburg, C. (1995) *Implementing a School-to-Work Transition System: a Rochester, New York, case study* (Rochester, National Center on Education and the Economy).

Statistics Canada (1995) 1991 *Adult Education and Training Survey* (Ottawa, Employment and Immigration Canada).

Statistics Canada (1996) *Reading the Future: a portrait of literacy in Canada* (Ottawa, National Literacy Secretariat, Human Resource Development Canada and Statistics Canada).

Taylor, A. (1996) Education for 'post-industrial' purposes: understanding the context of change in Alberta Schools, Ed.D. thesis (Journal Graduate Department of Education, University of Toronto).

Theobald, S. (1997) Out of school, out of work, *The Toronto Star*, 28 May, p. C1–2.

Tough, A. (1978) Major learning efforts: recent research and future directions, *Adult Education*, pp. 250–263.

Tough, A. (1979) *The Adult's Learning Projects: a fresh approach to theory and practice in adult education*, 2nd edition (Toronto, OISE Press).

Tuijnman, A.C. (1989) *Recurrent Education, Earnings and Well-being: a fifty-year longitudinal study of a cohort of Swedish men* (Stockholm, Almqvist and Wiksell).

Tuijnman, A.C. (1992) The expansion of adult education and training in Europe: trends and issues, *International Review of Education*, 38, pp. 673–692.

US Department of Education (1996) *Condition of Education* (Washington, DC, US Government Printing Office).

US Department of Labor, Bureau of Labor Statistics (1994) *Employer-provided Formal Training* (Washington, DC, US Department of Labor).

US Department of Labor, Bureau of Labor Statistics (1996) *The 1995 Survey of 29 Employer-provided Training* (Washington, DC, US Department of Labor).

Chapter 4

Social capital, human capital and the learning society

Tom Schuller and John Field

Introduction

The idea of a learning society assumes that certain types of social arrangements are more likely to promote lifelong learning than others. Yet although the idea of a learning society has been widely and enthusiastically embraced by politicians and educationists, there has been little debate over the precise types of social arrangement that promote communication, reflexivity and mutual learning over time (Ranson, 1994; European Commission, 1995). Specific studies of learning within social institutions such as the family or the workplace have rarely been accompanied by a wider conceptual framework on societal learning.

This chapter considers the potential of one such conceptual framework, that of social capital. As developed by James Coleman and others, the idea of social capital has come to play an important role in helping explain educational attainment (Coleman, 1988, 1994). For Coleman, the concept of social capital complements that of human capital; indeed, it helps explain variations in the levels of human capital in any given society. Coleman's conclusion is, briefly, that high levels of human capital tend to arise when individuals can draw on:

> the set of resources that inhere in family relations and in community social organisation and that . . . can constitute an important advantage for children and adolescents in the development of their human capital.
> (Coleman, 1994: 300)

This is an appealing conclusion, not least because it directs attention to such 'soft' variables as social networks and values, rather than focusing primarily upon the 'hard' variables that tend to form the bedrock of human capital thinking. This chapter therefore considers the relationship between human

This is an edited version of an article published in *International Journal of Lifelong Education* 17, 4 (1998): 226–235.

and social capital, not only in respect of the educational attainment of school-leavers, but more widely in the context of the learning society.

Human capital: a two-edged instrument?

It was in the 1960s that Theodor Schultz and Gary Becker developed Adam Smith's original notion that investment in education and skill formation was as significant a factor in economic growth as investment in physical plant and equipment, and the phrase 'human capital' was born. It has been immensely influential at all sorts of levels, including that of political imagery.

James Coleman, one of the originators of the term 'social capital', observes that:

> Probably the most important and most original development in the economics of education in the past 30 years has been the idea that the concept of physical capital as embodied in tools, machines and other productive equipment can be extended to include human capital as well. Just as physical capital is created by changes in materials to form tools that facilitate production, human capital is created by changes in persons that bring about skills and capabilities that make them able to act in new ways.
>
> (Coleman, 1988: S100)

Since Becker and Schultz, huge amounts of research and analysis have been built on the notion of human capital (see e.g. Carnoy, 1995). In particular, economists have focused on rates of return to different types of investment in human capital, which may be calculated in such a way as to allow aid donors and other investors to make informed decisions about where to focus their efforts. But how appropriate is this approach, particularly when examined in the broad context of the learning society?

Measurement of human capital has always been a problem. Highly sophisticated econometric analyses of the effect of human capital investment are often founded on the assumption that human capital can be measured simply by the number of years' schooling. More plausible is the use of qualifications as a measure but here again there are serious question marks against the intrinsic validity of such measures (e.g. Mulligan and Sala-i-Martin, 1995). The assumptions on which towers of statistical analysis about the relationship between education and economic success are built are often heroic to the point of stupidity. Given the power of human capital, in theory and practice, there is a remarkable dearth of serious instruments by which the nature and quality of the investment are measured.

It is important that we do not project on to human capital theory blame for a whole range of unpalatable developments, which arise largely from political choices and not from the nature of the theory. Nevertheless, there are serious objections. One is the intrinsic merit of education as a consumption good, to persist for a moment longer with the economic vocabulary. People do, and should, value learning as something that they enjoy, even if the value is consumed once the act of learning is over. Very obviously, people buy books, CDs, computers and the other accoutrements that designate the professional learner; and they still spend money on traditional courses and appear to enjoy them. We are not aware of any attempt to incorporate such educational consumption into the human capital model; rather, these activities are treated by economists primarily as a form of leisure spending with little relevance to productivity and competitiveness. This can be criticized on at least three grounds: first, that it ignores evidence of 'spillover' or transfer between one learning domain and another; second, that it is based on a partial picture of economic activity, excluding such areas as voluntary engagement or domestic labour; and third, that it treats quality of life issues as at best intangible, at worst peripheral.

The second major objection is more of a tactical one, but none the less important for that. The more the language of investment dominates, the more it is accepted not only as rational in its own terms but even as the only language, the more difficult it will be for learning activities that cannot show a visible return, and especially a quick return, to justify themselves. This is a serious problem in an accountancy-driven society. It incidentally adds a question mark against the otherwise very interesting, if somewhat impracticable, objective – one of five – of the European Union's Year of Lifelong Learning, to make investment in human resources as regular a feature of company balance sheets as investment in physical assets.

These objections notwithstanding, human capital remains an immensely powerful analytical notion. But it is time to ask whether it may not have achieved, at least implicitly, a dominance that partially undermines its contemporary utility. The narrowness of its measures, of input and output, arguably has a distorting effect on real investment patterns. In particular, it concentrates on individuals, since it is individuals who spend the years in school and to whom qualifications are awarded, and to the extent that it does this it ignores the wider social context within which much learning takes place, and the relationships – personal and institutional – that actually constitute the vehicles or channels through which learning takes place. It is precisely this relational domain that forms the object of social capital analysis.

Social capital: three conceptions

The notion of social capital has already acquired currency in the USA, but is only starting to do so in the UK. Robert Putnam defines social capital as 'the features of social life – networks, norms and trust – that enable participants to act together more effectively to pursue shared objectives' (Putnam,

1996: 66). This is indeed broad, but he proceeds quickly to give this empirical substance, drawing on extensive time-budget surveys of Americans in succeeding decades: 1965, 1975 and 1985. Most forms of collective political participation, both in the direct sense of political such as working for a political party or more broadly such as attending meetings about town or school affairs, have declined by between a quarter and a half. These findings are complemented by opinion surveys, which show a decline in the last two decades of social trust. Only nationality groups and hobby clubs are reported to run counter to this trend (for a fuller account, see Putnam, 1995).

Putnam examines possible causes for this civic disengagement. He looks for a possible explanation to such items as longer working hours, participation by women in the workforce, or the decline of traditional communities through slum clearances. The main conclusion is that the 'culprit' is television. He contrasts newspaper reading, which is positively associated with participation, and television, where 'each hour spent viewing is associated with less social trust and less group membership'. Television privatizes leisure time, and therefore erodes social capital. He finds, surprisingly, that although participation is usually associated with higher levels of education, and educational levels have increased, the decline in social capital has affected all levels:

> The mysterious disengagement of the last quarter century seems to have afflicted all educational strata in our society, whether they have graduate education or did not finish high school.
>
> (Putnam, 1996: 67)

On this he concludes that the rise in education has mitigated what would otherwise have been an even steeper decline, but it has not succeeded in reversing it.

Putnam's approach is overtly normative. His indicators of active engagement are selective (he excludes environmentalist movements, and other types of engagement that European investigators show to appeal to younger adults). But his deployment of empirical data is substantial and compelling as an identification of a significant trend. The failure of rising educational levels to halt the decline in social capital is a powerful indication of a rather different form of instrumentalism than that which is usually pointed to. Moreover, the differentiation, crude as it is, between different types of mass media – some as positively informative, and encouraging participation, others as sapping social energies – opens up important avenues for exploration in relation to the information society.

Although he draws on earlier uses of the term, James Coleman can probably claim to be the real originator of the concept of social capital, so we can turn to him with some expectation of a starting definition. He acknowledges the diversity, if not the diffuseness, of the concept.

> Social capital is defined by its function. It is not a single entity but a variety of different entities, with two elements in common: they all consist of some aspect of social structures, and they facilitate certain actions of actors – whether persons or corporate actors – within the structure.
>
> (Coleman, 1988: S98)

Coleman goes on to specify three forms of social capital. The first deals with the level of trust that exists in the social environment and the actual extent of obligations held. Social capital is high where people trust each other, and where this trust is exercised by the mutual acceptance of obligations. Coleman gives the example of Egyptian markets where neighbouring traders help each other by bringing commissions or providing finance without entering into legal or financial contracts. The second form concerns information channels; here Coleman cites a university as a place where social capital is maintained by colleagues supplying each other with ideas and information. Third, norms and sanctions constitute social capital where they encourage or constrain people to work for a common good, forgoing immediate self-interest.

Coleman then turns to examining the effect of social capital in creating human capital, in the family and in the community. Family background plays a large part in educational achievement; first through financial capital – the wealth that provides school materials, a place to study at home and so on; and second through human capital, measured approximately by parental levels of education and influencing the child's cognitive environment. To this Coleman adds social capital, defined in terms of the relationship between parents and children. By this he means not so much the emotional relationship as the amount of effort parents put directly into their children's learning. At the community level, social capital involves the extent to which parents reinforce each other's norms, and the closeness of parents' relations with community institutions. Where households move frequently, and little social interchange occurs between the adult members of the community, social capital is likely to be low. This may occur even where financial and human capital levels are high. Coleman uses this to explain why Catholic and Baptist schools in poor but relatively stable neighbourhoods often outperform many private schools: 'the choice of private school for many of these parents is an individualistic one, and, although they back their children with extensive human capital, they send their children to school denuded of social capital' (Coleman, 1988: S114).

Both authors are quite explicit about the normative content of their conceptualizations. The emphases are different, with Putnam seeking to regenerate political health and Coleman to explain the effects of social relationships, but both give primacy to the role of norms. Second, there is a clear commitment to collective values. Coleman, for example, does not pause to consider whether the imposition of norms by the Catholic church, aligning itself with parents to achieve educational success, might through its authoritarianism undermine nonconforming forms of social capital.

Third, both call into question the value of human capital when it is divorced from wider social relations. They challenge the individualism and the assumed rationality of orthodox human capital approaches. Coleman draws on economistic notions of utility maximization as well as on sociological models of socialized behaviour, but he concludes by identifying social capital as a public good, and pointing out that the social structural conditions that overcome the problems of supplying it as a public good – strong families and strong communities – are less in evidence than in the past, and we can therefore expect a decline in human capital as a consequence. Finally, both offer rather different sets of specific measures by which the accumulation or erosion of social capital can be assessed. These certainly have their weaknesses, but they make a striking contrast with the narrowness of the assumptions made in most human capital computations.

Twins, siblings or enemies?

Now for a brief exploration of the relationship(s) between human and social capital. This means pointing to differences; however, the purpose is not to substitute social capital for human capital, as some kind of friendlier, more collective form of investment. To argue along these lines would be to fall into the trap of counterproductive dichotomizing. Nor, incidentally, does the whole argument in favour of bringing social capital into the equation avoid issues about power and conflict; these remain to be worked through.

Here is an initial summary of the differences from the discussion thus far:

- Human capital focuses on the individual agent, social capital on networks and relationships.
- Human capital assumes economic rationality, and transparency of information; social capital assumes that most things are seen through lenses of values and norms that are socially shaped.
- Human capital measures inputs by reference to duration of education or numbers of qualification; social capital by the strength of mutual obligation and civic engagement.
- Human capital measures output in terms of individual income or productivity levels; social capital in terms of quality of life.

The relationship between human and social capital is not necessarily an antagonistic one, conceptually or practically. But in what ways is it conceivable that we might have an expansion of human capital, as conventionally measured, and a decline in social capital? Coleman's example is one of highly educated parents failing to convert their human capital into social capital by not building it into their parental relationships. This is a matter of neglect, rather than active erosion of social capital. Another example, closer to the current theme, might be called the Walkman nightmare version of the learning society (Schuller, 1997). This is the dystopia of whole series of individuals permanently plugged into their personal training programmes, but with no sense of the value of learning as something shared with others, including friends, colleagues, families or their wider social milieu. Human capital rises, as they are guided to higher and higher qualifications, but at the expense of the means of personal communication and relationships. To some extent this is satire, but if human capital accumulation does occur independently of such social contexts it will be, at best, of very limited social and economic value, and it may well be actively erosive.

In this case, the relationships are personal ones. But it would be wrong to conceive of social capital as only about maintaining these kind of relationships, crucial though they are to many forms of effective learning. A second type of relationship is the institutional, the way in which different institutions (educational and non-educational) communicate, collaborate or compete with each other (healthy competition being as much of a valid relationship as fruitful collaboration). There is much food for thought here, analytically and politically: how do we construct or maintain institutional relationships that support rather than impede learning? But there is a third form of relationship, which illustrates well the difference and the complementarity of human and social capital.

This in turn brings us to the long-running debate about specialized versus general knowledge. In one form it runs parallel with the history of human capital theory, since one of the early theoretical distinctions was between general and specific skills, and who should be expected to invest in these. But it can have a wider sense. There have been many arguments, notably in relation to English higher education, about undue specialization. The critique is powerful, but has often taken the form of a rather unreflecting condemnation of specialization *per se*, leading to another counterproductive dichotomy. Of course specialized skills and knowledge are needed; the issue is the balance between them and wider forms of knowledge. The point, though, is not just that a balance is needed. It is that the claim of more generalist knowledge must be not just that it covers more areas, for this would leave it open to the jibe that a generalist is someone who knows less and less about more and more. Its essential value depends on the ability it confers to see the relationships between these different areas. Without that relational knowledge, generalism loses its cutting edge.

How does this fit with the point that human capital theory has already made a distinction between general and specific skills? The short answer is that 'general' in this sense is equivalent to transferable; they are the skills that are usable in several contexts, but may still be highly specialized. But social capital cannot be characterized as the metaknowledge that enables an individual awareness of the relationships between other skills and know-ledges to emerge. It refers rather to the ways in which diverse areas of knowledge, or skills, are pieced together by more than one person, not neces-sarily operating at the same level but complementing each other at least to the extent that makes forms of learning possible that would not otherwise have been so. For this to work, it requires norms to operate, implicitly or explicitly.

An operational typology

We now turn to the specific ways in which social capital may influence life-long learning. Coleman's chief interest has been in the effects of social relationships upon young people's attainment in schools, and as we have seen his argument is essentially that high social capital tends to favour high levels of attainment among the young. Our typology is concerned with aspects of lifelong learning, and not solely with learning among school pupils; this is expressed in the three grids, which try to relate levels of social capital as defined by Coleman to levels of achievement in the schools system; to levels of participation in continuing education (defined as any formal adult education and training programmes); and levels of participation in non-formal education (defined as learning that takes place during social interaction that is primarily undertaken for non-educational purposes).

In the case of schoolchildren, Coleman's findings are that high levels of social capital are normally associated with high levels of educational attain-ment; conversely, low levels of social capital usually lead to low levels of educational attainment. The virtuous circle in this relationship is therefore found in quadrant B of our grid, while the vicious circle is located in the outer reaches of quadrant C (Figure 4.1). Among the UK regions, Northern Ireland appears to provide a strong empirical demonstration of Coleman's thesis: levels of social capital are high (as indicated by family structures, church and other voluntary society membership, or levels of charitable giving) and so are levels of schools attainment (as expressed in GCSE and GCE results (Field and Schuller, 1995)), so that this small and reasonably compact UK region seems to sit in quadrant B.

Things become more complicated when we come to consider lifelong learning as a whole, and not simply the initial school cycle. Coleman's thesis may hold good for school attainment, where family, church and other social networks function to reinforce the message given by teachers to young people. It is likely that similar processes will operate in the case of contin-uing education, as measured by levels of participation in adult education and training (Figure 4.2)? Taking Northern Ireland once more as an illustrative empirical example, we find that a compact UK region with comparatively high levels of social capital is also characterized by very low rates of partici-pation in continuing education (Field and Schuller, 1995; Sargant, 1997);

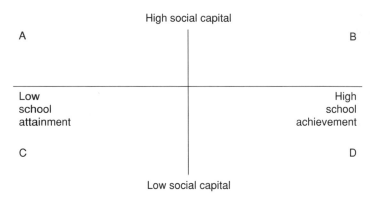

Figure 4.1 Social capital and human capital – initial education.

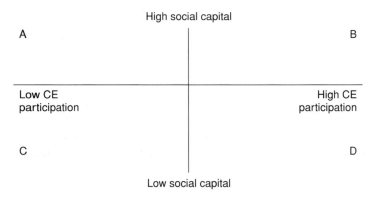

Figure 4.2 Social capital and human capital – continuing education and training.

it therefore falls into quadrant A. What appears to happen in this case is that formal adult education and training – particularly in their certificated forms – are comparatively unimportant to actors who can draw on other resources to gain access to employment or promotion or any benefits associated with lifelong learning.

If access to social capital appears to discourage adults from participating in formal education and training, its relationship to informal learning is likely to be different again. While membership of close social networks may be expected to produce high volume flows of information, and foster mutual approaches to problem solving, they may also restrict the range of actors (and hence expertise) from whom information is sought. Thus, the owners of family businesses will typically seek advice and financial information within personal networks, but may have poor networking with such external

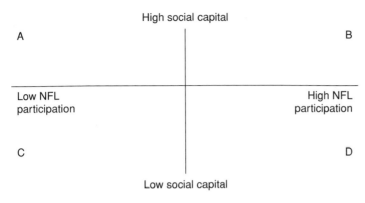

Figure 4.3 Social capital and human capital – non-formal learning.

and unknown (personally) actors as bank managers. Moreover, close networks can sometimes also lead to the screening and even hoarding of information (and including information about valuable sources of expertise) in an attempt to gain or maintain competitive advantage; as Baldacchino (1995: 271) puts it, 'face-to-face relations are complemented by back-to-back relations'. More recently, in the context of globalizing tendencies, the link between space and social capital is being further uncoupled, so that one may share few relations of reciprocity and trust with neighbours and kin, yet engage in and construct close social networks and institutions that are remote and perhaps even short-lived (Beck, 1997). As the example of the Walkman dystopia shows, though, this is by no means a unilinear process. Furthermore, measuring non-formal learning is – by definition – an awkward business. Nevertheless, it seems plausible to suggest that high levels of social capital lead, in general, to higher-than-average levels of informal and non-formal learning (Figure 4.3). Whereas formal learning is associated with the development of routinized systems of transmitting and recognizing knowledge and skills, less formal types of learning are promoted by the pooling of information and sharing of capacities that arise when levels of trust, reciprocity and common norms are high. To pursue the example of Northern Ireland once more, the evidence available is consistent with this view (see also Moreland, 1993); provisionally, we would place this compact UK region somewhere within quadrant B.

This typology remains somewhat hesitant and incomplete, but it does appear to be suggestive. More work certainly needs to be done to identify empirical examples of communities (spatial, occupational or values-oriented) that have comparatively low social capital in relation to lifelong learning, quadrants C and D are as yet underexplored. We are as yet unclear about the impact of scale (cf. Baldacchino, 1995): while it may be possible to generalize about social capital in Northern Ireland, it is more difficult to extend this approach to larger social systems. We are also aware of the risks of implying a simple dichotomy between low and high levels of social capital. This in turn generates further difficulties of analysis and coherence, which are easily overlooked in creating – largely for heuristic purposes – the provisional typology outlined above.

Conclusion: some further questions

Some of the social capital terminology is distinctly woolly, especially the last two measures listed above: mutual obligation and quality of life. The task is to develop measures – and policies – that will stand up. This is the challenge that the human capital approach has met forcefully and head-on, with its calculations of rates of return to education at all levels and in all countries, best known in the corporate work of the World Bank.

The first set of questions is therefore about measurement. What kind of constructive critique can be mounted of the measures used in respect of human capital? And how do we pursue the development of adequate measures for assessing the accumulation or erosion of social capital? It might be helpful here to think not of alternative and competing sets of measures, but of nested sets, from the narrowest qualification-focused to the broadest set of social indicators, each fulfilling different roles. There may be trade-offs between specificity and focus on the one hand, and contextualization and scope on the other. Building such a nested structure should help to avoid the quantitative spuriousness of the human capital approach on the one hand, and the overinclusive vagueness of social capital on the other.

The second set of questions concerns the nature of the relationships that form the essence of the social capital concept, and have more of a practical or policy-related character. Attention here might concentrate on three areas. The first is the personal: what are the kinds of context and culture that promote communication and mutual learning as part of the fabric of everyday life? This is surely at the heart of a learning society. Second, what kinds of institutional relationship are most supportive of learning? These will definitely be plural; in some instances, collaboration may be the appropriate mode of coexistence, but in others competitive relationships will be the ones that most actively foster learning. The need is to sort out which is which, and what are the most fruitful forms of competition and collaboration. Finally, relationships between different knowledge areas merit further reflection. Rather than accumulating certificates as individual pieces of evidence of human capital, we need to ask what the balance is across the portfolios held by individuals and by groups, so that the awards are related to the social units that are to deploy the knowledge and skills.

References

Baldacchino, G. (1995) Labour formation in small developing states: a conceptual review. *Compare*, 25(3), 263–278.
Beck, U. (ed.) (1997) *Kinder der Freiheit* (Frankfurt: Suhrkamp Verlag).
Becker, G. (1964) *Human Capital, a Theoretical and Empirical Analysis, with Special Reference to Education* (New York: Columbia University Press).
Carnoy, M. (1995) *Encyclopedia of Economics of Education*, 2nd edn (Oxford: Pergamon Press).
Coleman, J. (1988) Social capital in the creation of human capital. *American Journal of Sociology*, 94 (Suppl.), S95–120.
Coleman, J. (1994) *Foundations of Social Theory* (Cambridge, MA: Belknap).
European Commission (1995) *Teaching and Learning: Towards the Learning Society* (Luxembourg: Office for Official Publications).
Field, J. and Schuller, T. (1995) Is there less adult learning in Scotland and Northern Ireland? A quantitative analysis. *Scottish Journal of Adult and Continuing Education*, 2(2), 71–80.
Moreland, R. (1993) Towards a learning society: a study of formal, non-formal and informal adult learning opportunities. D.Phil. thesis, University of Ulster at Jordanstown.
Mulligan, C. and Sala-i-Martin, I. (1995) *Measuring Human Capital*, Centre for Economic Policy Research, Discussion Paper 1149 (London: CEPR).
Putnam, R. (1995) Tuning in, tuning out: the strange disappearance of social capital in America. *PS: Political Science & Politics*, 28(4), 664–683.
Putnam, R. (1996) Who killed civic America. *Prospect*, March, 66–72.
Ranson, S. (1994) *Towards a Learning Society* (London: Cassell).
Sargant, N. (ed.) (1997) *The Learning Divide* (Leicester: National Institute for Adult Continuing Education).
Schuller, T. (1997) Building social capital: steps towards a learning society. *Scottish Affairs*, 18, 77–91.
Schultz, T. (1963) *The Economic Value of Education* (New York: Columbia University Press).

Chapter 5

The comparative dimension in continuous vocational training

A preliminary framework

*Isabelle Darmon, Carlos Frade and
Kari Hadjivassiliou*

Introduction

Continuous vocational training (CVT) as an identified and formalised field
of policy and practice is a recent creation, and by no means a settled
one. Informal training in the workplace, as well as codified training
through apprenticeship, has, of course, existed for centuries in most European countries, where it was associated with forms of control of access
to the crafts and to mechanisms of social promotion at work (Winterton
and Winterton, 1994). However, even though structures of social dialogue
and funding were initiated by the state and established both in France in
1959 and in Britain in 1964, CVT has taken on a radically different
aspect in the last 30 years, and mostly in the last 15 years, during which it
has become associated with a different kind of change, that is, *change
and restructuring for competitiveness and flexibility.* Although the rationales
of social promotion, and even that of permanent education as a right
still survive, clearly the rationale just mentioned has become dominant and
has meant a change in the main players as well, as the *enterprise* became
the key decision maker in relation to the implementation and use made of
CVT. This change has slowly evolved throughout Europe (Kaiserbruger
et al., 1996).

Thus CVT has become a sphere of its own over the last decades, with its
legislative and bargaining frameworks, its markets and providers, its quality
standards, and has become an issue of considerable expenditure. Directly
linked to the search for competitiveness and the problem of unemployment,
CVT has become an issue in European and national policy, as well as an
object of formal or informal bargaining between policy makers, social partners, and within companies themselves. In short, *CVT is everything but a
neutral and mechanistic response of companies to objective market pressures and
technological changes.* It has become a key sphere of negotiations (in the broad

This is an edited version of a chapter published in F. Coffield (ed.) (1998), *Why's the Beer
Always Stronger Up North?*, Bristol: Policy Press.

sense of the term) at different levels, which themselves reveal emerging or renewed forms of regulation, or at least 'social checks'.

To compare CVT innovations in Britain, France and Spain, which is one of the purposes of the Tavistock study on *Innovations in CVT in the workplace*, of which this chapter is a contribution, is to analyse evolving modes of *regulation and compromise (or accommodation)* within three societies that have all been subjected to deregulation, although arguably to very varying extents. This chapter sets out the preliminary steps towards what could become a framework for transnational comparisons of CVT, and draws on previous comparative research done by the Tavistock Institute (see especially, Frade and Darmon, 1996 and 1997; Darmon *et al.*, 1996). In the section on levels of analysis in the comparative framework, the main rationales for a framework emphasising the policy background of CVT and CVT as a sphere of negotiation are explained, and the implications for a transnational comparison are drawn out. In the third section we review the main trends of the national configurations of CVT in each of the countries in this study. Finally, we outline the implications of the framework for the transnational comparison of training innovations at the level of the firm.

In the rest of this chapter we will refer to 'company training' when discussing the *object* of analysis; we will refer to CVT or 'continuing training' when discussing *policies*. CVT is broader than just company training in most countries – in Britain, where there is no official definition, CVT seems to encompass training for the unemployed in official texts; in France CVT – as defined by the 1971 law and subsequent amendments – includes company training, the right to training leave, and special fixed-term contracts for young people including the provision of vocational training in firms and in schools; in Spain, CVT – as defined by the National Tripartite Agreement – includes company training, the 'individual remunerated training permit' and theoretical training in the apprenticeship contract.

Levels of analysis in the comparative framework

The last three decades have seen dramatic changes in international competition, in the capital ownership of production, in modes of production, and as a result, in employment structures and conditions, forms of work organisation, and skills. The industrial, social, and educational patrimonies of old Europe, which had started to be established in the second half of the nineteenth century and had been consolidated in the after-war period, have been deeply shaken by this international turmoil. Change and flexibility have become masterwords in our societies. In that context, company training has been seen *both* as an instrument for and as a buffer against change, an *ambiguous status* that denies the concept any neutrality.

With these international trends concerning all European countries (and indeed all Western countries), and with the elaboration of European-level responses in terms of regulation and deregulation of competition, quality norms, and consumer protection, one may doubt whether company training, increasingly considered as an instrument for business strategy, may not be more influenced by these trends at the international and European level rather than shaped by the national context. The setting up of international quality standards in some sectors has led, for example, to new training requirements for the workforce of these sectors that have given rise in some interesting cases to training modules being elaborated jointly by the profession in various European countries, or to the transfer of sectoral training from one country to another (see, for example, Tavistock Institute *et al.*, 1996). However, these very examples have also exposed the complexity of joint efforts and of transfer processes because of national specificities.

In fact, because of the scale of the changes that have occurred in the last three decades, and of the challenges they have brought to the industrial base and to the welfare systems in our societies, governments have tended to harness efforts for competitiveness and to engage in reforms of the welfare state that have meant high levels of intervention and dramatic changes in the legislative and regulatory frameworks. And these reforms have profoundly affected the role assigned to education and training. Hence it is argued that a transnational comparison of what shapes company training has to start with a *comparison of national policies* – and we would add, not only with education and training policies, but with the wider economic and social policy and the associated regulatory framework. Sectoral deregulation policies, as well as the deregulation of industrial relations and of the labour market all have a crucial bearing on company training.

This acknowledgement of the primary relevance of the national policy level in comparative research has been vindicated by the regulation school (e.g. see Leborgne and Lipietz, 1990). Although we share some of their key assumptions, we would tend to analyse the general trends in Western societies as more than just a crisis in Fordist modes of production, and refer more generally to globalisation, massive unemployment and the crisis of the welfare states as the major interrelated trends that Western societies have to face. Second, instead of having an almost exclusive focus on distinct national 'models' of response, we emphasise not only the communality of the policy trends but also the different national responses on the basis of diverse national institutional mixes and traditions. Thus, we argue, all countries have followed a deregulatory path, but some more intensively and extensively than others; likewise, the importance of 'checks' to this process is very much to do with national traditions. As we shall see, the institutional arrangements, dominant orientations, and forms of company training are strongly determined by deregulation and counterbalancing policies.

Thus, the second level of analysis is that of the 'CVT *sphere*' at a national level as a sphere of new social 'compromise' within the deregulation context.

The various actors, their interests and the *dominant* terms of the debates are described for each national configuration – these various aspects being quite strongly shaped by the extent to which deregulation policies have been applied and how they have been checked.

Finally, the third level of analysis, that of the firm itself, will provide a particular instance of company policy, which, again, cannot be considered as a mechanistic response to a set of given objective conditions, but as a particular instance of social 'compromise', marked by company-, sector-, 'territory'-specific characteristics, to be sure, but nevertheless feeding into the wider negotiations taking place in our societies.

Thus the approach developed in this chapter seeks to avoid the trap into which in our view too many comparative exercises fall. Too often such comparative exercises are mere mechanical juxtapositions, and seem to be, perhaps unwillingly, underpinned by an axiom that elements or components of innovations have meaning and function in themselves, that is, independently of the *configuration* within which such components are actually included. To this atomistic view we wish to oppose a *systemic view* according to which *the relationships between innovation components and the system within which such components function is far more important than the components taken by themselves*. As will be developed below, for example, the 'compromise' taking place around company training in the UK is *wholly encompassed by economic values* – the dominant one being the free-play of the markets. In contrast, company training in France and mostly in Spain will be analysed as a 'social compromise' between increasingly dominant market values and still legitimate and powerful social forces, acting as guarantors of employee protection, promotion, and rights, as well as of more general solidarity embracing the unemployed.

Deregulation policies, social checks and CVT in Britain, France and Spain: a preliminary analysis

In this section we explore the national configurations at a preliminary stage, against the backdrop of common trends towards *economic deregulation, deregulation of the labour markets* as well as *decentralisation and deregulation of industrial relations*; we are primarily relying on a review of the literature, and on previous research carried out by the Tavistock Institute (especially Frade and Darmon, 1996), on preliminary interviews for the fieldwork in this project, as well as on recent fieldwork carried out for related projects. This analysis, however, will be adjusted after completion of the case-study work in Britain, France and Spain, specifically planned for this study.

United Kingdom

In comparing dominant policy trends, we would tend to locate the UK at one end of the spectrum, whereas Spain would be at the opposite end. The peculiarity of UK policies, most authors agree, is that the economic aim has become an overarching and dominant concern. Policy priorities have been set up in the UK according to this dominant economic concern, and welfare-social protection in particular has been subordinated to it, to the extent that 'even where attempts are made to incorporate social regeneration more centrally into programmes the change of emphasis shifts because *it is integrated into a business oriented vision*' (Cochrane, 1994: 123; emphasis added).

Deregulation of the labour market in the UK has practically touched upon all those processes that are considered to hinder the free working of the supply-side factors in relation to the labour and production process, including any form of association, and particularly trade union power; wage regulations and pay-bargaining arrangements, the objective being to individualise pay bargaining – here institutions that influenced pay in the public sector have been removed; likewise, wage councils agreements that covered some 2.5 million workers were also abolished (Mullard, 1995).

UK regulatory framework

According to different studies the regulatory framework in the UK has been based upon a major institutional strategy and a chief institutional instrument, namely, the promotion of an *enterprise culture* and the creation of what have been called *quasi-markets*. The latter are constituted by quasi-markets internal to a socio-economic sector – for example, the 'provider market' in the National Health Service, the internal market in education (in continuing training, the main relevant institutions are Training and Enterprise Councils (TECs) and Local Enterprise Companies (LECs) in Scotland). The regulatory framework is also characterised by the *complete decentralisation of industrial relations* (no obligation for employers to recognise unions, no obligation to bargain, no obligation to set up elected bodies representative of staff), although some of the Conservative reforms in that area are likely to be reversed by the new Labour government.

Regulatory framework for company training

The company training sphere is itself characterised by its extreme decentralisation, as a result of deregulation policies in this area as well. In 1964, in a totally different context of skill shortages, the Conservative government set up a statutory framework in the Industrial Training Act to establish tripartite Industry Training Boards (ITBs) in various sectors. The following administration (Labour) implemented the new framework and the related levy on all employers. However, pressures (mostly from small and medium-sized enterprises (SMEs)) in the 1970s and the new Conservative agenda from 1979 led to a complete overhaul of the system: 'Since . . . 1979, the emphasis has moved from tri-partism and statutory training provision towards employer-led and voluntary arrangements for training' (Winterton and Winterton, 1994). The Employment and Training Act of 1981 abolished 17 out of the 24 ITBs and established 90 (now 120) non-statutory Industry Training Organisations (ITOs) in their place, which were employer-led bodies with no obligation to involve trade unions.

However, the pervasion of the training sphere by the enterprise culture has been more far-reaching than the deregulation of institutional arrangements, and has also shaped the aims and the contents of company training, in a move that concerned the whole of education and training. As is well known, this evolution started before the 1979 Conservative government with the famous 'Great Debate' in education initiated by the then Labour Prime Minister, James Callaghan. From that time onwards, education was to be 'publicly redefined as a mere instrument of the economy' (Frade, 1996). In terms of content, this came to be achieved through 'radical vocationalism' and the assessment of competences defined by educationalists and employers (unions were also invited to take part in most cases).

The overall concern with training for flexibility and adaptation to business circumstances, although ironically delivered through a system usually described as extremely bureaucratic, is best understood when reading official statements such as the definitions provided by the UK in a European Commission publication on CVT (Ant et al., 1996):

> Initial vocational training aims to provide young people with training leading to National Vocational Qualifications (NVQs) and with the broad-based skills necessary to become *flexible and self reliant employees.* CVT follows this initial vocational training phase and is designed to respond to the needs of the individuals and employers *in adapting to changing responsibilities, employment patterns, work roles, technological change and innovation.*
>
> (authors' emphasis)

Although other rationales for company training exist, we will argue in the next section that they share key assumptions regarding the nature of the labour market and of company flexibility. In contrast to practice in Spain and France, British companies do not make a compulsory contribution to the training of the unemployed. This is left to companies' 'corporate social responsibility' strategies, and hence to the discretion of scattered initiatives.

Spain

At the opposite end of the spectrum is Spain, where the *social* aim of the policies of the last two decades has been as important as the *economic* aim. The special situation of Spain is due to the coming of a democratic regime and, with it, the need to develop the emerging, status-influenced rather than universally-oriented, welfare state created during the previous 40-year-long political period. Thus, whereas France and the UK already enjoyed a universal welfare state by the mid-1970s, Spain had to develop and *universalise* it – a task that was to be an essential aspect of the legitimisation of the new democracy. As a result of this, monetarist and deregulatory policies in Spain went hand in hand with welfare-social protection policies that have established universal services in the areas of health, education and the protection of elderly people.

As compared with the UK, deregulation of the labour market started timidly is Spain in the early 1980s, with legislation allowing the hiring of workers on temporary contracts (1984). Partly, this timid beginning can be attributed to the fact that labour costs in Spain throughout the 1980s were lower than in other industrialised countries (Almeda and Sarasa, 1996), but also to the power and legitimacy of the unions, which were fundamental in bringing democracy. Deregulatory policies began to be pursued in a more determined way in the 1990s, particularly with the reform of the labour market in 1994. Legislation since 1990 has considerably weakened employment protection, particularly with the creation of different modalities of temporary and apprenticeship contracts. The 1994 Act also allows those companies that are in a difficult economic situation to leave branch agreements. Further deregulation, together with other compensatory measures, has been undertaken as part of the national agreement between employers and unions at the beginning of 1997.

Spain's regulatory framework

The construction of a democratic political regime and the development of democratic institutions have constituted the main change in Spain over the last two decades. Devolution of power to the autonomous nationalities and regions has undoubtedly been the most important political process, so that a genuine process of political and socio-economic decentralisation took place, changing profoundly the structure of the previous centralist and authoritarian state. Another crucial process, as mentioned above, has been the reconstruction and development of the welfare state. Overall, the Spanish regulatory framework can be characterised by the decentralisation of powers to the regions and to the localities as well (note that this is utterly contrary to the process undergone by Britain over the last decade); conflicts about overlapping competencies by central, regional and local governments; lack of appropriate co-ordination structures to deal with such problems; a civil society whose strongest institutions are the family, foundations and charities, particularly the Church, and a voluntary sector that is increasingly more important.

The 1994 reforms of the socialist government cannot be understood if decoupled from a parallel review of industrial relations, and indeed as we shall see below, social dialogue structures are a key ingredient of the Spanish regulatory framework.

Industrial relations are quite recent in Spain since free unions only re-emerged after Franco's death. The major concern then became the consolidation of democracy, and governments until 1984 helped with the development of structures involving the social partners. After 1984 and the first reforms of the labour market, the 'moderation pacts' that had prevailed until then gave way to a less consensual social compromise that evolved into outright conflict between 1988 and 1992 as the socialist government led a so-called 'rigour' policy. At the same time centralised bargaining was supplemented by sectoral and territorial bargaining. The 1994 Act on the reform of the labour market confirmed this trend by transferring key areas of labour legislation (including Franco's professional ordinances – i.e. sectoral labour regulations) to branch and company negotiation. Collaboration over training could be significant as an important step in the evolution of industrial relations and thus constitutes – here again – a sphere of high stakes.

Regulatory framework for company training

Collective bargaining also gained strength within continuing training: in December 1992 a national tripartite agreement was signed which some key principles and practices (see Durán López *et al.*, 1994). Among the most important of these, the agreement establishment that:

• the tax for vocational training, levied on both employers and employees, should, as a mandatory duty arising from the 'principle of solidarity', devote 50 per cent of the funds thus collected to the *Instituto Nacional de Empleo* (INEM) for the training of the unemployed, while the remaining 50 per cent will be devoted to continuing training;
• continuing training should be considered both as an economic factor and as a means of promoting the professional and social development of the employees;
• continuing training is a responsibility of both employers and employees, whereas the role of the government is to support and facilitate the process, and to collaborate on more specific aspects such as the use of the networks of public centres of vocational training.

The importance of the solidarity principle as an essential foundation of the Spanish regulatory framework is thus made manifest. The FORCEM, the institution in charge of allocating the mutalised funds upon presentation of individual or collective company and sectoral training plans, is jointly managed by employers and unions and governed on the basis of consensus. Sectoral and regional commissions were also set up.

France

In France there have been, over the last two decades, 'two voices', as it were, arguing for competitiveness and social solidarity respectively. Since the late 1970s, and apart from the 1981–2 period, policies have been strongly directed at modernising and restoring the competitiveness of the French economy through the enterprise and market principles, and this policy has been accompanied by a social discourse. It has been argued by some economists, however, that employment policies were, to a large extent, subordinated to these economic goals. Nevertheless, the concern about the rise of job insecurity, poverty and exclusion amidst fears of a social divide, brought about policies for monitoring and limiting deregulation, and for extending and increasing social protection to populations 'missed' by sectoral policies and social security institutions. Combating exclusion has become a major national concern, a major topic in government discourse, and has led to the definition and implementation of solidarity principles and mechanisms.

'Flexibility' became the keyword for companies, employer representatives and, of course, for government since the early 1980s. Although this tendency has by no means been as actively promoted by French governments as in the UK, it has in practice been supported by it (Gautié, 1993: 87). Thus the Labour Law (*droit du travail*) has grown over the past years to include more and more derogatory measures: new labour contracts have been offered particularly to young and long-term unemployed people, and in general more flexible labour contracts have been permitted (Join-Lambert, 1994). While these deregulatory measures were progressively taking place, although not without hesitations and U-turns, regulations were issued aiming at avoiding abuse and making firms more socially responsible (obligation of *plans sociaux*, parity of conditions for part-time staff etc.).

France's regulatory framework

According to different studies, the last 15 years have been marked, apart from a short-lived nationalisation policy, by a *relative* weakening of the state in the economic sphere. This has been translated into a *decentralisation* of the state, which has been arguably more important over the last few years. In particular, the regions have acquired powers to formulate and implement policy in the field of vocational training. It has been argued that the way of doing things in France, that is, the policy-making process, is 'statist in style, corporatist in form and pluralistic in practice' (Freeman, quoted in Hantrais,

1996: 52), a description that seems to capture the spirit of the French regulatory framework. In terms of employment policies, the government has retained responsibility until recently (*loi quinquennale* of 1993, in which some of its prerogatives were decentralised at a regional level), and is still prominent in the education field. The structures for *implementing* policy are, at least in theory, largely decentralised to *collectivités territoriales* and to both sides of the industry, although the state takes the lead when negotiation at this last level is not conclusive.

Framework for company training

The framework for continuous training is in many ways a reflection of these more general evolutions. Donzelot (1984) recalls how all the laws on 'social guarantees' since the beginning of the 1970s, including the one on continuous training in 1971, stemmed from the realisation after 1968 of the necessity of less centralised and 'ideological' fora, and of more local decentralised procedures to tackle the desire of the French to '*changer la vie*' in a concrete and everyday fashion (in this the successive governments have been following Delors' inspiration). The 1971 law thus established the company (and to a lesser extent the branch) as the place of negotiation, decision making and implementation of continuous training. On the other hand, the already mentioned concern with both promoting modernisation *and* addressing social cohesion was already present in the 1971 law, and was re-emphasised in the new 1991 provisions. This is apparent in the various arrangements of the law both in terms of funding (1.5 per cent of the company payroll has to be spent on training their staff and the young unemployed – or paid to a mutualising fund) and of the objectives outlined by the Code of Labour: 'ensure economic efficiency' . . . 'combat social exclusion and promote social advancement' . . . 'foster cultural development'.

The evolution of the framework for continuing training also reflects the evolution of the role of the state: the initiative was taken by the social partners who agreed on an 'interprofessional agreement' in 1970, which was then translated into law and the same procedure occurred again in 1990/91 – the social partners have a general responsibility for initiating policy in the field. Moreover, the evolution of state intervention in the economy more as a catalyst than as a prescribing authority has been very much felt in the area of company training, for example, with the setting up of '*Contrats d'Etudes Previsionelles*' (studies funded by the government and agreed with the sectoral social partners helping to identify the likely evolution of employment and skill requirements in a given sector and leading to training policy in that sector).

The terms of the debate and the nature of the social 'compromise' over company training

In order to understand what shapes company training in a comparative way, we have argued that we should look at company training as *a sphere that both reflects and promotes new 'compromises'*. Our review of national configurations has shown that the common trends towards economic and labour market deregulation, as well as the decentralisation of regulatory frameworks, had exerted contrary pressures on company training, but that these pressures nevertheless meant that training had become a key area of formal and informal negotiation. Company training studied at the level of the firm is bound to be underpinned by these conflicting rationales and the case-study work about to take place in the three countries will have to assess exactly in what terms the question of company training is posed at the level of the firm, both to illustrate and to adjust our more global understanding. In the three countries considered it looks as if flexibility, be it labour market or internal functional flexibility, has become an imperative for which only compensations can be negotiated – company training having become a key element in this compensation strategy set out by unions and/or public authorities. We have also argued, however, that company training was both used/claimed as an instrument for change and as a buffer against change – and the analysis at enterprise level should provide instances of both.

In the UK, as has been said above, the concern for competitiveness is shared by government, employers and unions and has come to *steer* not only the approach to company training but also to initial education and training.

In broad terms, the drive for competence-based vocational training promoted by the government, as well as the exhortations of the Confederation of British Industry (CBI) are met by the dramatic change of attitude of the Trades Union Congress (TUC) (and affiliated unions) over the last decade. There are indeed disagreements, the unions advocating qualification-oriented training, the recognition of qualification in pay, and ultimately the establishment of a right to training and of a levy on employers. Employer bodies, and above all individual companies, might be much less concerned with the actual qualifications, and more with the immediate relevance of training to their business needs.

Despite these disagreements, we would argue that the approach has become consensual at the policy level. Training is an important component of an emerging discourse dominated by 'one voice', wholly encompassed by economic values, on the need for '*flexibility and employability*', flexibility being understood both as 'external' (i.e. having to do with hiring and firing, outsourcing, subcontracting etc.) and 'internal' (i.e. flexibility of working times, internal mobility of workers, multi-skilling etc.). The complete deregulation of the labour market is a fact acknowledged by all actors in the field, including the unions, and the re-establishment of a minimum wage and of union recognition requirements will not fundamentally change this fact.

'*There is no going back*', union representatives told us in recent fieldwork. Thus this new discourse on flexibility and employability legitimises the already well-advanced shift of the burden of responsibility for education, training and employment on to the *individual*, and implicitly denies any notion of objective structural problems such as lack of jobs, and the increasing proportion of poorly paid, untrained, routine and insecure jobs. It also legitimises the domination of labour market relevance as *the* criterion of the 'good', to the detriment of any educative or developmental goal.

It must be said that this *pensée unique* has been reached within a context where unions have been considerably weakened, where they have had to fight for their survival as meaningful social actors and have had (and still do) to rethink their strategies. More and more unions are entering so-called 'partnership approaches' with employers; there are union 'mergers'; a chief concern is to raise membership. In very general terms, and with notable differences from one sector to another, unions have tried to squeeze into a scene largely dominated by employer concerns, and to found a new legitimacy based on economic 'realism' and managerial competence.

The nature of the consensus also needs to be looked at in a closer fashion, as it may not address the large disparities that exist between sectors and segments of the workforce:

- Economic deregulation and deregulation of the labour markets have not hit all sectors in the same ways. Some actors particularly in industry still enjoy relatively stable and 'rich' industrial relations, steady investment, good levels of pay and social benefits, and have remained relatively impervious to *external* flexibility (i.e. to outsourcing, resorting to short-term and temporary contracts etc.). In such contexts, such as the chemical industry, for example, the trade-off seems perfectly plausible: 'The unions have agreed to multi-skilling where workers are trained to the appropriate national standards and competences, which are seen as protecting workers from skill dilution' (Winterton and Winterton, 1994: 20–23).

At the other side of the spectrum, the service sectors in particular have been fully experimenting with the joint effects of economic and labour market deregulation; the pressure for cost cutting and profitability has been such that even in sectors such as banking, where the industrial and social patrimony had been relatively conservative and peaceful until the late 1980s, a complete change of culture and work organisation took place (a process not yet completed) accompanied by massive redundancies, increased centralisation of decision and Taylorisation of part of the work, and polarisation of the workforce (core/periphery, highly skilled/deskilled, etc.). In these circumstances, and with the looming prospect of a strong decline in the numbers employed over the next 10 years (current estimates are of a decrease of more than 25 per cent) the flexibility/employability balance does not appear so much a trade-off as a trap.

- The discourse on flexibility and employability does not take enough account of the current processes of polarisation of the workforce into, on the one hand, a high-skilled core, able to bear and take advantage of labour market flexibility; and, on the other hand, a less skilled or unskilled periphery, on which labour market flexibility is imposed, and for which training 'for employability' is pure rhetoric.
- Finally, even within this rationale of employability and flexibility, there is a need for serious reflection on the most suitable institutional arrangements. The current voluntaristic and business-led system takes a short-term view of business requirements while the development of broad-based education rather than narrow vocational training might be more suitable for these very interests (for a critical discussion of this issue, see Forrester et al., 1995).

In France, as could be expected, the same disparities between sectors, company sizes and sections of the workforce are to be found. However, our concern here is with the *dominant* terms of the social 'compromise', and the case-studies will help identify the extents and variations in its application. In a first approximation, one might say that the dominant trend is towards a *trade-off between flexibility and security of employment*. Hence, despite current trends towards training for employability, the efforts of the government, of the social partners, and of the education and training institutions involved in company training have been towards improving the relationship between training and *employment*. This 'compromise', which takes place in a configuration where economic competitiveness is primary but where solidarity and employee protection are legitimate and effective checks, acknowledges the deficits of a system that up until the mid-1980s was in many ways a 'repair system' in that companies hit by economic deregulation and restructuring were calling for the help of the state and in particular for funding for the retraining of employees once it was 'too late'. This led to a new focus for government policy in the mid-1980s and an impulse towards anticipation of employment and qualification requirements in each sector as well as within companies, a focus of government policy on SMEs and the less qualified workforce, and a renewed impulse towards employer/union co-operation.

The critical mass and system of compulsory funding of company training, the bipartite structures set up to monitor employment and training (*Commissions Paritaires pour l'Emploi, Fonds d'Assurance Formation*), and finally the substantial impulse given by the anticipation studies funded by the government have led to company training becoming a key forum of discussion and planning, in which overall consensus prevails – in that field – between government, employers, and unions, under the pressure of public opinion.

(This is of course not the case in other areas of negotiation.) *Internal* flexibility is thus promoted, as well as qualifying training especially for the lower skilled and for the young unemployed. However, while there has been substantial progress in a number of sectors, and although innovative agreements have been signed at branch level, similar disparities to the ones encountered in the UK continue to exist: the sectors most concerned by the flexibility of the labour market (such as retail chain stores, hotel and catering, etc.) have traditionally had a seasonal, low-skilled, low-paid workforce, and apart from one or two large companies improving their image and addressing turnover problems through company training, the general picture is at odds with the type of social 'compromise' described above.

Similarly SMEs, although some of them have benefited from the sectoral structuring of the organisation of company training (the *Fonds d'Assurance Formation* providing advice for identification of training needs, for the design of a *cahier des charges*, for the choice of a training provider etc.), are still largely out of the described social 'compromise' – as anticipation is difficult for them, and training often impossible to organise (especially as the French law favours off-the-job training).

In Spain as we have hinted above, company training is part of a wholesale restructuring of the regulations and conditions of employment. In particular, the National Tripartite Agreement on continuing training was signed only months before the 1994 labour market reform, and the relationships between employers and unions on continuous training thus both provide a test for the increased role of social partners in employment matters, and are probably affected by the parallel negotiation on pay scales and work conditions in each sector as a result of the abolition of the professional ordinances. Inevitably as more sectoral labour agreements are being prepared, the issue of linking company training with qualifications and pay is likely to be raised. (This will be one of the issues to explore further in the fieldwork.)

The use of company training as an instrument for change has been a particularly visible strategy in Spain in recent years. The available literature still depicts Spain as a 'modernising' country, and the recent setting up of a review and a complete overhaul of the vocational training system is read as a national strategy for qualifications on a par with the rest of Europe (see, for example, Ant et al., 1996; Brandsma et al., 1996; Kaiserbruger, 1997). Company training is seen first as a means for Spain to acquire a skilled labour force and as a means for companies to meet their immediate needs (two aims that can be contradictory). This is especially visible through the comprehensiveness of the system put in place: the compulsory contribution, the mutualisation principle, the award of funding of company training only after reviewing company training plans, and above all the institutional arrangements facilitating the participation of very small enterprises through collective training plans on a local or sectoral basis. All of these are innovative arrangements piloted and monitored on a bipartite basis, which demonstrate the basic consensus of the social partners on a national strategy of modernisation and qualifications.

The unions are keen, as in Britain and France, but perhaps with more emphasis in Spain, to translate these acquired qualifications into job promotions. One of the problems is the fact that bargaining over classifications is proving a very lengthy process; the translation of this aspiration for recognition of qualifications into career paths is by no means an established procedure. The other rising issue on the training agenda is training for employment preservation and anticipation. Partly because of the recent nature of the framework for in-company training, and partly because the strategy of the unions that have a key role to play in the elaboration of this 'compromise' is still unclear to us, it is difficult to summarise the nature of the 'social compromise' being elaborated around training; this will have to be further explored in the fieldwork.

Conclusion

This chapter set out to show that studying innovation in company training on a cross-national basis means comparing emerging 'compromises' within increasingly flexible and deregulated environments. Company training is at the core of change, since it is used as an instrument for cultural change in companies, as a new form of internal communication, and as a support for the adaptation of the workforce to company needs. It is also considered a buffer against change, through the qualification of individuals, through the anticipation of employment trends and skill requirements. The fact that company training can fulfil both these roles emphasises its suitability for supporting 'compromise'. However, the nature and workability of these 'compromises' very much depend on the relative strength of the institutional actors. 'Industrial patrimonies' in given sectors and companies might be more conducive than others to accommodation. But policy, whether interventionist or not, is still policy, and plays a key role both indirectly through providing checks more or less on deregulation and directly through initiating an institutional framework of negotiation.

It is clear, for example, that the British 'compromise' is underpinned by shared assumptions regarding the flexibility of the labour market and is therefore totally encompassed by economic values, a configuration that is at odds with the French and Spanish contexts. The French 'social compromise' reflects a concern for checking flexibility, as well as for organising solidarity (e.g. with the levy paying for the training of unemployed young people). The more recent framework for company training in Spain seems to have been built from the recognition of the special difficulties there are in drawing very small enterprises and some categories of the workforce within the social 'compromise'. This recognition has led to an attempt at designing the framework on the principles of equity and universality of the social 'compromise' offered by company training, whatever it may be.

References

Almeda, E. and Sarasa, S. (1996) 'Spain: growth to diversity', in V. George and P. Taylor-Gooby (eds) *European welfare policy*, London: Macmillan.

Ant, M., Kintzele, J., van Haecht, A. and Walther, R. (eds) (1996) *Access, quality and volume of continuing vocational training in Europe*, Berlin: Luchterhand.

Brandsma, J., Kessler, F. and Munch, J. (eds) (1996) *Continuing vocational training: Europe, Japan and the United States*, Utrecht: LEMMA BV.

Cochrane, A. (1994) 'Restructuring the local welfare state', in R. Burrows and B. Loader (eds) *Towards a post-Fordist welfare state?*, London: Routledge.

Darmon, I., Frade, C., Boukhabous, Z. and Danau, D. (1996) Leonardo project 'PRISM', first report, London: Tavistock Institute.

Donzelot, J. (1984) 'L'invention du social', Essai sur le déclin des passions politiques, Paris: Fayard.

Durán López, F., Alcaide Castro, M., González Rendón, M. and Flórez Saborido, I. (1994) *La formación profesional continua en España*, Madrid: Ministerio de Trabajo y Seguridad Social.

Forrester, K., Payne, J. and Ward, K. (1995) 'Lifelong education and the workplace: a critical analysis', *International Journal of Lifelong Education*, 14(4) (July–Aug.), 292–305.

Frade, C. (1996) *Education and training policies in the UK*, the DELILAH Project, TSER Programme, Brussels: DGXII, EC.

Frade, C. and Darmon, I. (1996) *For the development of a comparative framework in research on social exclusion*, Working Paper, London: Tavistock Institute.

Frade, C. and Darmon, I. (1997) 'Social exclusion: towards a framework for understanding and policy', *Annual Review 1996–7*, London: Tavistock Institute, 51–57.

Gautié, J. (1993) *Les politiques de l'emploi*, Vuibert, Points Forts Economie.

Hantrais, L. (1996) 'France: squaring the welfare triangle', in V. George and P. Taylor-Gooby (eds) *European welfare policy*, London: Macmillan.

Join-Lambert, M.-T. (1994) *Politiques sociales*, Presses de la Fondation Nationale des Sciences Politiques et Dalloz.

Kaiserbruger, D. (1997) *Négocier la flexibilité, pratiques en Europe*, Les Editions d'organisation.

Kaiserbruger, D., Pincot, B. and Terrier, M. (1996) *Le développement de la formation continue dans les PME: analyse comparative des dispositifs allemands et français*, Délégation à la Formation Professionelle, Paris: Ministère du Travail et des Affairs Sociales.

Leborgne, D. and Lipietz, A. (1990) 'How to avoid two tier Europe', *Labour and Society*, 15(2).

Mullard, M. (1995) 'Economic policy options', in M. Mullard (ed.) *Policy making in Britain*, London: Routledge.

Tavistock Institute, Danish Technological Institute, Bernard Brunches Consultants (1996) *Final evaluation of the FORCE programme*, vol. 1, London: Tavistock Institute.

Winterton, J. and Winterton, R. (1994) *Collective bargaining and consultation over continuing vocational training*, Moorfoot, Sheffield: Employment Department.

Chapter 6

Post-school education and training policy in developmental states

The cases of Taiwan and South Korea

Francis Green, Donna James, David Ashton and Johnny Sung

Introduction

The historical transformation of certain societies in East Asia continues to fascinate scholarly and popular observers. The emergence of the first-tier 'miracles' of South Korea, Taiwan, Hong Kong and Singapore has been variously attributed to early adoption of an export-oriented industrialization strategy, to sound macroeconomics including a high savings ratio, to market-complementing industrial policies and to a culture of hard work (e.g. Stiglitz, 1996). Often highlighted, but rarely explored, in accounts of the East Asian miracles is the role of education and training. High levels of educational attainment and skill formation are recounted, and a simple correlation is made between economic and educational success. With the latter accorded a causal role, one has the proposition that the miracles were 'HRD (Human Resource Development)-led'. Influential in this perspective is the finding from cross-country, econometric studies that show that high primary and secondary school enrolments in 1960 can explain the experience of higher growth rates in later decades (World Bank, 1993; Benhabib and Spiegel, 1994).

This chapter explores the articulation of the town transformations of the economy and of the skill formation systems in the larger leading East Asian 'miracle' economies, namely South Korea and Taiwan, with reference in particular to skill formation after compulsory schooling. We start from the proposition that the success with economic growth cannot be understood simply as a supply-side phenomenon. Rather we shall argue that the distinctive characteristic of policy formation in these two countries is the manner in which, over time, both the demand for and the supply of skills for industry were influenced by the state, and co-ordinated as part of the development strategy. We propose that this co-ordination bestowed a continuing competitive advantage for these East Asian economies that goes some way to

This is an edited version of an article published in *Journal of Education Policy* 14, 3 (1999): 301–315.

explaining their capacity to sustain high rates of growth over long periods. We also discuss the development of contradictory tendencies for policy formation in the current period, as the economies converge on the frontiers of technology.

In the second section we set out the bare bones of the model of skill formation that we believe applies in varying degrees in the leading Tiger economies of East Asia. Since we draw heavily on the theory of the developmental state (e.g. Wade, 1990; Castells, 1992), while we attempt to extend this theory, we refer to the model as a 'developmental skill formation system'. We have set out to examine the applicability of this model, through a series of semi-structured interviews with policy makers and observers and through a synthesis of their responses with published and unpublished literature. We argue elsewhere, in a more extensive analysis, that the developmental skill formation model applies, with varying degrees of approximation, to the study of all skill formation policies in the four leading East Asian 'miracle' economies (Ashton et al., 1999). Moreover, there is some recent evidence of diffusion of certain elements of a developmental skill formation policy, towards other developing countries in the South East Asian region and elsewhere. The third section summarizes our findings in respect of Taiwan and South Korea. The last section concludes with a discussion of the distinctiveness of policy making in these countries, and a consideration of how far this model is sustainable in the current era.

Developmental skill formation

The education and training systems of South Korea and Taiwan have been developed in the wake of pre-Second World War Japanese colonial domination. School and university systems often had to start from scratch because the previous rudimentary education system was primarily driven by Japanese national priorities, and unsurprisingly was not appropriate in the newly liberated countries. Moreover, in the absence of any strong occupational traditions with associated apprenticeships, it was also necessary to develop quickly a system of post-school skill formation to match the transforming economy. The rapid changes that took place in ensuing decades stand in contrast to the comparatively slow evolution of education and training systems in the West (Green, 1990). Above all, Western systems developed with a great deal of autonomy from the process of industrialization of the economy. In the East Asian 'miracle' economies, the key to the sustainability of the miracle, and in particular their move from low value-added production to high value-added production lay precisely in the control exercised by the developmental state. Defining features of developmental states are their ability to act independently of immediate interest groups, and their imperative to seek legitimacy in the face of external threats through economic growth (Cumings, 1987).

In developmental states, processes of education and training policy making have a distinct character. First, the state influences employers' demands for skills, via an early emphasis on state industries, through its strong influence over employers and through the direction of the economy in general. For example, when in the 1970s South Korea's President Park decided on a strategy of investment in heavy industry, he was also acutely aware of the relevant skills that would be required in the workforce. Similarly in Taiwan, the skill requirements of state-initiated investment in heavy industry during the 1970s were anticipated and met by new tertiary technology institutes and by expansion of university science and engineering departments. Second, the state can flexibly use several mechanisms to ensure an adequate supply of skills. This flexibility derives from the fact that education and training policies are linked at the top with the formation of economic policies, through particular institutional mechanisms. With some 'inside' knowledge and a relatively effective civil service able to read the likely skill demands of the economy, the government is able to plan strategically a supply of skills. The institutional mechanisms, originally set up within an authoritarian state, also allow a large degree of central control over schools, universities and training institutes, thus permitting plans to be made effective. Finally, a consequence of these features is that there is a relatively close connection between the stage of economic growth and the development of the education and training systems.

Inevitably, this sketch is simplified. It obscures the conflicts that have arisen, and the mistakes that have been made, and is no more than an 'ideal' description of what we believe to have been the dominant force for change in the recent era. Whether the development skill formation model can continue to be dominant is a matter for discussion, to which we return in the concluding section.

Mechanisms

The influence of the governments of South Korea and Taiwan on the direction of economic growth, via their trade and industry policies, is a matter of historical record and will not be discussed in detail here. In the case of South Korea, Amsden (1989) for example has shown how the state became a key player assisting the process of adoption of borrowed technology, through a systematic protectionist strategy and collaboration with the Chaebol (Korean conglomerates) based on export-driven incentives. Although early commentators were wont to attribute Taiwan's success to free-market policies, the state-led nature of its development, as identified for example by Wade (1990), is also now accepted by modern commentators. The impact of state-led policies on skills demands is generally implicit. The mechanisms for co-ordinating education and training policy are, however, less well known. In Taiwan, the main institution for linking the supply of skilled workers with current and future demands of industry, has always been the central economic policy-making body, which since 1978 has been the Council for Economic Planning and Development (CEPD). The CEPD works with the government to generate the industrial strategy and ensures that other ministries toe the same line to meet the objectives of the economic plans. The CEPD also has the responsibility of ensuring that the educational and training system delivers appropriately trained personnel.

It was in the mid-1960s that manpower plans were becoming explicitly linked with formal economic plans. For example, in 1966 the (predecessor of the) CEPD initiated an increase in vocational and industrial education, corresponding to plans that involved Taiwan beginning to move up the value-added ladder. In the early 1970s it initiated an expansion of engineering and natural science departments in universities, in view of its extensive plans for industrialization of the economy. In recent times, the CEPD played an important part in the development of the Asia Pacific Regional Operations Centre in Taiwan, by ensuring that there is an emphasis on enhancing continuing education, innovation and the quality of education. While the CEPD is probably not as powerful as it used to be, if only because the legislature has gained some influence at the expense of the executive, our interview evidence confirmed that it still holds much more influence than other ministries, and retains control over manpower planning. The Manpower Planning Department, which is part of the CEPD, carries out the detailed planning and policy execution. This central focus is then supplemented by other mechanisms. While the centralized Ministry of Education controls the supply of education, the Council for Labour Affairs has the responsibility for public vocational training. Another key institution is the National Youth Commission, which monitors the supply of very highly qualified manpower. An important activity since the late 1980s is providing incentives to highly educated Taiwanese scientists and engineers, now living in the United States, to return. These scientists were much less in demand in earlier economic stages than in the present stage when Taiwanese industry needs to be more innovative (not just adapting existing technologies). Helping to seal the top-down sway of all these institutions has been the pervasive influence of the Kuomintang party, which until recent times has been virtually indistinguishable from the state.

In South Korea, the Economic Planning Board (established in 1961) has performed the function of the main linking mechanism. It was called a board in order to distinguish itself from ministries, and demonstrate its overarching control. It had three major roles: to plan and formulate economic policy programmes, to co-ordinate economic and other policies by the ministries, and to evaluate policy programmes (KDI/World Bank/UNECA, 1996). It formulated a series of five-year economic plans, in the light of which skill formation policies were drawn up and implemented. For example, just as in Taiwan, the EPB anticipated skill shortages in the 1970s in the course of the second five-year plan; it initiated an expansion of science and technical education, beefed up the promotion of vocational education in schools and set up a public training system to provide both skilled craftsmen and operatives. Because of its overarching role and power, and because of the unassailable position of economic development (with national defence) as the primary goal of government, the EPB could largely achieve its objectives. The EPB has been supported by an infrastructure of government research and strategic planning agencies, two notable ones being the Korean Development Institute and the Korean Educational Development Institute. In addition the EPB has been further strengthened by advisory support from the President's officials in the Blue House. Indeed, direct presidential concern with skill formation has been a notable feature in South Korea.

Even though this institutional structure has remained in place for more than three decades, there have been changes, not least with the onset of political democratization and economic modernization. In the 1990s the EPB has less power than previously although its waning power may not be as dramatic as the Korean government may want the World Trade Organization and other OECD members to believe. The 'normalization' of the functions of the EPB was highlighted when it was merged in 1994 with the Ministry of Finance into the Ministry of Finance and Economy (MOFE). Disagreements between ministries can now emerge, which might previously have been suppressed by a more powerful 'superministry'. Yet the MOFE still has substantial authority over other ministries. For example, with regard to the recent education reforms proposed by the Ministry of Education, it was reported to us that the MOFE 'strongly urged people in the Ministry of Education to take these actions', and it was clear that they broadly expected compliance. The linkages between economic and educational planning have been in place to prepare for future manpower requirements. These linkages can only be successful if there are tools to implement required changes. In the case of South Korea, the high demand for education has made the job a case of limiting and directing this demand through the use of quotas based on predictions made from manpower plans and made possible through the Ministry of Education's centralized control over private and public education mentioned above. Implementation of the quotas has been through the school and college admission and examination systems. Selective funding is also used to promote certain fields of study. For example, Information Technology is now being emphasized so funds are being increased in this area while funds are being withheld from other fields. The use of entrance quotas for level and field of study is widespread. The quotas are set through requests from certain ministries who work from their own manpower predictions. Thus the Ministry of Science and Technology approaches the Ministry of Education for changes in the science quotas while the Ministry of Industry and Commerce will demand changes in the quotas of particular industrial areas. The Ministry of Education considers these requests in the light of overall strategy.

The development of post-school education and training policy

In order to understand the focus and the evolution of post-school skill formation policies, it is necessary briefly to describe the schooling outcomes. First, in both countries there was not only a relatively high initial participation in primary education (in 1960, the participation rate was 60 per cent in impoverished South Korea, 67 per cent in Taiwan compared, say, with 22 per cent in Pakistan), there was a rapid increase in school participation over the next two decades. By 1990 south Korea's population over 15 had received an average of nearly ten years' schooling, and Taiwan eight years. (The OECD average was nine years.) In both countries the public showed a large appetite for education, due to the egalitarian nature of the systems and high economic returns and in part to Confucian norms. Both governments have retained strict control over the system, even though it has been mainly financed through private contributions. The product in both countries is a basic education across the vast majority of the young population. Second, in both countries the government influenced the form of education in order to meet what it judged to be the economy's needs as it began to move away from exclusively low value-added production methods. Both governments channelled large numbers of secondary students into vocational education, despite this being highly unpopular with aspiring parents. Taiwan in particular, sent 57 per cent through the vocational route in 1970, rising to a peak of 72 per cent in 1990 (Chang, 1996).

The high participation in schooling and the emphasis on vocational education, both have implications for skill formation after school. On one hand, the high participation in schooling fuelled the social demand for higher education places. The problem facing governments has not been how to motivate higher education – indeed, a perennial social problem is the 'examination hell' endured by teenagers in their struggle to get admitted into higher-ranking universities. The objective, rather, has been to delay opening the floodgates to mass higher education until the economy has sufficiently matured, if it ever will, to require mass proportions of graduates. A further problem of recent concern to both governments has been the quality of higher education – whether it is producing sufficient creative skills for a new economy premised on innovation as the main source of competitive advantage. The high proportions in vocational education have served to supply some of the traditional skills needed in industry, especially when industry did not benefit from a legacy of craft-trained personnel. As we shall see, private sector training has been slow to develop in both countries, with employers resisting government attempts to induce them to increase training.

The large inflows of graduates from the vocational high schools meant that the training problem did not lead to widespread skill shortages. Nevertheless in both countries the governments anticipated early on, largely as a result of the mechanisms described above, that there would be a need for new supplies of industrial skills, beyond what could be taught in vocational high schools.

Taiwan

Beginning in the late 1960s, and complementing the stress on vocational education, manpower plans in Taiwan turned to the question of training. Rapid export-oriented industrialization in the 1960s was beginning to raise the demand for skilled labour. The abundant supply of unskilled labour was also drying up. Several measures were taken to pursue the goal of a training policy, including signing a mutual agreement with the United Nations, implementing a new form of apprenticeship training, introducing skills tests and skills competitions, and proposing the establishment of nine public and private training institutes (San and Chen, 1988). During the period of the second plan (the late 1960s), an in-plant planning programme was carried out in state-owned enterprises in which training and recruitment needs were predicted from forecasts of business development. The state was concerned that training would be needed to realize fully the benefits of the expansion in compulsory education. By the third plan (1971), the state intended not only to continue to use the state-owned enterprises to forge new industrial development but also to guide private industry in successful training. The plan was explicit that the in-plant planning programme was to be used in state-owned enterprises to demonstrate its value to the private sector (Economic Planning Council, 1971: 50).

Other attempts were made in the early 1970s to increase the commitment and financial contribution to training of private industry. In 1972 the Vocational Training Fund Statute was promulgated. The idea behind the statute was based on research conducted into the use of levies in other developing and developed countries (principally Britain). The statute required that all public and private enterprises with over 40 employees should contribute to a Vocational Training Fund through a levy of at least 1.5 per cent of the payroll. Enterprises that conducted in-service training would be reimbursed (up to 80 per cent) by the Fund. There were doubts about the implementation of the statute while it ran and by 1974, during difficulties caused by the first oil crisis, criticism of the levy by industry rose to such a level that it was repealed. Both political and economic problems contributed to the state giving in to business pressure over the levy issue. The cost of the administration of the levy has also been cited for its unpopularity. Even though the levy was withdrawn, an increase in in-plant training during and after the levy period is reported (San and Chen, 1988). However, public training had to be continued and financed by the government, which took the view that in-plant training remained insufficient.

The levy was reinstated in principle by the Vocational Training Act of 1983. However, as a result of interministry infighting, this levy was neither promoted nor implemented. While the Council for Labour Affairs had included a levy in the Act, the Manpower Planning Department (MPD) within the Council for Economic Planning and Development did not want to implement it. So the state concentrated on the provision of training at public training centres. It was undoubtedly well advised to do so, because the Taiwanese economy was then, and still is, overwhelmingly dominated by small and medium-sized enterprises (SMEs). It is likely that a renewed programme would have been overwhelmed by administrative costs and bureaucratic rigidities. Only within the larger companies is there any substantive training in Taiwan. Note, however, that informal learning is an alternative vital form of skill formation in many Taiwanese SMEs. With high turnover, an entrepreneurial culture and a plentiful supply of vocationally educated new recruits, lack of formal in-plant training has hardly proved a major handicap hitherto.

Following the state-initiated moves into heavy industry during the late 1960s, which intensified after 1973 during the period of the ten major construction projects, vocational education was expanded to tertiary level with the establishment of the National Taiwan Institute of Technology. This completed the full system of vocational education – vocational school, junior college and the institute of technology. Further institutes of technology were also established. Not only would the institutes provide technologists to meet the increasing demands of industrialization (the development of heavy industry), but they would also promote the image of vocational education by offering opportunities (and a Bachelor's degree) at the tertiary level. As export-oriented industrialization progressed, more labour was needed and the third manpower plan promoted the full utilization of women workers, and their education and training. There were also proposals to increase the amount of private investment in education, and to expand engineering and natural science departments at the university and college levels (Economic Planning Council, 1971: 37). The proportions of students in science and engineering were raised from 28 per cent in 1969–70 to 40 per cent in 1981–2, and slightly more since then (Law, 1994). In 1979 the Science and Technology Development Programme addressed manpower at the tertiary levels in response to the increasing capital- and skill-intensive industrialization occurring in the wake of the oil-shocks. The emphasis was on university education and post-graduate education and on the key technologies that it was anticipated industry should acquire (Li, 1988). The total numbers in higher education were steadily allowed to rise: by the mid-1990s some three out of every five high school graduates were going on to enrol in some form of higher education.

Thus, to summarize the development of skill formation practices and policies in Taiwan since the 1960s, a manpower policy and system was adopted and placed under the control of the Council for Economic Planning and Development. The needs of the developing economy were assessed by the CEPD and passed on to the MPD. Vocational education was expanded at the expense of the popular academic education. Technical institutes provided more incentives for people to follow the vocational route and provided technician training. Tertiary and secondary education was restricted in the early years while semi-skilled labour was in demand. Later, more focus and resources were also given to science and technology. Vocational training was increasingly emphasized through public training centres; however, the state was unable to shift much responsibility for training to the private sector.

South Korea

While Taiwan was unusually successful in its drive to raise proportions in vocational education, the South Korean government was less efficacious (or at least less pressing). Though it successfully lifted vocational education to 47 per cent of all pupils in the 1970s, this proportion fell steadily thereafter (Korean Educational Development Institute, 1994). The public accepted vocational high schools in that they fulfilled the pent-up demand for education, but they were still not as popular as academic education. The government produced propaganda to promote vocational education and training, stressing the relatively high economic returns. The entrance examination for vocational high schools was set earlier than for the academic high schools. The intention was that more students would accept places in vocational schools rather than have to potentially take a year out if they failed in academic high school examinations (Gill and Ihm, 1996). The declared goal, which was to have two-thirds of high school students in vocational high schools, was never reached; but the government's power was still sufficient to ensure very substantial numbers of vocationally educated graduates from the school system.

Given this outcome on vocational education, the government turned at successive moments to attempt to install and upgrade a vocational training system. Even in the late 1960s (when South Korea was still a very low-income nation), the government anticipated the advent of skill shortages with industralization by starting up a public training system, primarily to provide skilled craftsmen and operatives. The government took the lead, since enterprises were unwilling to provide or did not accept the need for training (Ministry of Education/Korean Educational Development Institute, 1996). Well-equipped public vocational training institutes were founded and, with financial support from the World Bank and the International Labour Organization, the Central Vocational Training Institute was established. In addition, some in-plant training was directly subsidized by government in a scheme that ran from 1968 to 1971.

In the 1970s, during the launch of the 'Heavy Chemical and Industrialization Plan', the promotion of training as well as vocational education became the key policies to provide the new industries with the semi-skilled and skilled labour required. Some policies were even supervised by the Blue House itself down to the smallest detail. President Park was convinced that the very success of the HCIP was reliant on the right manpower mix, and tried to persuade private business to support it. Thus, the vocational education and training plans and the HCIP were seen as 'a kind of package' with the aim of producing graduates to go straight into the factories. In 1972, the Ministry of Science and Technology predicted that there would be a shortage of skilled labour in their science and technical manpower forecast. It was felt that the manpower needs of the HCIP would not be met by public training centres alone (Lee, 1996). The government enacted the Special Measures Law for Vocational Training in 1974, under which companies of over 500 employees were required to train 15 per cent of the workforce. The penalty for non-compliance was a fine. From 1976 lowering the threshold to 300 employees expanded the coverage, while at the same time the penalty was referred to as a levy. The first effects of the levy were judged very favourable. It raised awareness of training needs and the numbers receiving training increased substantially: the years 1972 to 1976 saw altogether 177,388 craftsmen coming out of in-plant training centres, while over 1977 to 1981 the output was 337,388 craftsmen (Lee, 1990).

Yet it is possible to detect, from the start of the 1980s, increasing signs of strain in the Korean skill formation system. As the process of industrialization was being broadened to include more high technology sectors, and as the economy was starting to be opened to more direct global influence, there was increasing recognition of the need for change. This was reflected in the founding of the Presidential Commission for Education Reform in 1985. For the most part, however, the system remained unchanged till the mid-1990s. The government preferred to attempt to create the needed skills using the existing institutions, rather than commit the funding to extensive reforms (Ministry of Education, 1996). In the fourth five-year plan (1977–81), forecasts for technical manpower by KDI again revealed that there would be a shortage of skilled manpower. At the same time, the beginning of pressure from trading partners for liberalization as well as the pressure from the second-tier NIEs, required increased internationalization and a move into higher value-added technological products. Yet the main response was through the enlargement of public training institutes (Kim, 1993), because the initially successful levy scheme began to fail. The numbers receiving in-plant training fell by two-thirds in the mid-1980s. By lowering the size threshold in 1990 to 150 employees the scheme was broadened to include more employers, but by 1992 only 16 per cent of establishments covered by the scheme actually did any training, and only 8 per cent did enough to be exempted entirely from the levy. Despite an increase in the levy to 0.6 per cent of the wage bill, the rest chose to pay up and draw skilled or semi-skilled workers as necessary from the public training centres.

Training levy schemes like South Korea's have been utilized in a number of countries, or particular sectors of countries, but usually have had a relatively short lifespan owing to opposition from employers. The distinguishing feature of the Korean system is that it remained *in situ* for two decades, and is being replaced only by an enlarged system on similar principles. This longevity is no doubt attributable in part to the power of the Korean developmental state to resist opposition from sections of employers. *Internal* diagnoses of the failure of the levy to meet its objectives primarily emphasize the rigid bureaucratic control of training, rather than the still comparatively low size of the levy. In addition, the underlying demand for formal training was limited where, as in the majority of Korean enterprises, a well-educated labour force was engaged in mass-production processes using comparatively low-skilled methods. This concentration on Fordist production methods may also help to explain too the other main feature of the levy system, namely that the training it did support was at a low level. Even by 1991, some 95 per cent of private training was for Assistant Craftsmen, which is the lowest skill level.

Attempts to introduce an apprenticeship scheme along the lines of the German dual system, and to train a cadre of 'Meister' who can provide in-house training have also not worked well (Jeong, 1995). Primarily, this was because they did not have the same institutional infrastructure as in Germany, argued to be an important adjunct of the dual system (Streeck, 1991); another factor was an overly rigid bureaucratic control of the scheme. Policies for higher technical skills were, however, less problematic since they did not rely so much on the coercion or consent of employers. To some extent the need for more technicians to support the engineers and professionals could be met by the junior colleges (Lee, 1983). The number of these colleges increased during the period of the fourth plan (1976–81), and throughout the 1970s they churned our ever-increasing numbers of applied science graduates. By 1980, more than one in three junior college students were studying engineering or the natural sciences.

It was in the 1970s that the tide of demand for education reached the tertiary level with considerable force. The government curbed this demand by the addition of the nationwide Preliminary Examination for College Entrance to the individual entrance examinations held by universities from 1969 to 1979 (Gill and Ihm, 1996). For some time, private tutoring was prohibited, as a response to the social problem caused by excessive competition for tertiary places. But supply was raised partly by the opening of new air and correspondence universities. In 1980, however, it was resolved to elicit an increased supply of graduates by the simple expedient of a partial lifting of the floodgates to enrolment in existing universities and by setting up some new technical universities (polytechnic colleges). Tertiary enrolments grew at an annual rate of 18.3 per cent from 1980 to 1985 (Jung, 1996). Even though limits were placed on the numbers graduating, and even though enrolments were slowed to a growth of only 2 per cent in the late 1980s, the early 1980s cohort of graduates was released on to the labour market only to find – not surprisingly – that not all of them were wanted. Graduate employment rates fell sharply and, a few years on in the late 1980s, wage premiums for graduates and the implied ex-post-marginal rate of return also dropped (R yoo et al., 1993; Jung, 1996). The returns to higher education nevertheless remained relatively high, and were still estimated to exceed the returns to other levels of education. Come the 1990s and tertiary enrolments again picked up, with the numbers rising at more than 5 per cent a year: by 1995 55 per cent of the school-leaving cohort went on to enrol in tertiary education. Thus the government was easily able to obtain a sufficient cadre of university-educated personnel to work in the now advanced sectors of the Korean economy. But it became increasingly concerned about the quality of the graduates, and with potential quantitative excess. At the recent seminar on the future of Korean education organized by the Korean Development Institute, the spectre was raised of a near-universal participation in higher education early in the new millennium.

Conclusion: is the developmental skill formation model still sustainable?

Part of the reason for this fear of having too many graduates may lie in the evident trend (to be found in both countries) towards a loosening of the controlling ties of the developmental state. No longer are the governments able to withstand so easily the pressures of public demand, nor can they influence the private sector so easily. Are they losing control?

We have found that, hitherto, the 'developmental' nature of the state in both Taiwan and South Korea has fostered a relatively close linkage between the economic system and the skill formation system. The close linkage was remarkable considering the extraordinarily rapid economic transformations that were taking place. At the same time, it was because education and training policies were able to keep up with and occasionally anticipate the changing economy that no period of drastic skill shortages ever emerged to block the continuation of economic growth and the transformation to higher value-added economic sectors. We propose, in effect, that the political and institutional mechanisms put in place by the ruling elites proved, despite their problems, to be superior in terms of flexibility to any scenario that might have ensued in a more market-driven skill formation system. In this instance, the superiority of state action cannot therefore be reduced merely to a case of internalizing an external benefit (which has been the argument of the World Bank (1993)).

Broadly speaking, the mechanisms we describe involve strategic co-ordination at the top levels of government between economic and skill formation policies. An overarching body – the CEPD in Taiwan and the EPB in South Korea – has the job of delivering this strategy and the power to bring other ministries into line with it. Strong centralized control enables the state to ensure delivery of its skills plans at the ground floor, whether in schools, universities or public training centres. Within this framework, the tertiary institutions, both academic and vocational and the public training centres, have been built up over the last two decades; while demonstrable economic need (as expressed in economic and manpower plans) was not always the only factor leading to changes, it was always a major consideration. The chief problem in the system has been the attenuated ability of the state to compel employers to train their workers. In Taiwan the state was able to promote enterprise training where it was itself the owner, but this facility has disappeared with successive privatization of industry. In both countries a levy was tried early on in the development process. While in South Korea the levy had a short-term success and has endured, it was dropped in Taiwan, where the economy is dominated by small-scale enterprises that have expressed little interest in formal training.

The current era is witnessing changes that may undermine the usefulness of the developmental skill formation model in coming decades. It is widely argued that there needs to be changes in the skill formation system. As these economies approach maturity and as the 'knowledge age' dominates national competitiveness, deficiencies in the quality of education and in the provision for lifelong learning have been highlighted. There is also the trend towards an opening up and democratization of political and economic life in both South Korea and Taiwan, which may limit the state's power to pursue strategic objectives.

Consider some of the changes now proposed or under way. In South Korea, the chief means of securing improved education quality is to be through greater diversification via funding incentives. Universities are to be induced to provide more varied, innovative and flexible courses, and to set their own (diverse) entrance criteria. A credit bank system is to be introduced in order to promote flexibility for student learning and to permit lifelong learning. Public vocational training is to receive more funding still and to be integrated more with vocational education. As regards private training, the old levy system is being phased out, and replaced as part of a new Employment Insurance System. The new system is still to work on the principle that enterprises are taxed and get reimbursed if they provide training; however, the bureaucratic control is to be much looser, greater diversity among providers is encouraged, and more scope for individual choice fostered. Finally,

at the upper end of the spectrum, strategic efforts are being made to invig-
orate the research capacity of industry by increasing the capacity of universities to deliver Research and Development manpower and co-operation with
industry.

In Taiwan, the government has announced no major education reform,
but nevertheless still aims systematically to address skills supply issues as part
of its economic strategy. It currently has a 'Manpower Development Plan
for Crossing the Millennium', a part of its 'National Plan for Crossing the
Millennium', which is linked to the Asia Pacific Regional Operations Centre
and plans to improve national competitiveness. The government has plans
for piecemeal reforms in schools, and is continually exercised by the social
problem of excess pressures from the university entrance exam. As for universities, it is likely they will continue to expand, driven partly by public
demand, with the intention of allowing more choice. However, the main
preoccupation is with vocational training, where the deficiencies of the
private sector are recognized. The government aims to deliver new and better
public training programmes – particularly in targeted areas such as comput-
erization and industrial automation – and an improved infrastructure of skills
testing and certification.

The changes in Taiwan represent a case of continued improvements on
an already successful public system. The changes in South Korea, which will
no doubt be slowed down by the financial crisis of 1997 and its aftermath,
amount to a very substantial reform of a skill formation system that is already
looked up to by many observers in the West. At the heart of this paradox
there are certain contradictory tendencies in the political economy of skill
formation in both South Korea and Taiwan. Confucian culture has left its
imprint on the educational system in the form of an emphasis on rote
learning. While this has facilitated high levels of achievement in the basics,
mathematics, science and language, which in turn has prepared young people
well for further trainng in craft and intermediate-level skills, this approach
is now being seriously challenged. With the emphasis in the knowledge
intensive industries on creativity there is a real fear, expressed in current
policy debates, about the adequacy of an educational system that so far has
served these societies well. The persistence of rote learning as the normal
pedagogy is deep seated, hard to challenge, and could, it is argued, have
potentially damaging effects on economic growth. In both societies there is
concern that unless their education systems, at the highest level, can introduce a more creative, research-based tradition, they will lose out in the field
of industrial research and development.

A further tension lies in the mechanisms for linking education and training systems with trade and industry policies. The threats to the continuance
of these mechanisms come from two sources. One is the international
community, especially the major Western powers. As the tigers have become

important players on the world stage, they have come under increasing pressure since the mid-1980s from international institutions to open up their markets and deregulate. In South Korea there has been some reduction in the power of the Economic Planning Board, and the monopolistic dominance of the Chaebol has sharply constrained the government's privatization policy. The external pressure was brought to a head in late 1997 by the need to borrow urgently from the International Monetary Fund to try to shore up confidence in Korea's weak financial system. Moreover, given the increasing regional integration of economies in East Asia, other countries with less pressing internal structural problems cannot avoid region-wide financial crises. It is likely that in the future governments will have somewhat less ability than hitherto to determine the industrial direction of the economy. Further external pressure comes from the integration of the People's Republic of China and other low-income countries into the world economy. The proximity of the mainland and the cultural closeness may prove an especially difficult problem for the Taiwanese authorities whatever the political future holds: as governments hold less power over indigenous capital, the hand of the more internationally-oriented fractions of capital is strengthened by the alternative strategy of exploiting abroad its ability to manage very low-cost, low-skilled labour. The sandwich problem – being pressed between the older industrial countries and the very low-wage countries – is a very real concern for the governments of the tiger economies.

The other threat to the linking mechanisms comes from within countries. Internal pressures for democratizing of society may lead to a looser control over employers and the various skill formation institutions. These institutions are likely to come under increasing pressures from other sources – such as unions and professional bodies – and increasingly agencies may resist the impositions of central government control. Government itself might need to accede to popular pressures – in South Korea, for example, participation in higher education continues a seemingly inexorable upward trend in response to social demand.

Any weakening of the links between the skill formation system and the economy could be both a problem and a blessing, given the need for more creative forms of learning. Among the respondents we questioned on this issue the typical view was that there was a need for more creative and imaginative workforces if companies are to maintain their edge in world markets. To provide workers with yet higher levels of skill and creativity it is argued that the education and training institutions require more autonomy to respond, in appropriate ways, to the requirements of employers. The current direction of government policy is to accept this diagnosis and reduce central regulation, thereby providing greater local autonomy. In South Korea the authorities are thereby attempting to make a virtue out of necessity. Yet by decentralizing and providing this autonomy the state runs the risk of losing its control over education and training and hence over the supply of skills that has been so important a part of their policies hitherto.

On the other hand there remains in both societies a legacy of concern with the long-term strategic direction of the economy. To assume that, once catch-up is complete, future growth will proceed along a global trajectory that is determined outside national boundaries would be an historical abstraction. The contradictions associated with catch-up are real; nevertheless there has always been a large dose of historical common sense in the method of simple extrapolation from the past. The trick of future forecasting is to recognize the contradictions of the existing mode of economic growth, as well as the continuity of politico-economic processes that hitherto have proved successful in their own terms. The willingness of policy makers to integrate the education and training system within a strategy for economic growth, and the mechanisms for doing so, remain much stronger in Taiwan and South Korea than even now in the West. In Britain, it is now held, at least by the political authorities, that education policy is a branch of economic policy. Whether or not this is broadly accepted as a normative goal for education – as it is in Taiwan and South Korea – a strategic approach to education and training policy formation is likely to have limited impact if at the same time the state has no strategic aims for the economy. As long as Western states like Britain cede to individual employers alone the ability to determine the direction of skills formation – what may be termed the market-based approach to skill formation – it remains likely that they will experience in this respect a source of competitive disadvantage in relation to states that intervene strategically.

References

Amsden, A.H. (1989) *Asia's Next Giant* (New York: Oxford University Press).

Ashton, D., Green, F., James, D. and Sung, J. (1999) *Education and Training for Development in Asia. The Political Economy of Skill Formation in East Asian Newly Industrialised Economics* (London: Routledge).

Benhabib, J. and Spiegel, M.M. (1994) The role of human capital in economic development. Evidence from aggregate cross-country data, *Journal of Monetary Economics* 34, 143–173.

Castells, M. (1992) Four Asian tigers with a dragon head: A comparative analysis of the state, economy and society in the Asian Pacific Rim, in *States and Development in the Pacific Fim* by R.P. Applebaum and J. Henderson, 50–70 (London: Sage Publications).

Chang, P. (1996) *Manpower planning in the R.O.C. on Taiwan*, mimeo, CEPD.

Cumings, B. (1987) The origins and development of the Northeast Asian political economy: Industrial sectors, product cycles and political consequences, in Frederick C. Deyo (ed.) *The Political Economy of the New Asian Industrialism*, 44–83 (Ithaca and London: Cornell University Press).

Economic Planning Council, Manpower Planning Department (1971) *The Republic of China's Third Manpower Development Plan of China* (Taipei: MPD).

Green, A. (1990) *Education and State Formation: The Rise of Education Systems in England, France and the USA* (London: Macmillan).

Gill, I.S. and Ihm, C. (1996) Vocational education and training reforms in Korea: Constraints and innovations, in *KDI/World Bank/UNECA International Development Exchange Program*, Study Tour on Economic Development and Human Capital in Korea, Oct. 6–12.

Jeong, J. (1995) The failure of recent state vocational training policies in Korea from a comparative perspective, *British Journal of Industrial Relations*, 33 (2), 237–252.

Jung, J. (1996) *Educational expansion and economic returns to college education in Korea*, KIET Occasional Paper No. 22 (Seoul: Korea Institution for Industrial Economics and Trade).

KDI/World Bank/UNECA (1996) Institutional mechanism, in *International Development Exchange Program*, Study Tour on Economic Development and Human Capital in Korea, Oct. 6–12.

Kim, J. (1993) Vocational training in Korea, with emphasis on large scale enterprises, in B.C. Sanyal, Kim Jae Woong, Tun Lwin, A. Arcelo and M. Bray (eds) *Education, Employment and Human Resource Development: Report of a Sub-regional Workshop*, Seoul, Republic of Korea, 2–12 June 1992 (Paris: UNESCO).

Korean Educational Development Institute (1994) *Educational Indicators in Korea* (Seoul: MOE).

Law, W. (1994) The higher education systems of the People's Republic of China and the Republic of China: A comparative study, Ph.D. thesis University of London, Institute of Education.

Lee, J. (1996) *Human resource development strategy: The case of Korean vocational training*, mimeo, Korea Development Institute.

Lee, K. (1983) *Human Resources Planning in the Republic of Korea: Improving Technical Education and Vocational Training*, Washington, DC: World Bank Staff Working Papers No. 554.

Lee, M. (1990) *Technical/Vocational Education System: A Comparison of Pakistan and South Korea* (Pak/88/007) ILO/UNDP/Government of Pakistan.

Li, K.T. (1988) *The Evolution of Policy Behind Taiwan's Development Success* (New Haven and London: Yale University Press).

Ministry of Education [S.K.] (1996) *Education in Korea 1995–1996* (Seoul: Ministry of Education).

Ministry of Education/Korean Educational Development Institute (1996) *The Korean Education System: Background Report to the OECD* (Seoul: Ministry of Education/Korean Educational Development Institute).

R yoo, J., Nam, Y. and Camoy, M. (1993) Changing rates of return to education over time: A Korean case study, *Economics of Education Review* 12 (1), 71–80.

San, G. and Chen, C. (1988) *In-service Training in Taiwan ROC*, CIER Economic Monograph Series No. 20 (Taipei: Chung-hua Institution for Economic Research).

Stiglitz, J.E. (1996) Some lessons from the East Asian miracle. *The World Bank Research Observer* 11 (2), 151–177.

Streeck, W. (1991) On the institutional conditions of diversified quality production, in Egon Matzner and Wolfgang Streeck (eds) *Beyond Keynesianism. The Socio-Economics of Production and Full Employment* (Cheltenham: Edward Elgar).

Wade, R. (1990) *Governing the Market: Economic Theory and the Role of Government in East Asian Industrialization* (Princeton, NJ: Princeton University Press).

World Bank (1993) *The East Asian Miracle: Economic Growth and Public Policy* (Oxford: Oxford University Press).

Chapter 7

Lifelong learning and welfare reform

Colin Griffin

Introduction

It has long been recognized that lifelong education can be thought of as either concept or policy, at least in terms of analytic philosophy (Lawson, 1982). Whether or not we accept this kind of either/or logic, there is no doubt that the shifting emphasis away from education to learning in the lifelong context *does* signify some kind of substantive development away from a conceptual to a policy-oriented approach.

Lifelong learning has been incorporated into the policy discourse at the national and international level and the transition from principle to practice, or from policy formulation to policy implementation, is already under way. In his opening address to a recent conference of the European Commission (EC), Allan Larsson summarized the current situation in these terms:

> The fact is that 1999 is a crucial year for life long learning. 1999 is the year when the principle of life long learning will move from being merely a popular conference theme, a matter of good intentions, to becoming a matter of firm commitments by governments, in all the Member States, across the European Union.
>
> (Larsson, 1999)

In fact, the principle of lifelong learning, as far as the EC is concerned, is one of employment policies and 'continuous reskilling of the workforce', with associated tax and other incentives, the objective of this being the 'common economic health' of member states. As was the case with the Commission's general approach to lifelong learning and the learning society, the focus is strongly on training, so that it is no longer *education*, but *learning* itself, that is being incorporated into economic and employment policy.

This shift away from education towards learning really must be construed in policy terms and this too is coming to be recognized, albeit rather slowly.

This is an edited version of an article published in *International Journal of Lifelong Education* 18, 6 (1999): 431–452.

Thus, in a recent exploration of the politics of the new learning environment, Geoffrey Elliott begins to unravel the policy significance of the abandonment of education as social *policy* in favour of individual learning as government *strategy*:

> My suspicion is that there is a growing movement in education which purports to privilege empowerment of the individual learner, alongside large-scale policy initiatives on the part of multi-national industries and governments, thereby clouding the real impact of government policies of the Right throughout Europe and else-where which are anti-educational in that they are in effect disempowering learners through resource starvation, market-driven policies and sycophantic campaigns which offer the illusion that action is being taken to promote learning.
>
> (Elliott, 1999: 26)

This somewhat convoluted suspicion can readily be translated into terms of policy analysis: what has driven 'education' out and 'learning' in is not only the forces of technology and globalization, together with the changing role of the state, as identified in an earlier article (Griffin, 1999). What fuels Elliott's suspicion is that education policy is something that the government is no longer prepared to fund as it used to be under the social democratic conditions of the welfare state. Individual learning, however, whereby the costs are borne largely by learners themselves, is the 'illusion' represented by the retreat from policy to strategy. This was implicit in Griffin, 1999, but it was also noted that the association of lifelong learning with the reform of the welfare state was sometimes quite explicitly made: 'learning . . . will be at the heart of the government's welfare reform programme' (DfEE, 1998a: 6).

If it is indeed the case that lifelong learning is part of the government's strategy to reform the welfare state, then it could be argued that learning to do without welfare is what lifelong learning is really about. And in this sense, lifelong learning policies really *are* anti-educational in the sense that they are intended as a kind of smokescreen to disguise the systematic dismantling of the welfare state and the social democratic basis of state education systems.

In the recent article (Griffin, 1999), it was suggested that two approaches to lifelong learning have emerged in the policy literature. Whereas international organizations such as UNESCO (1996), the OECD (1996) and the EC (1996) project what was called a *social democratic* approach to lifelong learning and the learning society, national governments and bodies in Britain at least (NAGCELL, 1997; DfEE, 1998a) project an idea of lifelong learning that reflects a *neo-liberal welfare reform* policy approach, which can be contexted in the so-called crisis of the welfare state in Britain and other countries.

The distinction lies between an approach to lifelong learning that reflects the continuing and redistributive role of the state, and one that envisages a minimal role for the state and a view of lifelong learning that has more to do with lifestyle, culture, consumption and civil society. In short, the social democratic version continues to project lifelong learning in the form of educational and training provision as a welfare function of the state. On the other hand, the welfare reform version sees lifelong learning as a strategy for replacing a provision model of education by one reflecting the centrality of learning in the lives of individuals and in the culture of society itself. Such a model is therefore consistent with a policy of withdrawing state support from a whole range of social benefits and other social welfare services, which is what Elliott's suspicions amount to.

Why there should be this kind of distinction to make between the policy approaches of international organizations and those of national governments (and there is no reason to suppose that Britain is alone in this respect) is interesting in itself, but will not be pursued in detail here. Suffice it to say that international organizations are not accountable to taxpayers in the way that national governments are in democratic societies. This chapter is concerned with identifying the elements of the second of these approaches and therefore with the proposition that, in policy terms, lifelong learning and the learning society may be construed as strategies for the reform of the welfare state.

Education and learning

It has also been recognized that the distinction between education and learning is crucial to any understanding of lifelong learning as education policy and the failure to make it has brought about the confusion between various perspectives on lifelong learning:

> Let us put aside the familiar confusion and sometimes calculated obfusca-
> tion between education, provided by increasingly various forms of teach-
> ing and study support, and the learning that education is intended to foster
> but which can and often does also occur without deliberate educational
> intent. We need an operational understanding of 'lifelong learning' in the
> context of 'the learning society' and reinforced by 'learning organizations'
> to be able to see how postgraduate and postexperience education relate
> to lifelong learning. 1996, the European Year of Lifelong Learning, saw
> something of a climax to the rhetorical debate on these matters. To some
> extent, the old European debate of the early 1970s on recurrent and per-
> manent education is coming together with and being reinvigorated by
> new interest in the learning organization and learning society.
> (Duke, 1997: 83)

The two approaches to lifelong learning being distinguished here do, to some extent, represent alternative 'operational understandings' of the distinction between learning and education: the argument here is that we need to see this in terms of *policy* and *strategy* on the part of governments and international agencies, rather than as simply a 'rhetorical debate'.

Terms such as 'lifelong learning' or the 'learning society' have, in effect, been hijacked by advocates of an education model in order to make the case for particular sectors of provision, such as higher education (Burgess, 1997; DfEE, 1997; Watson 1998) or community development (Moreland and Lovett, 1997). These are representative examples of the social democratic policy of lifelong learning, seeking to achieve redistributive educational provision through increased educational opportunity, be it formal, informal or non-formal. They are recognizable social welfare ideologies of education. Adult education, for example, will be seen as a fundamental strategy for life-long learning by its practitioners and, for many, there will be little to choose between two names for the same thing. Indeed, the confusion of education and learning has sometimes led to the supposition that *either* could be an object of policy. This is said to have been the case in the USA, for example, during the development of the post-industrial period:

> With the changing social conditions of the 1960s, new ways of thinking about adult education began to appear under labels such as lifelong education, lifelong learning, and recurrent education. Each of these in some way reflected an attempt to make adult education an object of public policy.
>
> (Stubblefield and Keane, 1990: 35)

It is evident, however, that the *learning* focus of lifelong learning could never have been an object of public policy in the same way that the *provision* one could. It is being argued here, on the contrary, that this way of thinking about lifelong learning should be understood more in terms of the *withdrawal* of the state from public policy making as part of a strategy to reform the welfare state.

Distinguishing between learning and education is crucial to the analysis of the two approaches to lifelong learning that are being identified here. The social democratic one can always be reduced to the case for securing more educational opportunity by way of structural provision along the lines of traditional *educational* divisions. It is, above everything else, a *provision* approach, lending itself therefore to traditional welfare policy analysis, as described in Griffin (1999). However, as has been suggested, there is a sense in which learning, as distinct from education, could not be an object of social policy at all. The conceptual distinction between learning and education must be maintained if we are to make any sense of the issues raised by the learning society and lifelong learning. For one thing, learning is something we *attribute* to people without being able to *mandate* it or secure it in the way that social policy must presume, to some degree at least: learning eludes social policy because it cannot, like educational provision, be directly controlled. At the level of government strategy, people may be variously persuaded, cajoled, bribed, threatened or shamed into becoming active individual learners: their learning cannot be mandated.

Education itself has been represented as an archetypal project of modernity, expressed as a form of social welfare policy. But in conditions of *reflexive* modernity, it has been suggested that:

> human learning cannot be objectively 'controlled', as many expert professionals tend to assume. Human learning is a very complex activity which is in the first place 'meaningful' to the actors involved. This implies that learning activities are always affected by the way learners define the situation in which they find themselves. Definitions of the situation are rooted in biographical trajectories which are both unique and common. They are unique because every single individual processes her experiences in a unique way. They are common, because single individuals process their experiences with the help of interpretations provided by others.
>
> (Wildemeersch, 1998: 8)

If this reflexive view of learning is taken, it is beyond the reach of policy. It becomes, in a way, depoliticized and repositioned away from social welfare provision into lifestyle, culture, organizations and civil society itself. According to such a view, the attribution of learning to a learner, traditionally the role of the professional educator, is an act of *interpretation* rather than of measurement (Bauman, 1987), and to confuse measurement with interpretation is a form of reductionism. The social democratic approach is reductionist in this sense, in that it reduces learning to what can be measured (because 'controlled') in terms of the outcomes of policy.

This can be illustrated by, for example, the view of CEDEFOP, an education and training body of the EU. In a recent policy statement (Cresson, 1996) the traditional ('modernist') view of the connection between education and training on the one hand and social democracy and progress on the other is restated. Anticipating the recommendations of the EC White Paper (EC, 1996), the context of policy is seen as one of increasing competitiveness and growth, individualized learning, accessible training, updated knowledge and combating social exclusion. The focus is upon social problems of employment and labour market skills, and upon the European dimension. The recommendations of the White Paper were in terms of the acquisition of knowledge, links between schools and business, the need to combat social exclusion, community languages and tax breaks for training. Lifelong learning itself is approached as a *style* of learning, as well as a 'seamless web' of organization, in which the worlds of education, training and work are more closely linked. Indeed, links and 'bridges' constitute a major element of lifelong learning policy rhetoric.

The *policy objective* of lifelong learning remains, for Europe at least, that of economic growth and increased productivity and competitiveness. However, the need for flexibility in employment, together with the new instability of work, is linked with that for increased training in order to limit social exclusion, and advance social mobility and cohesion. In summary, this is a reductionist model of lifelong learning as a form of progressive and redistributive *education* policy, in global market conditions, and from the perspective of the industrialized countries of the world as they move through the post-industrial era.

Another reductionist model of lifelong learning policy is the one that is often associated with the study of adult participation in learning activities.

The adult participation model

Studies of the degree to which adults participate in learning activities are one of the most characteristic examples of the redistributive social democratic approach to lifelong learning policy, focusing as they do upon *barriers* to participation. Such barriers are usually of a social structural nature, but there is often reference to issues of the unequal distribution of cultural capital too. It is usually taken for granted that the level of adult participation in learning is a measure of the degree to which a 'learning society' is becoming a reality. There has been, in fact, a 'silent explosion' of adult learning, according to a recent six-country comparative study of adult learning (Belanger and Tuijnman, 1997: ch. 1). This is brought out in other such participation studies, both comparative (Belanger and Valdivielso, 1997) and national (DfEE, 1998b). The question remains, however, whether policies for lifelong learning, or the identification of a learning society, could follow from any such survey.

These studies represent a reductionist model in that they deal with measurement rather than interpretation, and although sometimes presented within a multidisciplinary framework, the key discipline of policy analysis is not adequately represented, if at all, even where policy contexts or implications are suggested. They also represent a particular, if somewhat heterogeneous, sector, that of adult education and adult learning. Thus, although they add considerably to our knowledge about adults' participation and non-participation in education, they do little more than make a case for removing barriers to participation and expanding provision. They are also generally lacking in any analytical or critical perspective with regard to policy issues, particularly in the industrialized countries, which are precisely those in which welfare policies have often collapsed:

> Although some progress has been made in the preceding two decades, since the term 'lifelong learning' became popular in the industrialized countries, much remains to be done. A major gap in the provision of

lifelong learning concerns the adults. If the lifelong learning target is defined as reaching at least secondary level education for all, some 76 million adults in the OECD countries need to be reached. Adult learning targets are defined more modestly in developing countries, but still represent a huge task. The question is not only one of resources but also concerns appropriate policies and practices.

(Belanger and Tuijnman, 1997: 245)

It seems to follow from this that there is no distinction to be made between a 'learning society' and one that is simply better educated and trained.

This kind of conception of lifelong learning and the learning society is very problematic, not only because it is reductionist, but because from a policy analysis perspective, many issues remain unaddressed:

- The nature of the connection between education, training and economic development is by no means straightforward or thoroughly understood.
- The widespread failure of welfare policies and the worldwide crisis of the welfare state have led to a general retreat from policy making on the part of governments.
- On the other hand, it would be a mistake to suppose that globalization and market economics have resulted in a complete loss of control on the part of the state.

These are the kinds of issue that generations of social welfare policy analysts have posed, and which need to be addressed as a condition of any analysis of lifelong learning *as* policy. What we learn from such analysis is that there is no straightforward connection between, for instance, the identification of need and the formulation of policies to address it: this is precisely the reason why so many welfare policies have been abandoned or have failed.

There is, then, a general problem involved in attempting to derive conclusions about policy from participation studies, or indeed from any basis in the study of post-industrial society, technological determinism, or the global economy. The only conclusions that could be derived from such studies are those concerning the expansion of educational provision along the lines of the kind of social democratic approach identified in Griffin (1999).

There also exists a good deal of conceptual confusion over the idea of a learning society, not least in that it is associated with lifelong learning itself. The former, however, is a *collective* concept, whereas lifelong learning is something usually attributed to *individuals*. As a result, it is possible to analyse these ideas from any number of positions, and over the last few years, they have been. The learning society and lifelong learning have been analysed as concept (*Journal of Education Policy*, 1997), myth and ideology (Hughes and Tight, 1995; Strain and Field, 1997), rhetoric (Griffin, 1998), economy (Strain, 1998), and so on. All of these analyses reflect a social democratic approach to educational provision: as with the adult participation model, the main problem is said to be that the learning society doesn't exist. They all rather beg the question of whether it *could* exist, and if so, what are the political dynamics around its existence: these are critical analyses, but they tend to focus upon 'learning' and 'society' in a reductionist way from the perspective of policy analysis. The challenge is from post-industrial society or even from postmodernism itself (Usher *et al.*, 1997), and it is a challenge to educational provision and practice.

In a model of lifelong learning that is not only post-industrial or post-modern but *post-welfare*, we have another kind of account of the new 'grand narrative' of learning that is apparently displacing the modernist project of education. Policy analysis provides another perspective, and a more critical one with respect to globalism, technology and the market, and the other taken-for-granted elements of the social democratic approach. For example, from this perspective, lifelong learning could be conceived as a function of the grand narrative of social welfare reform. Perhaps lifelong learning is little more than a relatively cheaper and more effective means of solving the kinds of social problem that the welfare state was intended to address but has failed to solve, such as poverty, exclusion, disaffection, and their social and economic effects?

In order to explore the neo-liberal welfare reform approach to lifelong learning, however, it is necessary to look again at the distinction between education and learning upon which it rests.

Function and provision

The social democratic approach to lifelong learning was described as reductionist because it reduced statements about learning to statements about education, substituted measurement for meaning, and generally confused the concept of the 'learning society' with that of a better-educated and trained one. The welfare reform approach, however, maintains a clear separation between education provision and the function of learning in individual and social life.

This distinction may be used to locate a whole range of models of lifelong learning and the learning society. It has already been suggested that a reflexive concept of learning both distances it from education and puts it beyond the reach of social policy, at least in the sense in which social policy is conventionally understood. Nevertheless, any concept of learning has a social dimension, and the role of learning in the welfare reform approach to lifelong learning can perhaps be best understood by thinking of learning as a *function* of individual and social life. At present, evolutionary theories of learning are much to the fore (they mirror the technological determinism also to be found in the policy literature), seeing learning as a function of survival or growth in both individual and social terms. 'There is no alter-

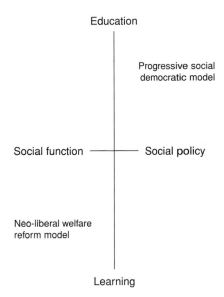

Figure 7.1 Education and learning.

native' is the phrase often used in the rhetoric of lifelong learning policy discourse, precisely as it is in the discourse of welfare state reform: globalism, technology and the market having apparently narrowed our scope for individual choice. As will be suggested, however, individual lifestyle choice is fundamental to our life in postmodern times and this is where learning is increasingly coming to be positioned: this is what our models now suggest.

So there are two dimensions to reflect in locating the two broad models of lifelong learning in relation to each other: along one lies education and learning, and along the other social policy and social function.

Figure 7.1 locates the neo-liberal welfare reform models of lifelong learning in the bottom left-hand corner, signifying that they are concerned with learning rather than education and with learning as a *function* of individual and social life, rather than as an object of public policy. Our other models, which are really education policy models of lifelong learning, appear at the top right-hand corner of the diagram, being concerned with the *provision* of education and training opportunities.

Thus, reference to a 'learning society' or a 'learning culture', or to any of the discourses that emphasize the need for a change in people's attitudes, values, beliefs and lifestyles towards the place of learning in their individual and social lives, can be located here. It refers more, therefore, to learning as 'a way of life' rather than to the provision of opportunities for education and training, and it could therefore be identified as a feature of postmodern society. This is not only because it reflects the knowledge base of production and economy, and therefore people's working lives, but also because of the significance of learning for new patterns of lifestyle, consumption and culture. As will be seen, theorists have already begun to take account of this in the literature of adult education, if not of lifelong learning itself.

As for the other two sectors of Figure 7.1, the top left-hand one might be occupied by a sociological account of the function of education systems in society. It could therefore be filled by the study of education as socialization, control, selection, or mobility and so on, either from a functionalist or a more phenomenological perspective. In the bottom right-hand corner of the figure lies the issue with which this chapter is primarily concerned, that of the sense in which learning *could* be an object of policy, with its objectives as attainable as any other object of policy. If this *is* the case, then lifelong learning is just another name for the provision of education and training opportunity, and the learning society just another name for a better-educated and trained one. If not, then lifelong learning refers to learning as a *function* of individual, social and cultural life, and in this sense it could not be an object of policy of such.

Policy and strategy

Failure to distinguish between policy and strategy is another source of confusion about lifelong learning. But these concepts need to be separated and distinguished in exactly the same way as those of education and learning themselves. For while it is impossible for lifelong learning to be an object of public policy in the conventional sense, it does not follow that governments and other agencies are powerless to promote opportunities for *learning* as a function of individual and social life.

The role of states and governments in the face of globalism, the market and the new technologies has changed. And even though they will no doubt continue to retain national control over significant aspects of policy, nevertheless it has become apparent that their role with regard to many social and economic functions has become much more *strategic* and less oriented towards old-style *policy* making. Embracing the market and the global economy entails that the role of the state is much more one of enabling or making possible certain economic conditions, rather than rigidly controlling and mandating the outcomes of policy. The retreat from command to free-market economies is not only an economic but a social revolution, so that the role of the state with regard to individuals is better described as one of managing autonomy and permitting the widest possible scope for lifestyle choices. At least, this is the typical situation of those states, such as Britain, where reform of the welfare state reflects quite a wide political consensus.

The difference between policy and strategy can be illustrated by the difference between educational policies for schooling and strategies for the learning society. Schooling is an object of national policy because it is subject to compulsion and regulation in every possible way: with regard to participation, curriculum, professional and administrative control of every aspect of the process. School education is a classic instance of policy formulation, and lifelong learning a classic instance of governmental strategy. Since learning *as such* cannot be mandated or controlled, the strategic role of governments can only be one of creating the conditions in which as many people as possible have opportunities to learn. The welfare reform model by no means implies that governments are impotent in respect of learning, or that there is not much that they can do to encourage it.

In fact, since the 1970s and 1980s there has been a tradition of regarding such initiatives as recurrent education, paid educational leave, workbased learning and so on, as *strategies* to achieve the learning society or lifelong learning itself (Houghton and Richardson, 1974; Flude and Parrott, 1979; Himmelstrup *et al.*, 1981; Titmus, 1981). Adult education has, in fact, often been thought of in strategic rather than in policy terms, certainly by governments themselves. This has never been true of schooling, which is much less often thought of in relation to lifelong learning, and continues to be neglected in this respect of national policy, at least in Britain. Again, there is somewhat of a contrast here with the work of international agencies such as the UNESCO Institute for Education, which has maintained a tradition of including school education systems in the conceptualization of lifelong *education* at least (Dave, 1976; Skager and Dave, 1977; Cropley, 1977; Ingram, 1979). This tradition is, however, as the stress on lifelong education suggests, a social democratic model of education provision. This point might also be suggestive in terms of the alternative approaches to lifelong learning policy that are being explored here: as has been suggested, there is a detectable difference between policies of national states and international organizations with respect to the *scope* of policy in relation to strategy. Such organizations are not, in the way that national governments are, subject to political pressures to reduce the role of the state in respect of welfare provision generally.

Thus, the strategic role of post-welfare states is one of managing markets, choice and autonomy, and they do not formulate *policies* in relation to lifelong learning in the way some of the adult participation models, and many other lifelong learning discourses, seem to suggest. The reason why they do not is not only because of the impossibility of formulating learning as an object of public policy, but also because the political choice is *not to do so*. The strategy of governments is to create the conditions in which people, families, communities and organizations are most *likely* to learn for themselves, thus obviating the need for education policy in the traditional sense. This is a characteristic function of governments in post-welfare conditions.

Markets and quasi-markets

One of the most characteristic features of the classical market in goods and services is the principle of *caveat emptor* ('buyer beware'). This means simply that market choices are assumed to be made on the most rational possible basis, on the fullest possible information. Market rationality entails that mistakes made in market choices cannot be retrieved. In the case of education and welfare services, however, this has rarely been the case: consumer protection, in the form of quality assurance, public standards, transparency, and a host of other publicly funded mechanisms to curb the free operations of the market, are taken for granted as essential conditions for its role in post-welfare society. Thus in the case of health, housing, pensions, insurance and so on, governments curb markets with consumer protection that is an object of *policy*, that is, it is not on the voluntary basis of consumer protection in the rest of the market for goods and services. The policy literature of lifelong learning in the welfare reform model reflects this *quasi-market*, and not that of an economic market in the *laissez-faire* or classical sense.

The social democratic, or reductionist, approach thus continues to make traditional, but rather simplistic, assumptions about a 'market' in adult education on the basis of post-welfare conditions such as vocationalism, deregulation and competition in industrialized societies: 'The notion of the adult education market . . . is central to an understanding of the new policy context of adult education in many industrialized countries' (Tuijnman and van der Kamp, 1992: 210). This is a version of the adult participation model of lifelong learning, with policy conclusions derived from assumptions about policy that have long been challenged in the policy discourse itself. In so far as lifelong learning is conceived as a welfare function of society, which it clearly is in these kinds of models, it has proved more appropriate to think in terms of quasi-markets, rather than markets *as such*.

The characteristics of quasi-markets have been described in a classic source as follows:

> They are 'markets' because they replace monoplastic state providers with competitive independent ones. They are 'quasi' because they differ from conventional markets in a number of key ways. The differences are on both the supply and the demand side. On the supply side, as with conventional markets, there is competition between productive enterprises or service suppliers. Thus . . . there are independent institutions (schools, universities, residential homes, housing associations, private landlords) competing for customers. However, in contrast to conventional markets, all these organisations are not necessarily out to maximise their profits; nor are they necessarily privately owned.
>
> (Le Grand and Bartlett, 1993: 10)

This is a supply-side analysis of quasi-markets, which undoubtedly better fits the situation of lifelong learning suppliers more accurately than a conventional market analysis. We shall see that the demand-side perspective also offers more to our understanding of lifelong learning as policy later.

The need for an alternative to conventional market analysis in education has also been usefully formulated in terms of an 'administered market', an idea that reflects the point made above about consumer protection and, like the 'quasi-market', more accurately expresses the situation in lifelong learning policy than the conventional market idea:

> The market is a political creation, designed for political purposes, in this case to redistribute power in order to redirect society away from social democracy and towards a neoliberal order. The market in education is not the classical market of perfect competition but an administered market. Exchange is carefully regulated, with, for example, stringent controls placed upon professional powers to redistribute resources and admissions. The market is thus an institution which is constituted by government and underwritten by legislation to define the relative powers and contractual responsibilities of participants.
>
> (Ranson, 1994: 97)

Thus, the concept of the 'administered' market expresses the changing role of the state in a way that the classical model of the market does not: it represents the government's *strategic* role in ensuring the transition from a command to a market economy, and from a welfare state to a neo-liberal order. In so far as lifelong learning strategies are analysed in this way, then lifelong learning itself is implicated in the reform of welfare, and the retreat from policy making to strategic role can be understood in terms that both reflect the essentially *political* nature of the process, and the *reality* of it. These policy analysis perspectives, derived from welfare and educational policy contexts, are a fundamental element in the various neo-liberal welfare reform models of lifelong learning with which this chapter is concerned.

This point may be illustrated by returning to the demand-side perspective of quasi-markets mentioned above, in the form of an important example from the social democratic or reductionist model of lifelong learning policy, that of vouchers and similar consumer-oriented participation schemes:

> On the demand side, consumer purchasing power is not expressed in money terms in a quasi-market. Instead either it takes the form of an earmarked budget or 'voucher' confined to the purchase of a specific service allocated to users, or it is centralised in a single state purchasing agency.
>
> (Le Grand and Bartlett, 1993: 10)

Voucher schemes for education and other kinds of welfare provision are highly characteristic of the neo-liberal welfare reform policies of states such as Britain, and have certainly been attempted with varying degrees of success, not least in adult education (Jarvis *et al.*, 1998) They are an example of the strategic approach to lifelong learning, which incorporates significant aspects of quasi-market and administered market policy models.

The consumer credit model

A recent study of lifelong learning accounts embodies both the strategic and 'culture change' elements of the neo-liberal welfare reform approach, arguing that a shift towards a new 'mass culture' of learning can be achieved through consumer credit models of participation and provision. The role of Individual Lifelong Learning Accounts (ILLAs) has been described in relation to policies for economic and social welfare policy reform:

> As ILLAs come on stream, there will be major opportunities for using them in tandem with other areas of Government policy: savings policy, regional and national devolution; the whole set of learning policies – those which come under the heading of the University of Industry, those relating to records of achievement, and training time off for 16+ school leavers in employment, to name but a few.
>
> (Smith and Spurling, 1997: 78)

There could not be a clearer example of the integration of lifelong learning strategy into neo-liberal welfare reform policy. It is essentially a 'banking' model of education, bringing to full fruition the idea of Freire (1972) in that it does not shift the concept of education away from provision towards the learning function, but suggests at the same time that some kind of 'cultural' shift as necessary. This can be interpreted as the need to shift people's dependency upon the welfare state to provide educational and other services, towards a consumer credit system whereby individuals take responsibility for their own lives in every possible context.

The ILLA is

> held by individuals at banks or other financial institutions as a lifelong store of value; is dedicated to the purchase of learning, whether of services or materials; is owned only by individuals. Only they have the say on withdrawals; can be used to buy learning at any stage in a person's life; is separate from any other current or deposit accounts the individual may hold.
>
> (Freire, 1972: 16)

The basic financial functions of ILLAs are saving, borrowing and credit. This clearly reduces learning to a commodity in classical quasi-market conditions.

It is therefore a social democratic model in respect of its reductionism. But it also lays stress upon the key elements of the neo-liberal welfare reform approach: culture, lifestyle and consumption.

Policy conclusions are based on the need to move from the current culture of learning (based upon a participation model) towards 'a mass culture for lifelong learning', and it is this element that identifies the consumer credit model with welfare reform policies of the state. However, it remains basically a participation and provision model of learning culture, in which learning itself can be thought of as an object of social and public policy. Not only that, but culture change itself is conceptualized as subject to policy, so that if people's attitudes to learning do not spontaneously change, they must be made to, for reasons that are by now familiar in the analysis of the neo-liberal model: competition, globalization, technology and the social threats these bring with them:

> The task of changing to a mass culture of lifelong learning is a huge challenge. It is tempting to hope that it could happen naturally, but we believe it will not – certainly not on any acceptable time scale. So the change has to be *made*, and the reasons for it are compelling ... Two factors come together to make the case for change: the threat to the UK economy from globalisation; and the ever-growing threat of social exclusion for a large minority of UK citizens.
>
> (Smith and Spurling, 1997: 7)

Thus, the consumer credit model of lifelong learning policy reflects the reductionism and provision-based social democratic model, on a typically nationalistic basis. But its political rhetoric is that of neo-liberalism, in so far that it invokes elements of culture, lifestyle and consumerism in its analysis of the need for culture change, attempting to reconcile the extreme individualism of learning accounts with a concept of mass culture, by way of quasi-market strategies urged upon the government. It is the kind of position that might be located in the bottom right-hand corner of Figure 7.1. On the one hand, it sees a major role for social policy in changing attitudes and values, and on the other it sees learning in highly individualistic terms and in terms of people's attitudes towards it. In other words, in terms of the figure, it is a hybrid, and represents above all the view that learning can (and must be 'made') an object of public policy. But this is the sector of the diagram where, above all, the hypothesis of lifelong learning as policy is tested, both for rhetoric and substance.

The neo-liberal welfare reform approach, as has been seen, lays stress upon aspects of culture, lifestyle and consumption, and the need for changing these, in the way that social democratic or wholly reductionist models tend not to. This is the case even though the same policy/strategy objectives may be envisaged: globalization, markets, risk, social disorder,

competition, technology. These can be summarized as the ills and consequences of post-industrialism. But if we assume, on the contrary, that
learning cannot be an object of policy in the same way that educational
provision can, and if we assume that *political* changes are also under way,
then a model of policy to reflect these elements can be identified. The fact
is, much of the policy discourse of lifelong learning is both apolitical and
deterministic at the same time: it is the language of inevitability in the face
of technological and global change. Paradoxically, at the same time, the
discourse is one of individual choice, lifestyle and consumption, and these
elements of the neo-liberal model will now be examined.

The cultural/lifestyle model

If learning is a complex activity, associated with meaning and interpretation, then it is difficult to conceive it in policy terms. If it is a matter of
attribution, and if it is a function of human life and social existence then
it must be a central attribute of culture and lifestyle. Social democratic
approaches to lifelong learning policy reduce learning to education and make
learning a commodity, to be secured in market or quasi-market conditions.
But, as has been seen in the consumer credit model described above, such
an approach is constantly infiltrated by cultural elements in the course of
the rhetoric around it, so that changing culture itself becomes an object of
public policy. The 'life events' and 'barriers' of participation studies (DfEE,
1998b) become transformed into lifestyle and consumption patterns for a
quite different approach to lifelong learning.

   In postmodern analysis, the significance of lifestyle for adult education has
been recognized, and the relation between learning and consumption begun
to be conceptualized. Culture as the practice of learning may be contrasted
with culture as an object of policy, and this is an important element in any
neo-liberal welfare reform model:

> In the postmodern, the educational is recast as the cultivation of design
> through experience, both conditional upon and responsive to contem-
> porary socio-economic and cultural fragmentation. Learning does not
> simplistically derive from experience, rather, experience and learning
> are mutually positioned in an interactive dynamic. Learning becomes
> the experience gained through consumption and novelty, which then
> produces new experience. Consequently, the boundaries defining 'accept-
> able' learning break down – in lifestyle practices learning can be found
> anywhere in a multiplicity of sites of learning.
>
> (Usher, Bryant and Johnston, 1997: 107)

This kind of non-reductionist model of lifelong learning clearly removes it
from the realms of social policy and into the world of strategy, markets and

individual lifestyle practices. This has implications for the role of the reflective educational practitioner, as Wildemeersch (1998) has observed, and for the social status of authority figures such as educationists themselves, as Bauman (1987) suggests. This is a significant development of postmodern society:

> Educational practitioners rather than being the source/producers of knowledge/taste become facilitators helping to interpret everybody's knowledge and helping to open up possibilities for further experience. They become part of the 'culture' industry, vendors in the educational hypermarket. In a reversal of modernist education, the consumer (the learner) rather than the producer (educator) is articulated as having greater significance and power.
>
> (Usher *et al.*, 1997: 107–108)

Although we need to bear in mind the differences between markets, quasi-markets and hypermarkets amidst all these analogies, it is apparent that this is a model of learning far removed from the social democratic approach, and as much in tune with the consequences of postwelfarism as postmodernism. It is a culture and lifestyle practice made possible by the socio-economic and technological conditions of society and *not* one that could be produced by social policy.

However, as soon as we begin to think of lifestyle we begin to think of class, which remains a completely unexamined idea on the part of advocates of a 'mass' learning culture 'for all'. There are major divisions in any way that 'culture' could be conceived and they need to be taken into account in an analysis of lifelong learning policy. The 'culture industry' is a targeted rather than an undifferentiated field, and lifestyle practices reflect the divisions of class and culture:

> [K]nowledge becomes important: knowledge of new goods, their social and cultural value, and how to use them appropriately. This is particularly the case with aspiring groups who adopt a learning mode towards consumption and the cultivation of a lifestyle. It is for groups such as the new middle class, the new working class and the new rich or upper class, that the consumer-culture magazines, newspapers, books, television and radio programmes which stress self-improvement, self-development, personal transformation, how to manage property, relationships and ambitions, how to construct a fulfilling lifestyle, are most relevant.
>
> (Featherstone, 1991: 19)

So there are links between learning, culture and class that are central to our understanding of learning in this kind of analysis. As Featherstone goes on to put it: 'The new petit bourgeois therefore adopts a learning mode to life: he is constantly educating himself in the field of taste, style, lifestyle' (91).

The idea of the 'learning mode', associated with culture, class and lifestyle, is another major element in the neo-liberal welfare reform approach to life-long learning policy. It removes the idea of the 'learning society' a long way from that of the better-educated and trained society that is characteristic of the social democratic approach to lifelong learning. Such analyses of consumer culture and postmodernism therefore lay great stress upon patterns of consumption and leisure, and it is not difficult to reconceptualize the strategic role of the state in relation to such social and economic changes as these. They owe much to the reconceptualization of commodities and consumption away from the economic to the social and symbolic level of analysis associated, for example, with Baudrillard (1998).

The leisure/consumption model

Field (1996) has argued that adult education and training can be regarded as a form of consumption in four respects: affluence and increasing exercise of choice on the part of most adults; a more consumer-oriented public policy; the market nature of adult education provision; the dominance of human capital theory in educational thinking (Field, 1996: 137–138). Field is criti-cal of the approach taken by writers such as Featherstone, at least as far as adult education is concerned, arguing that it neglects the degree to which patterns of consumption indicate *individual* practices of individuation and differentiation, in favour of an analysis based upon the identities of groups. Writing from within a provision and participation perspective, Field provides a critique of the neo-liberal perspective, reflecting therefore much more of a social democratic viewpoint:

> Consumption is, I believe, to some extent a useful perspective from which we can examine aspects of the education of adults. It is only one among a number of perspectives, and its value is bound to vary between different sectors, levels and styles of provision. Yet compared with production, reproduction and citizenship, consumption's place in the study of adult education is consistently downplayed by both scholars and practitioners.
>
> (Field, 1996: 146)

Field is here primarily concerned with open learning in adult education, rather than with lifelong learning policy analysis, but he argues that adult education and training provide a 'test case' for the consumer culture hypoth-esis, and that there may be a 'loose fit' between consumer culture theory and adult learning.

Patterns of leisure, as well as of working life, have changed, as has what *counts*, not only as leisure but work and learning itself. This needs to be reflected in the analysis. The crisis of the welfare state not only affects the economy of adult education and training, as Field says, but it goes much deeper. This chapter will therefore conclude with a brief review of responses to the crisis of welfare in so far as these might have a bearing upon policy models of lifelong learning.

The crisis of welfare

It has been observed that even in those cases where a 'postmodern' aware-ness of issues for lifelong learning are concerned, these are rarely contexted in the general crisis of the welfare state. And yet, of all the projects of moder-nity, it is the welfare state that is the most identifying and characteristic.

So, how is what has been called a neo-liberal welfare reform approach to lifelong-learning policy related to the kinds of developments that are usually taken to constitute the postmodern condition? We are now in a position to identify and distinguish the elements of the approach as follows:

- A stress upon *learning* as distinct from and not reducible to *educational provision*.
- A stress upon learning as an attribute or function of people's *lifestyles* rather than as a function of *educational provision*.
- A stress upon learning as an aspect of *culture*, rather than upon educa-tion as a function of the social *structure*.
- A stress upon learning in the *lifeworld* of meaning and action, rather than upon learning in the education *system*.
- A stress upon the *strategic* role of the *state*, rather than upon the role of the state in educational *policy making*.
- A stress upon learning as a form of *consumption* on the part of indi-viduals, rather than upon the *institutional* framework of educational provision.
- A stress upon the policy-derived formulation of *quasi-markets* in which learning is contexted, rather than upon the *market* of classical economics.
- A stress upon the *management* of learning-related activities, rather than upon the *direction* and *control* of such activities, such as continues to be the case with the state in relation to schooling.
- A stress upon the *integration* of individuals' lives, in terms of their social, economic and recreative and *leisure* activities, rather than upon the *divi-sion* of lives into *private* and *public roles*.

These then are the elements of the neo-liberal approach to lifelong learn-ing policy, in contrast with those of the social democratic approach usually associated with the international agencies, which promote such policy. Ideas such as the 'learning society', the 'learning culture', the 'learning revolution' or whatever, could only be operationalized in these terms. Whether such cultures, or such societies could be 'made' to exist is problematic, since so many of the elements of the model refer to what are essentially *spontaneous* aspects of life and learning. To construct them as objects of public policy in any meaningful sense would be contradictory and self-defeating. This is why, from a cultural perspective on learning, the social democratic approach is reductionist: because it reduces the individual and social *function* of learning to the measurable outcomes of educational *provision*.

The policy literature of lifelong learning contains elements of both approaches, in greater or lesser proportions. But what identifies the neo-liberal welfare reform approach most clearly is the integration and implication of lifelong learning into the welfare reform policies of the state. Those nation states that, under the pressure of globalization, markets, technology and the pervading ideology of neo-liberalism, move away from policy interventions to strategic roles in relation to lifelong learning (if not in relation to schooling, education and training) are projecting it as the only alternative to a social welfare provision that can no longer be afforded and that, in any case, many believed to have failed. However, lifelong learning continues to be strategically positioned in relation to traditional welfare state concerns: the development of human capital, the need for social inclusion and common cultures or social consensus.

From a critical point of view, the near monopoly of social welfare functions on the part of the state is a relatively recent development in history (Barry, 1990). But it is the alleged failure of the welfare state, and of traditional education systems, to achieve the purposes for which they existed, that has often been an identifying characteristic of the 'post-modern'. The 'crisis of welfare', in which some models of lifelong learning policy have been contexted, has attracted some attention from policy analysis, so this chapter concludes with a brief account of one or two positions on the welfare state. These pose the question whether or not traditional forms of policy analysis are any longer relevant to our understanding of this particular project of modernity, or whether new analytic concepts are needed for this purpose.

> Recent interest in questions of modernity and postmodernity designates a series of intellectual disputes about the adequacy and legitimacy of theoretical and analytic traditions in the social sciences.
>
> (O'Brien and Penna, 1998: 206)

They have argued that the contribution of postmodernism to welfare state analysis has, in fact, been to expose it as a failed project, and that such states (and the social democratic politics that brought them into existence) have 'exclusions, discriminations and iniquities' in their foundations:

> [P]ostmodernism has questioned critically the integrative ideology of social policy, indicating that the problem of social and political inclusion is not equivalent to the extent to which a public sphere bestows

rights or entitlements on citizens as a means of mitigating their socio-economic disadvantage.

(O'Brien and Penna, 1998: 207)

If this view of the impact of postmodern analysis upon social welfare policy is taken, then it follows that there is little possibility of a social democratic or education provision model of lifelong learning achieving any more combating social exclusion than did the welfare state itself. In other words, the expansion of educational provision and opportunity will be just as likely to promote social *exclusion* as was to be found under any welfare system. In traditional policy analysis terms, social exclusion might be an *unintended consequence* of the implementation of a social democratic policy of lifelong learning.

On the other hand, we can, from a postmodern perspective, begin to think of the 'learning society' or the 'learning culture' as themselves 'integrative ideologies' of social policy. Following his theme of the permanent need people have to reconstruct community life on whatever basis, Bauman has said that:

Postmodernity does not necessarily mean the end, the discreditation or the rejection of modernity. Postmodernity is no more (but no less either) than the modern mind taking a long, attentive and sober look at itself, as its condition and its past works, not fully liking what it sees and sensing the urge to change.

(1991: 272)

According to Bauman, the 'postmodern political agenda' can be thought of in terms of the need to form social solidarities along new lines, after the collapse of the promise of social democracy, whether these are described as forms of 'neo-tribalism' or 'aesthetic communities', in the face of the fragmentation and social indifference of the market. The 'learning society' and the 'learning culture' are often represented, in the policy literature, as integrative strategies against social exclusion, and the consequences of the failure of social democratic policies to achieve their communal purposes. However, social democratic policy models continue to reflect faith in redistributive institutional provision, despite the failures of welfare. In Bauman's words: 'Modernity is still with us. It lives as the pressure of unfulfilled hopes and interests ossified in self-reproducing institutions' (Bauman, 1991: 270–271). It is in this spirit that so many post-compulsory education sector institutions have hijacked lifelong learning, namely, to better secure their own self-reproductive functions in a changing world.

It is possible to express the direction of policy models from education to learning and from provision to culture, in relation to the theorization of post-modern society. The progression from left to right in Figure 7.2 represents the

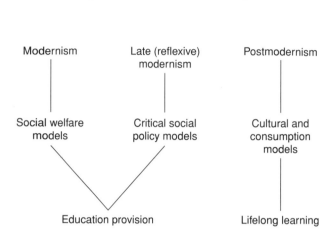

Figure 7.2 A social welfare critique.

movement from faith in the social welfare project through criticism of its effectiveness to its final 'crisis'. The critical social policy perspective has always
reflected a view of the welfare state as being founded in social inequality. In
educational terms, this has generally meant seeing education as social control.
Obviously, lifelong learning lends itself to this analysis in its social democratic construction as the expansion of education and training systems: there is
no more effective form of hegemonic social control than that achieved by way
of learning that is self-motivated, self-regulated and self-policed.

Peters and Marshall (1996) have attempted to outline the possibility of
'critical social policy in the postmodern condition'. They base this upon a
range of theoretical considerations, such as the cultural studies perspective,
Foucault's discourse analysis, reflexivity, modes of signification, new social
movement analysis, modes of production and information, new forms of state
surveillance, and so on. Nevertheless, the possibilities of framing critical
policy analysis in postmodern conditions remains problematic, especially if
'totalizing perspectives' are ruled out in such conditions:

> If critical social policy is not to remain mired in critique it must develop
> an offensive potential which means it must be able to go beyond the
> task of contesting meanings to provide alternative comprehensive policy
> frameworks. How it can perform this necessary service without invok-
> ing the dangers and risks of a totalizing perspective is still a critical
> question.
>
> (Peters and Marshall, 1996: 214)

Modern (nation) state	Postmodern (global) government
Policy	Strategy
Analysis: 1. Functional 2. Critical	Strategy analysis
Welfare	Markets and quasi-markets
Education	Lifelong learning

Figure 7.3 **The state educates; the learner learns.**

What all this illustrates as far as policy models of lifelong learning are concerned is that those who would criticize the social democratic approach must themselves have some kind of alternative to put forward that does not fall into the same traps. For example, if the social democratic model is reductionist, as far as learning is concerned, then what *is* a 'learning culture', and how would we recognize it if it existed?

Whatever the consequences of the attempt at postmodern critical policy analysis, it seems clear that the role of the state in respect of education continues to be a central issue. Until this changes virtually beyond recognition, then postmodern perspectives can only have a rather limited purchase. So far, there is little evidence that the control and surveillance functions of the state are diminishing, and probably for this reason the relevance of such perspectives remains small:

> There is clearly no such thing yet as a postmodern theory of education. However, there has been an increasing tendency for writers on education, both from the Left and the Right, to question many of those core

values and organizing concepts which have underpinned social democratic systems of state education in the postwar era and which post-
modernists have identified as typical products of modernity.

(Green, 1997: 8)

This can clearly be related to the kind of analysis of policy models of lifelong learning that have been identified here, in which the *possibilities* for
analysis are determined by such factors as the policy role of the state in
particular, stressed by the social democrats, but largely ignored (or relegated
to strategy) by the alternative, cultural model. This may be represented in
terms of Figure 7.3, in which the centrality of the role of the state can only
be expressed in *educational* rather than *learning* terms.

The role of the state, which is crucial in identifying possibilities for policy
analysis, is changing, and this does suggest that new analytic frameworks are
appropriate in understanding it. The shift away from old-style policy making
towards strategy formation has been identified as one key to understanding
lifelong learning in policy terms. This, in turn, creates the tensions between
the two policy approaches identified in this chapter. On the one hand, the
social democratic approach associated with international agencies continues
to project a redistributive welfare policy role for the state. On the other, in
the case of a national government such as that of Britain, where the reform
of the welfare state is a primary political objective, lifelong learning, and
other ways of achieving a 'learning society' or a 'learning culture', are to be
discovered in the policy literature. These, in turn, project lifelong learning
as a strategy of welfare reform, implicating it in the process and integrating
it with other reform strategies that have the effect of making individuals less
dependent upon the state. It follows that the stress moves away from unaf-
fordable institutional provision, and towards a concept of learning more
embedded in culture, lifestyle and consumption.

Conclusion

What these alternative approaches do, therefore, is to bring out the fundamentally different assumptions it is possible to make about learning and
education when the policy literature is analysed. Lifelong learning and the
learning society are often simply ways of integrating education policy into
wider policies for the reform of the welfare state. As has often been observed,
it is possible to position lifelong learning at several points along a continuum
running between utopian rhetoric to some fairly traditional arguments for
the expansion of education and training provision. Policy analysis of lifelong learning and the learning society needs to be based upon clear
distinctions between learning and education and between policy and strategy
on the part of the state. Above all, analysis is needed in terms of post-welfare,
as well as post-industrial or postmodern, society.

References

Barry, N.P. (1990) *Welfare* (Milton Keynes: Open University Press).

Baudrillard, J. (1998) *The Consumer Society: myths and structures* (London: Sage Publications).

Bauman, Z. (1987) *Legislators and Interpreters: on modernity and intellectuals* (Cambridge: Polity Press).

Bauman, Z. (1991) *Modernity and Ambivalence* (Cambridge: Polity Press).

Belanger, P. and Tuijnman, A. (eds) (1997) *New Patterns of Adult Learning: a six-country comparative study* (Oxford: Pergamon Press and UNESCO Institute for Education).

Belanger, P. and Valdivielso, S. (eds) (1997) *The Emergence of Learning Societies: who participates in adult learning?* (Oxford: Pergamon Press and UNESCO Institution for Education).

Burgess, R.G. (ed.) (1997) *Beyond the First Degree: graduate education, lifelong learning and careers* (Buckingham: SRHE and Open University Press).

Cresson, E. (1996) Towards a policy of lifelong learning. *Vocational Training 8/9 European Journal*, Dec. 1996 II/III CEDEFOP: 9–12.

Cropley, A.J. (1997) *Lifelong Education: a psychological analysis* (Oxford: Pergamon Press for UNESCO Institute for Education).

Dave, R.H. (ed.) (1976) *Foundations of Lifelong Education* (Oxford: Pergamon Press for UNESCO Institute for Education).

Department for Education and Employment (DfEE) (1997) *Higher Education in the Learning Society* (The Dearing Report) (London: The Stationery Office).

Department for Education and Employment (DfEE) (1998a) *The Learning Age: a renaissance for a new Britain* (Green Paper CM 3790) (London: The Stationery Office).

Department for Education and Employment (DfEE) (1998b) *National Adult Learning Survey 1997* (London: The Stationery Office).

Duke, C. (1997) Lifelong, postexperience, postgraduate – symphony or dichotomy? In R.G. Burgess (ed.) (1997) *Beyond the First Degree: graduate education, lifelong learning and careers* (Buckingham: SRHE and Open University Press).

Elliott, G. (1999) *Lifelong Learning: the politics of the new learning environment* (London: Jessica Kingsley).

European Commission (EC) (1996) *Teaching and Learning: towards the learning society* (White Paper on Education and Training) (Brussels: EC).

Featherstone, M. (1991) *Consumer Culture and Postmodernism* (London: Sage Publications).

Field, J. (1996) Open learning and consumer culture. In P. Raggatt, R. Edwards and N. Small (eds) (1996) *The Learning Society: challenges and trends* (London: Routledge in association with the Open University).

Flude, R. and Parrott, A. (1979) *Education and the Challenge of Change: a recurrent education strategy for Britain* (Milton Keynes: Open University Press).

Freire, P. (1972) *Pedagogy of the Oppressed* (Harmondsworth: Penguin Books).

Green, A. (1997) *Education, Globalisation and the Nation State* (London: Macmillan).

Griffin, C. (1998) Public rhetoric and public policy; analysing the difference for lifelong learning. In J. Holford, P. Jarvis and C. Griffin (eds) (1998) *International Perspectives on Lifelong Learning* (London: Kogan Page).

Griffin, C. (1999) Lifelong learning and social democracy. *International Journal of Lifelong Education*, 18, 329–342.

Himmelstrup, P. and others (eds) (1981) *Strategies for Lifelong Learning 1: a symposium of views from Europe and the USA* (Esbjerg: University Centre of South Jutland with Association for Recurrent Education).

Houghton, V. and Richardson, K. (eds) (1974) *Recurrent Education: a plea for lifelong learning* (London: Ward Lock Educational).

Hughes, C. and Tight, M. (1995) The myth of the learning society. *British Journal of Educational Studies*, 43 (3), 290–304.

Ingram, J.B. (1979) *Curriculum Integration and Lifelong Education* (Oxford: Pergamon Press for UNESCO Institute for Education).

Jarvis, P., Holford, J. and Griffin, C. (1998) A market for lifelong learning?: the voucher experience in the City of London. In J. Holford, P. Jarvis and C. Griffin (eds) *International Perspectives on Lifelong Learning* (London: Kogan Page).

Journal of Education Policy (1997) The Concept of the Learning Society Explored, 12 (6).

Larsson, A. (1999) Continuous learning for continuous change. Opening Address of the Competence for Europe Conference, Federal Ministries for Labour and Social Affairs, and for Education and Research, and the European Commission, 21 April 1999 (Berlin: European Commission).

Lawson, K. (1982) Lifelong education: concept or policy? *International Journal of Lifelong Education*, 1 (2), 97–108.

Le Grand, J. and Bartlett, W. (eds) (1993) *Quasi-Markets and Social Policy* (London: Macmillan).

Moreland, R. and Lovett, T. (1997) Lifelong learning and community development. *International Journal of Lifelong Education*, 16 (3), 201–216.

National Advisory Group for Continuing Education and Lifelong Learning (NAGCELL) (1997) *Learning for the Twenty-First Century* (The Fryer Report) (London: NAGCELL).

O'Brien, M. and Penna, S. (1998) *Theorising Welfare: enlightenment and modern society* (London: Sage Publications).

Organization for Economic Co-Operation and Development (OECD) (1996) *Lifelong Learning for All* (Paris: OECD).

Peters, M. and Marshall, J. (1996) *Individualism and Community: education and social policy in the postmodern condition* (London: Falmer Press).

Ranson, S. (1994) *Towards the Learning Society* (London: Cassell).

Skager, R. and Dave, R.H. (eds) (1977) *Curriculum Evaluation for Lifelong Education* (Oxford: Pergamon Press for UNESCO Institute for Education).

Smith, J. and Spurling, A. (1997) *Individual Lifelong Learning Accounts: towards a learning revolution* (Leicester: National Institute of Adult Continuing Education) (NIACE).

Strain, M. (1998) Towards an economy of lifelong learning: reconceptualising relations between learning and life. *British Journal of Educational Studies*, 40 (3), 264–277.

Strain, M. and Field, J. (1997) On the myth of the learning society. *British Journal of Education Studies*, 45 (2), 141–155.

Stubblefield, H.W. and Keane, P. (1990) The history of adult and continuing education. In S.B. Merriam and P. Cunningham (eds) (1990) *Handbook of Adult and Continuing Education* (San Francisco: Jossey-Bass).

Titmus, C. (1981) *Strategies for Adult Education: practices in Western Europe* (Milton Keynes: Open University Press).

Tuijnman, A. and van der Kamp, M. (eds) (1992) *Learning Across the Lifespan: theories, research, policies* (Oxford: Pergamon Press).

United Nations Educational, Scientific and Cultural Organization (UNESCO) (1996) *Learning: the treasure within* (The Delors Report) (Paris: UNESCO).

Usher, R., Bryant, I. and Johnston, R. (1997) *Adult Education and the Postmodern Challenge: learning beyond the limits* (London: Routledge).

Watson, D. (1998) *Lifelong Learning and the University: a post-Dearing agenda* (London: Falmer Press).

Wildemeersch, D. (1998) Lifelong learning and the significance of the interpretive professional (unpublished).

Chapter 8

Change of address?

Educating economics in vocational education and training

Jane Kenway

Introduction

My purposes in this chapter are threefold. My first is to offer an account of the ways in which economics has triumphed over education and particularly equity in Australia. I will focus on recent developments in vocational education and training (VET) to tell this particular narrative showing how educating is dropping out of vocational education and how the language of macro- and micro-economic reform and markets currently holds state and commonwealth governments and VET education policy makers under its sway. My second purpose is to show how educationally and possibly economically hollow this triumph is. I will do so by pointing to some of the problems that economic reductionism helps to cause and to some of the important human matters that it neglects – particularly matters of equity and ethics. My third purpose is to offer a conceptual framework for changing the address; for attending to matters of life chances and life choices, or what Giddens (1994: 114–115) calls 'emancipatory politics' and 'life politics'. The three main sections of the article are organised accordingly.

In offering this account I will attend to, yet also move away from, the many mini-narratives and narrowly focused debates that tend to dominate discussions of vocational education and training in both policy circles and mainstream publications. Instead, I will bring to the field several bodies of literature with which it seems largely unacquainted. It is my contention that this literature helps vocational education and training to see itself in a more powerful light; to look beyond the economic and properly recognise its rich potential to enhance the life of work and the work of life.

The triumph of economics

In this section I will offer a brief historical overview of the development of the Australian Training Reform Agenda, now called the Australian National

This is an edited version of an article published in *Journal of Education and Work*, 12, 2 (1999): 157–178.

Training Framework. I will then point to some of the key features associated with its progressive and regressive potential for workers generally and
for equity among workers particularly. Finally, I will explain how the government and management of VET has brought out its more regressive dimensions. Overall my argument is that economics has triumphed over education
and training, and so also over the full education of workers.

A little history about the Training Reform Agenda

The field of VET in Australia has been constituted and reconstituted several
times over the last decade and in May 1997 it was given yet another make-
over by the Commonwealth Liberal government, which was elected in 1996
(ANTA, 1997b). VET policies and practices are almost entirely different
from those that predominated in the 1970s and early 1980s. The system has
been thoroughly restructured and recultured. In the second half of the 1980s
the federal Labor government addressed the economic crisis through policies of 'structural adjustment'. Over the following decade a wide-ranging,
integrated, complicated and very ambitious policy agenda was pursued which
sought to integrate aspects of education, social and industry policy. Industry
protection was reduced, labour markets were partially deregulated and skill
formation was encouraged, all in the hope of improving international
competitiveness. Award restructuring and legislative and administrative
changes, such as the Training Guarantee Act, were to be used as mechanisms to change the organisation of work and training. The aim of the
then consensus between unions, government and employers that involved
co-operative tripartite planning was economic modernisation. This was to
result in industry development by making workers more skilled, flexible
and productive. Programmes of skill formation and the development of
credentialling pathways for lifelong learning (the Australian Qualifications
Framework (AQF)) were to effect an enterprising nation. But they were also
to offer workers a better deal. Economics had some heart.

Subsequently, in association with award restructuring and workplace
reform driven by the Australian Council of Trade Unions, a new body of
policy was developed under the rubric of the 'Training Reform Agenda'
(TRA). This involved:

- a National Framework for the Recognition of Training (NFROT);
- a competency-based approach to training and assessment, including the
  Recognition of Prior Learning (RPL);
- the Training Guarantee Act (which aimed to increase employers' investment in employee training);
- an open training market;
- bringing vocational and general education together, including the
  development of key competencies; and

- the Australian Vocational Certificate (AVC), a new, unified entry-level training system.

Under the recent Liberal government, this has become the National Training Framework (NTF), which seeks to be more simple and flexible ('user friendly') than its predecessor and to establish clearer links between training qualifications and the AQF, which includes schools and universities and provides certificates, diplomas and degrees (*Australian Qualifications Framework, Introduction to the AQF*, Curriculum Corporation, 1996).[1] It has two key components: new recognition arrangements and 'training packages' (*Australian Training*, ANTA, 1997b). These build on but also alter previous developments in ways designed to:

> grow a more competitive and effective market for vocational education and training. Such a market will promote increased opportunities for users of the system to choose providers, modes of training provision and for training organisations to have more flexibility to respond to clients. [and will] promote user choice.
>
> (*Assuring Quality and Choice in National Training*, ANTA, 1997a: 1)

An important part of the original TRA developed under Labor was the development of NFROT. This involved a nationally consistent means for recognising training programs, training providers, educational award courses and individual competencies. State authorities registered trainers and accredited courses. Under the Liberals this has been modified to become the Australian Recognition Framework, which involves a new approach to recognition. While the previous approach involved course registration and accreditation, the recent approach involves the registration of training organisations to enable them to provide their choice of 'products and services' associated with the Training Packages. Hence some organisations may offer a single service (e.g. skills recognition/assessment) and others may offer the entire raft including training, assessment and certification:

> Registered training organisations may include TAFE [Technical and Further Education] institutions, private providers, RPL agencies, group training companies, industry organisations and workplaces.
>
> (*Assuring Quality and Choice in National Training*, ANTA, 1997a)

'Mutual recognition' across the nation, quality assurance and greater freedom for providers are the justifications for this change (*Australian Recognition Framework*, ANTA, n.d.).

As part of award restructuring in the 1980s, a national uniform set of standards for comparing the skills required by different jobs in each industry and occupation was developed. The National Training Board (NTB), a Commonwealth/State body of government, industry and unions, drew up a national framework of competency standards (the Australian Standards Framework) for grading competencies. It provided the parameters within which recognised industry bodies developed competency standards specific to various industries, industry subsectors and occupations. It is used to determine industry skill needs and to provide criteria for defining individuals' skills consistent across states and territories and across industries. Competency standards are established by identifying workplace needs through a process of skills analyses and defining what is expected of workers through skills audits. Thus a *skills analysis* is undertaken to identify the skills required by a particular job. This is used to generate a skills register for each job. A *skills audit* is undertaken to identify the skills held by an individual. The skills of the individual can then be checked against the skills register developed from the analysis. Core or generic skills are identified, as well as more specific ones, in order to provide industry- or occupation-wide portability.

The most recent development in this area is the concept of Training Packages. These 'represent national products developed by industry to meet current and emerging skill needs' (*Training Packages*, ANTA, n.d.). Each industry will have a set of Training Packages specific to it. Through national Industry Training Advisory Bodies (ITABS) each industry will decide on what its priorities and needs are in this regard and the number of packages it has will depend on its subsectors. They will all consist of endorsed competency standards, assessment guidelines and qualifications. They may also include non-endorsed advice on learning strategies, assessment materials and professional development material. Training Packages will be available to all Registered Training Organisations to support different training pathways including those associated with schools and workplaces. The competency standards will be linked to the NTF and by extension the AQF. Individuals will be issued with Skills Passports to record their skills, competencies and qualifications.

Contexts of possibility for workers[2]

Along with award restructuring, the Training Reform Agenda originally included a range of progressive measures with the potential to improve students' and workers' access, participation and outcomes in both training and employment (see Seddon, 1994; Sedunary, 1995). It thus attracted the support of unions and of certain progressive groups in education circles alongside that of business and industry. Indeed, it produced some unexpected political alliances as well as some predictable opposition. So what were these progressive measures and have they been maintained under the Liberal government?

A national standards framework offered the potential to bring consistency and articulation to training programmes and the credential structures that certify various levels or stages of learning. The alignment of training curricula to a national standards framework provided a means for recognising learning in a way that allowed workers to move along career paths and from job to job in the labour market and to gain recognition for skills acquired overseas. These developments made it easier for training to be recognised consistently across all states and territories and to transfer credit between institutions and courses, for example, between TAFE colleges and universities. This national consistency and the provision of articulated pathways provided workers with a range of possibilities for mobility, geographic, educational and social. The national Training Reform Agenda sought to address educational elitism and, through a vocationally relevant curriculum, to attend to the needs of those particular students whom schools and universities systematically neglect (Ecclestone, 1997) and to attend to power differentials in the workplace by challenging the hierarchical binaries of education/training: academic/general education, working/learning, workers/bosses and so on (Sedunary, 1995). Parity of esteem and open access to credentials, knowledge and employment were the hopes inscribed in policy. Further, some of the associated policy documents also laid down some participation targets and guidelines for so-called target groups – the particularly disadvantaged (e.g. see Bagshaw, 1996; Sobski, 1996). Even though the Liberals do not exhibit much concern about such issues, these possibilities remain implicit in their policies. Indeed, the processes designed to ensure equity targets have been made more 'user-friendly' for all parties and thus allow for more portability.

But of course there is more to worker justice than mobility and, indeed, mobility may be hampered by other more subtle matters. However, a national standards framework also offered the potential to address some of the more subtle aspects of certain work-related injustices. First, it assisted the explicit recognition of skills that have traditionally been ignored or undervalued, providing an opportunity to challenge the gender and other biases in the description of skills. Related to this, the competency framework offers the opportunity for prior learning not developed within formal learning situations, but rather through life experience or work experience – whether voluntary, at home or in the paid workforce – to be recognised and acknowledged when they are relevant to, or necessary for, the performance of a job. Thus the competency-based approach can result in skills that were regarded as 'natural' to women or other specific groups being formally recognised. Second, jobs must have complete competency analyses associated with them and job applicants who fit a job description must be considered to be fully qualified for it. This transparency should make it more difficult for employers to discriminate; i.e. to deny employment or advancement on the basis of such things as gender, race or ethnicity. At this stage the Liberals have expressed little interest in such matters and, given their preparedness to hand over the development of Training Packages to industry, there are few signs that they will. To my knowledge, ITABS have not been instructed to pay particular attention to such matters in the process of developing packages and neither does it seem have the bodies responsible for accrediting providers.

For these and other reasons, the extent to which the potential noted here will ever be realised to any significant extent in Australia remains to be seen. Taylor and Henry argued that given Australia's history of successful progressive educational reform and the progressive potential of the policies and 'given what could be lost' (1994: 125) the best aspects of the policies should be supported. However, they predicted that:

> the very breadth and ambiguity of the policy agenda might very well serve to exacerbate regressive ends. If, for example, this does turn into an 'industrialists' agenda', if the 'new vocationalism turns out to be the old vocationalism with expanded territories', if the competencies movement becomes the graveyard of critical thought – then we would join with the critics in wanting to bury the new policies.

Over time, various critics focusing on a range of aspects of the TRA evident in this quotation have made the case that the potential was always exaggerated. Let us briefly name some of these lines of argument.

Realising potential for workers?

Some critics argue that the potential was always exaggerated due to institutional and educational problems associated with 'pathways'. They say that it was never possible to integrate systems that were systematically designed to function separately and unequally. They argue that TAFE and the expanding training sector could never hope to win against the entrenched privilege associated with the universities. Indeed, certain traditional universities have adopted a very elitist approach to credit transfer and RPL. While this has not been the case with all universities it is my observation that financial expediency rather than a commitment to the matters of principle alluded to earlier is what is encouraging many newer universities to consider the benefits of credit transfer.

Of course not all criticisms from the education sector arose from attempts to protect vested interests. Many critics were concerned about the quality of the educational experience offered by the modularised curricula associated with vocational competencies and competency-based assessments. The claims made here were many and varied and depended, for example, on the notions of competency involved, the critics' perceptions of the purposes of education, the particular learners that they had in mind and so on.[3] I will not canvas these debates here except to say that when reduced to the performance of work-related skills alone, such approaches to education and training certainly have their limits.

As Jackson (1997) argues, they fail to attend to many cultural, social, industrial and human aspects of work and workers. In so doing they do both employers and workers a disservice, for they inscribe narrowness and docility rather than creative and critical engagement. Further, many educators, particularly those in community-based adult education with its emphasis on adult literacy and basic education (often used as a stepping stone to further education by women), argued that competency assessments and modules went against their 'learner-centred, needs-based curriculum' (Angwin, 1994: 37). As Sue Willis has argued 'Common outcomes require uncommon provision' (Kenway and Willis, 1995). However, such arguments have largely proceeded unheeded by policy makers who sought educational change by policy edict rather than by dialogue. Hence dynamic grass-roots commitment was only ever generated in pockets in schools, TAFEs and adult education, and was never widespread.

The failure of policy makers to hear educators' voices in the debate meant that much of the educational potential of VET has remained unrealised and thus the barriers to educational mobility remain in place informally if not formally. In particular policy makers failed to include, involve, 're-educate' and support the educational communities whose support was originally vital to policy's implementation. Re-education was the key in many instances, as changing mindsets with regard to skill and worthwhile knowledge was quite basic to the entire process. Of course it could be argued that with the creation of the private provider market, gaining the support of the education sector did not matter. It would seem that many private providers did not have the above qualms of educators and were quite happy to provide the minimum curriculum for the maximum cost. We are yet to see the educational costs to all parties of the marginalisation of the education sector. However, this does not seem to be a concern of the Liberal government, which has further marginalised educators in its recent changes to policy in favour of employers and public servants.

Overall, the policy agenda failed to generate bottom-up support for top-down change in the education sector. Neither did it do a very good job of operating at the grass roots in workplaces with employers and employees, many of whom remained either unaware of its many dimensions or became overwhelmed by its complexities. It was certainly too centralised, too bureaucratised and acronymised, too concerned with matters technical and managerial and too remote from and insensitive to localities, institutions and people.

Finally, as other critics argued, training and award restructuring can only go so far when it comes to the supply of work and the ways in which it is organised and rewarded. The supply of skilled labour must be matched by the supply of jobs. Certainly industry investment and job-creation policies never matched the hopes that were invested in the TRA. Further, such policies were unable or implicitly unwilling to address the ways in which the labour market was being restructured by employers through the policies of deregulation of the centralised industrial arbitration system. The flexibility agenda, which was in part to enhance workers' conditions (and had particular potential for women; see Kenway and Willis, 1995), has largely been used by employers to minimise wage costs through numerical flexibility (increased use of casual and contract labour and of patterns of employment that are fine-tuned to the flow of work) and through wage and locational flexibility (home-work, out-work, off-shoring, etc.).

From the current evidence it would seem that whatever chances for justice and equity for workers that did exist under the Labor government are becoming more remote under the current Liberal government. The Liberal government has ended consensus with the unions and indeed is hostile to them and to job-creation policies, believing firmly in the trickle-down effect of economic expansion in a largely hands-off approach to equity, and in the miracle capacities of markets to address many entrenched social problems.

The most recent policies handed down under the Liberal government suggest that the triumph of economics over vocational education and training is now complete and that Taylor and Henry's fears about 'industrialists' agendas', 'old vocationalism' and 'the graveyard of critical thought' have been realised.

Certainly gestures towards workers' interests and equity remain. Witness the fact that one of the four objectives of the *National Strategy for VET for 1998–2003* (ANTA, 1997c) is 'achieving equitable outcomes'. Further, the following dot point in the *Annual National Priorities for 1998* is as follows: 'Provision of greater opportunities and improved outcomes for under-represented clients' (in *Australian Training*, ANTA, 1997b: 1). Indeed, the following remark is included in the *Issues to be addressed*:

> Considerable national effort and expenditure has been invested over the last ten to fifteen years to increase the participation in VET of targeted population groups in the emerging training market. Where the purchaser buys outputs, a key question will be how best to purchase activity to produce equitable outcomes.
>
> (*Australian Training*, ANTA, 1997: 4)

However, this bit of obfuscation suggests a rather limited agenda for improving the lot of 'targeted clients' through education and training. It is worth contrasting this approach with that suggested by Lim (1996) in the thoughtful and astute policy advice publication *More and Better Jobs for Women: an action guide*.

Of course while getting a better deal for workers was always high on the agenda for unions during the period of consensus for the purpose of economic modernisation, it was not always evident that the Labor government kept such matters to the fore. Its commitments to equity for 'targeted populations' were only ever token. And, as we have argued elsewhere, social justice and, for that matter, social policy were never equal partners; the former was always subordinated to economic policy (Fitzclarence and Kenway, 1993). Nonetheless, as indicated, VET was potentially both progressive and regressive. But it was Labor's broader management policies for vocational education and training that contained the most 'countervailing tendencies' and 'distorting effects' (Taylor and Henry, 1994: 106, 118). These have become more pronounced under the Liberals. Let me pursue this point a little.

Governmentality for economics

Beneath this body of VET policy, the bottom line under Labor and Liberal governments has been and remains simple: all education (but particularly VET) is to cost the state less and serve the economy and, by implication, employers and capital, more. This ambition is being achieved as a function of the master policy discourses of economic rationalism, human capital theory and increasing economic globalisation. As Taylor and Henry (1994) suggest, this combination alone is sufficient to reinscribe and exacerbate in post-industrial society the social divisions of industrial society. Further, as sociological studies of economic globalisation make clear, new international divisions of labour are emerging that pit third world workers against those in the first world (Castells, 1996). But the subordination of education and equity in VET to economics is also being achieved through three particular forms of governmentality, or what Foucault calls 'the conduct of conduct'; these are rationalisation, marketisation and corporatisation. It is these that are most clearly effecting the triumph of economics over education and equity in VET.

Rationalisation has mainly involved reductions in government funding ('efficiencies') to state-provided educational institutions. This is part of a general 'austerity' programme involving massive cuts in public sector spending. These reductions have, for example, led TAFE colleges to 'downsize', to seek 'opportunities for flexibility' (usually numerical) and non-state sources of funds. Business and industry are now increasing sources of revenue but equally importantly have become solitary sources of relevance. The preferences and needs of business and industry are now the only currency for TAFE, whose curricula are tailored (and Taylored) accordingly. This has had particular implications for gender equity. For example, with its courses dedicated largely to the notion of the skilled male worker, the TAFE college sector was always a 'male stronghold' in terms of purpose of culture, albeit with progressive pockets. Nonetheless this was being 'adjusted' slightly by policies for gender reform (equal opportunity and affirmative action initiatives) under Labor in the 1980s. However, rationalisation and mean and lean management have meant re-masculinisation as equity policies have a cost that governments no longer expect institutions to bear.

Marketisation, the second strategy of governmentality, proceeds hand in glove with rationalisation. Its modes of governmentality include privatisation, commericalisation, commodification and residualisation (see Kenway, 1994; Jakupec and McTaggart, 1996). In order to bring vocational education and training to heel in the late 1980s, the Commonwealth Labor government established an 'open training market' for the provision of curriculum. The established provider, TAFE, had to compete with private trainers for the provision of 'off the shelf' training modules to be sold to employers. The 'expansion of market mechanisms' is one of the *Annual National Priorities for 1998* announced in *Australian Training* (ANTA, 1997b: 1). Further, 'user choice' is now considered 'critical to the success' of Australia's VET system. It is defined as 'encouraging direct market-based relationships between individual providers and their clients' and as 'giving greater market power to clients to negotiate training that meets their needs and means that employers can use their own training providers' (*Australian Training*, ANTA, 1997b: 1).

Australia now has the phenomenon of 'tender teaching'. The curriculum is now commercialised and knowledge for work is commodified. With the 'client' for curriculum products understood mainly as the employer, knowledge for work is understood as what employers require. It is not necessarily the case that this is what is best for work or workers and neither is it necessarily the case that what a particular employer wants is good for the enterprise, industry or nation. Speaking of the tendering process in the adult and community education sector, Angwin says 'Tenders are called for funding future programs either annually or every few months resulting in an inability to develop coherent forward planning and tremendous uncertainty in the field' (1994: 39). She goes on to point to the end of professional collegiality and the 'creation of division rivalry and secrecy among providers' as they compete with each other for tenders.

My information suggests that Angwin's observations are also true of the VET sector with its increasing raft of private providers. However, with employers as the 'buyers with the bucks', private providers produce what sells. The Training Packages mentioned earlier are an example of an input/output model of education that plays down the significance of what happens in between. The fact that learning strategies, assessment materials and professional development materials are not to be endorsed by ITABs implies that content and process, learners and learning and teachers and teaching are less important than the front and back end. Therefore little encouragement exists for Registered Training Providers to take this middle seriously. Yet as all good teachers know, if a rich education is intended, ultimately it is the middle that matters. The market metanarrative cannot distinguish among products or among the different demands of customers; the same logic is applied to the exchange of simple goods as is applied to the exchange of complex services. While this has the benefit of simplicity, it is not clear to me that it is actually user-friendly or that it will actually assure quality. Without a serious miscarriage of notions of learning and teaching, a student purchasing education and training cannot be easily equated with a customer buying groceries.

The 'training market' model relies in large part on the willingness of employers to buy training programmes for their workers. This means that discriminatory practices can readily continue. As Wallace's recent research indicates, employers are most reluctant to provide training for women at lower levels of organisations (Wallace, 1999). Further, this 'user-pays' principle means that where employers are reluctant to train their workers, workers now have to pay more than ever for their own training.

The third key strategy of change is *corporatisation*. The key features of corporatisation are the application of business management principles to education and training management. This involves the apparently contradictory double moves of decentralisation and recentralisation, of autonomy and accountability. Within the centrally devised frameworks mentioned earlier, responsibility, stress and crisis are pushed down the line and away from governments to individual providers. However, these apparently flattened management structures still have a hierarchical command structure within which accountability is only ever steeply upwards.

Drawing their inspiration from Japanese management systems developed for the manufacturing sector after World War II, the ANTA that manages VET has adopted Continuous Improvement strategies for systematising and standardising 'production' and for improving quality and standards. Under the guise of quality assurance, a variation of TQM (total quality management), we have seen the development and application of a variety of technologies of control over the field that steer it ever more firmly in the interests of employers only.

Overall, VET is now caught in the grip of an 'economically correct' political lexicon in which vocational education's prime purposes are reduced to economic performance and industry needs. This lexicon restricts Australians' perceptions of the possibilities of current and future vocational education and minimises its capacity to address more complex matters associated with the altered context of working life and current forms of politics associated with life chances and choices. Their complexities are flattened out and reduced to the economic. This not only represents a triumph of economics over education, it represents a triumph of economics over sociability too, for it ignores the implications of a narrow focus on the economic for our social capital, fabric or glue; 'the processes between people which establish

networks, norms and social trust and facilitate coordination and coopera-
tion for mutual benefit' (Cox, 1995: 15). And it represents what Singer
(1993: 34) calls 'a triumph of economics over ethics'. It tends to ignore the
many disadvantages and insecurities for workers that are associated with
economic rationalism and economic globalisation. Let us briefly consider
some of these.

The altered contexts of working life and some associated problems

In my travels through and beyond the sociological literature about contemporary times, I have found the work of Giddens, Beck, Mckay, Singer and
Cox most helpful in attending to the complexities of the altered contexts
of working life. The British sociologist Anthony Giddens calls this era 'the
age of uncertainty' (1991). Hugh Mckay (1993), the Australian social
commentator, calls it the 'age of redefinition' and Ulrick Beck (1992), a
sociologist from Germany, talks of *Risk Society*. The Australian moral
philosopher Peter Singer (1993) asks us *How are we to Live?* and subtitles
his book *Ethics in an age of self-interest*, and Eva Cox (1995) invites us to
consider how we might work towards *A Truly Civil Society*. I will draw on
aspects of their work in addressing some of the problems associated with the
triumph of economics over vocational education and in considering further
the equity and ethical issues involved.

While I cannot adequately address them here, these altered conditions of
working life include the collapsing distinctions between space and time,
detraditionalisation and the rise of institutional reflexivity, i.e. the dynamics
of change effected through the generation and application of knowledge.
These involve the disembedding and re-embedding of social relations,
new forms of integration and fragmentation, the 'end of' tradition and
nature, manufactured uncertainty and radical doubt, generalised risk, and
over all what Giddens (1991) calls 'a runaway world of dislocation and uncertainty' (see further, Kenway, 1997). On the basis of his social surveys of
Australians over recent years, Mckay (1993) identifies seven main changes
that are features of Australia's age of redefinition and that might be said to
represent its move into a post-traditional order. These are the redefinition
of 'gender roles' – the changing nature of marriage and the family, rising unemployment and the changing nature of work and work ethics, the
'invention of invisible money' and changing habits and patterns of financial
exchange and consumption, the redistribution of household income, the
decline of the middle class and the widening gap between rich and poor,
the rise of multiculturalism and a crisis of notions of Australian identity
and finally, a change in the nature of government politics and the rise of
cynicism and confusion.

Productivism

Some of the issues associated with economic rationalism can be included in what Giddens refers to as the problem of overexpansion and 'productivism'. Productivism is:

> an ethos where work is autonomous and where the mechanisms of economic development substitute for growth and for the goal of living a happy life in harmony with others and with nature.
>
> (1994: 247)

As Giddens (1994), Beck (1992) and others argue, development has now come up against its own limits; it has turned back on itself and we are seeing the destructive effects of an emphasis on untrammelled growth and rampant industrialism. Crises have become normal, risk has been generalised and moral and ethical values have become repressed. The resultant problems now require novel solutions, which are increasingly difficult to find. The issue for governments and for us all, says Giddens, is not any more one of 'how much regulation and how much market but one of how to separate out productivity from productivism' (Giddens, 1994: 248).

Giddens calls for a critique of both the injustices that arise as a result of productivism and a 'retrieval of suppressed moral concerns'. Singer makes a similar call. He shows how 'the pursuit of self-interest (understood largely in terms of material wealth)' and 'the ideology of growth' (1993: 49) have become guiding imperatives at many levels in Western societies. These imperatives are evident in the ways in which countries and corporations engage with each other economically through to the ways in which individuals consume life-style goods and services. Explaining the 'paradox of hedonism', Singer (1993: 20) shows how consumption is mistakenly equated with fulfilment, but how little relationship there actually is between wealth and happiness, growth and a sense of fulfilment and plenty. Instead, the current approach to growth fuels an ongoing demand for more growth. He points out that 'we rarely reflect, either collectively or as individuals, on whether this dominant conception is a wise one. Does it truly offer the best lives for us all?'

For example, pointing to the 'time-poor' (those in full-time work) – the over-worked – Eva Cox (1995) makes the case that the ways in which they are currently using time are serious impediments to building social capital. She says that time is becoming ever-increasingly commodified through longer working hours, isolation in cars and through the increasing forms of work and leisure conducted 'alone' in front of screens. It is her view that this militates against building social capital and that this works against the social health of communities, organisations and indeed, the nation. It also, she suggests, works against economic productivity.

Change in broad structures of feeling

Most of us who are lucky enough to be employed are working in needy, greedy institutions insensitive to people's needs. As Sharon Johnson (1997: 114) argues:

> Australian workers have learned that people are not assets to be nurtured and developed, they are in fact expenses to be cut. The past decade of down-sizing and rationalisation has clearly destroyed an intrinsic under-standing between worker and manager. It has eroded the goodwill of employees to the point where they have become bitter, disillusioned, cynical and angry. At the personal level, the changing workplace proto-type and the evolution of a new psychological employment contract has left many employees angry.

Johnson goes on to describe 'angry workplaces' thus:

- Continuous change and upheaval within an organisation.
- Somehow the newest change just does not stick, the plans fall apart, change implementation becomes more difficult.
- Employees become 'me' centred. They need to know, 'what's in it for me?'
- Communication becomes strained. The new vision seems to fall on deaf ears. As time goes on employees become so fatigued and impassive about the next programme, the new customer service initiative, the process redesign, the next innovation that they switch off.
- Cynicism is rampant: 'it will never work, we've heard it all before'.
- High attrition as people jump ship and high absenteeism as people use up all their sick leave believing that the company owes them.
- Tension.
- A lack of energy.
- Employees seek meaning outside their jobs, in the family, in recreation, in hobbies or in other voluntary pursuits.

It is easy to see from this list why greedy institutions will eventually become less productive than those that seek to develop social capital. Indeed Cox (1995: 56) argues: 'We must put high priority into growing social capital by providing opportunities for trust and co-operation'. Even a hard-headed economic rationalist would have to acknowledge that such structures of feeling will cut into productivity and profits.

The rise of productivism and the loss of tradition is associated with the growth of individualism, with intensified searches for the means of self-aggrandisement, personal advantage and material accumulation. And along with 'manufactured uncertainty', high consequent risk and the paradox of hedonism, they are also associated with tension and emotional and moral disquiet, personal meaninglessness, existential isolation and a separation off from the moral resources needed to live a full life. There is a generalised sense of anxiety and meaninglessness. Even at the height of individual achievement and the 'peak' of individualised accumulation people are asking more often how satisfying it is to live this life.

The important thing about the work of people such as Cox and Singer is that it points to the ways in which individuals and groups are responding to wider social and cultural changes in the age of economic reductionism. It shows that we are suffering a loss of social cohesion, a loss of faith in our abilities to solve social problems and move forward. We have less trust, more conflict and more fear. Many of us are suffering a revolution of decreasing expectations. We are surrounded by risks but we take fewer risks. We try to manage risk rather than attend to its sources. Further, we have lost a sense of our own power to be different and to effect other sorts of change.

The sequestration of experience

Many of the existential and moral dilemmas that arise as a result of the changes noted above are 'sequestered away', separated out and become part of the institutionally and individually unaddressed and repressed (Giddens, 1991: 184–185). This process of the sequestration of experience, with its only focus on production and performance, gives individuals a sense of control, but one which is both spurious and rather dangerous. Moral and emotional issues that are put to one side by the individual or group will be repressed and thus will return in some form or other – often unpleasant.

As indicated above, VET is currently steeped in productivism, concentrating only on producing human capital and bracketing out social capital and moral, equity and ethical issues. Yet as we now see through examples, say, of worker suicide, outbreaks of workplace violence and work-related health problems, the repressed returns in unfortunate ways. Captains of industry and vocational education ignore, at their peril, these new structures and cultures of feeling.

Of course as Mckay (1993) points out, because we are living at the frontier of massive sociocultural and geopolitical change, feelings of alienation and uncertainty are understandable. However, his question is 'are we coping as well as we might?' (200). My question is 'how can education and training help workers to cope better?' Clearly answers to this question are many and might well include some of the issues that the progressive dimensions of Australia's TRA began to address before it was disengaged from its progressive elements. However, here I want to make mention of two forms of politics that have implications for VET policy and curriculum at all education levels and in all systems. If VET is to contribute to productivity rather than productivism, it must rise above the barren lexicon of economic reductionism, skills, instrumentalism and behaviourism (see Jackson, 1997), and it must treat its worker/learners as fully human and recognise the richness of the world of work. This means understanding it in educational, identity, social and cultural terms (see Casey, 1995; Probert and Mackey, 1996). One aspect of such a change of address would be to attend to emancipatory and life politics and to seriously consider their implications for worker education – on and off the job.

Two essential political and educational forms

My purpose in this part of the chapter is to explain emancipatory and life politics and the relationship between the two and to make some brief suggestions about their implications for VET. At this point I will not elaborate; that would fill another chapter. Giddens argues that contemporary times have generated two broad alternative political forms. He refers to these as 'emancipatory politics' – a politics of life chances, and 'life politics' – a politics of life decisions. I will consider each in turn.

Emancipatory politics: a politics of life chances

Emancipatory politics focuses on divisions between humans. It is about different life chances and is a politics of 'others'. Giddens (1991: 210) defines emancipatory politics as:

> a generic outlook concerned above all with liberating individuals and groups from constraints which adversely affect their life chances.

To Giddens such politics has either one or more of the following concerns: *exploitation* (the illegitimate monology of resources or desired goods from which others are denied access); *inequality* (differential access to material rewards); *oppression* (power applied by one group to limit the life chances of another); and matters of *marginalisation and exclusion* (1991: 211–214).

Giddens argues that emancipatory politics has an 'away from' rather than a 'towards' (Utopian) view of its work for change. In very general terms it seeks to 'shed the shackles of past tradition and custom permitting a transformative attitude towards the future' (1991: 211).

It seeks freedom from certain oppressive traditions and from the historic exercise of arbitrary power. It thus seeks to 'overcome the illegitimate domination of some individuals by others' and to eliminate or to reduce power differentials between them. In this regard it seeks to free the underprivileged from the material and other forms of deprivation that restrict their lives.

It is driven by an ethics of *justice* (norms of justice define what counts as exploitation, inequality and oppression) and *equality*. It is also driven by imperatives of *participation* and *autonomy*. It seeks to assist those who suffer any of the above to get more control over their own life circumstances, to help them to become capable of free and independent action in their life conditions and to be in the position to be able to make informed choices. Its purpose then is the creation of more autonomy of action, and it usually seeks some form of emancipation through some form of enlightenment.

In one way or another, state-provided education in Australia has always been concerned with the distribution and redistribution of life chances. However, at various times since the mid-1970s it has been much more explicit in its approaches with regard to a range of forms of exploitation, inequality, oppression, marginalisation and exclusion and particular social groups of students. While VET has certainly not been at the forefront of the field it has, as indicated earlier, attempted certain forms of redress. However, in recent times the move towards 'mean and lean' government has taken its toll on approaches to and support for emancipatory politics. To the extent that they exist, these are now minimalist both in scope and depth (on the issue of gender, see for example, Sobski (1996) and Schofield and Dryen (1997)). Ironically, this is occurring at the same time as, in the interests of greater productivity, managers are being encouraged to 'manage diversity' (see Liff and Wajcman, 1996).

Nonetheless, the dominant discourses of education policy and the broader culture have demonised, marginalised and repressed emancipatory politics under the dismissive rubric of 'political correctness'. Overall, this has meant that disadvantaged people cannot necessarily rely on education to help them to increase their autonomy, and their participation in and understanding of the power structures of working life. It also means that the advantaged are given less cause to consider the issues associated with oppressive traditions and the historical exercise of arbitrary power. Both worker and management education lose out here as such potential is stifled.

All minimalist approaches to equity are inadequate but their inadequacy becomes more apparent in these times as old inequalities continue and are exacerbated. For example, Mckay (1993: 133–155) shows how Australians are increasingly being 'divided by the dollar' as the amount and the nature of work and industrial relations change (84–110), as the gap between rich and poor becomes wider and more entrenched, as the middle class shrinks and loses its influence, as the number of poor increases dramatically to form an Australian underclass and as Australia's egalitarian dream recedes into our history. Mckay regretfully makes the case that Australia has yet to consider seriously the broad social implications of the 'rising tide of poverty'. The evidence seems conclusive that new work formations exacerbate inequality (see Adkins, 1997). Given the extent of over, under and out of work (Probert and Mackey, 1996), equity needs to be a key consideration in the ways in which we structure and organise work.

Of course, in a globalised world of collapsed space and time, notions of equity also take on global proportions. The life chances of Australians are profoundly affected by events elsewhere – by international labour markets, for example. On the other hand, equity concerns can no longer be understood only in terms of social groups. They now must also be seen as about relationships between rich and poor countries and different parts of the globe. The matter does not stop there either.

In vocational education, as elsewhere, it is often assumed that matters of equity only concern 'equity groups' or 'targeted populations' and those others who speak with and for them. This was always a faulty logic but current times are revealing the problems of this logic more starkly as a result of the notion of generalisability of high consequence risk. For example, as Singer (1993) argues, the costs and consequences of unemployment, poverty and their connections to racism now spill over on to all populations. While cities may be divided ghettoes of affluence and poverty and while those on the 'right side of the tracks' may feel that urban geography and security systems protect them from poverty-related crime and violence, history is showing them otherwise. They are losing their sense of security, their freedom of movement to and from work and their free choice of work location as the result of their fear of the violence and crime that arises from Western societies' sharpening schisms between rich and poor, black and white. As Mckay (1993: 222–229) demonstrates, on the one hand we are seeing as a result a 'retreat to the domestic cave' and 'the information club'. On the other hand, we are likely to see increasing class hostility from the disenfranchised, the further use of such means of escape as drugs, violence and crime and the expansion of ungovernable 'torrid zones'.

The reconfiguration of equity problems suggests that VET needs to reconfigure its approaches – again. As Connell (1995: 7) states:

> Progress in education requires building a culture of equity. In a culture of equity, all forms of injustice are automatically contested, and an ethic of mutual care, not the search for competitive advantage, is central to policy making.

Equally, the generalisability of risks suggests that VET needs to end the marginalisation of equity concerns.

Life politics: a politics of decisions about lifestyle

Emancipatory politics pre-exist and intersect with life politics, which I will now consider. Life politics is concerned with how we are able to understand our existence and how we are to live in the post-traditional, globally interdependent order. It recognises that what was once fixed by nature and tradition is now subject to decisions. It addresses new fields of action and aims for morally justifiable ways of living. It 'demands an encounter with specific moral dilemmas and forces us to raise existential issues which modernity has institutionally excluded' (Giddens, 1991: 9). A certain autonomy of action and of capacities to choose are the basic ingredients of life politics. It seeks to hold governments and other institutions to account; it builds up worker/citizens' capacities and rights.

So, for instance, life politics is concerned about issues associated with productivism, global ecology, nuclear war, violence on all fronts, global scarcity and abundance, the sanctity of human life, universal human rights, the preservation of the species and care for present and future generations of children. It attends to the shared high consequence risks of globalisation; these risks override the divisions of interest that motivate emancipatory politics.

Life politics is particularly interested in issues associated with the body and with the environment and of course both are of particular relevance to the world of work. It is interested in the ways in which abstract systems of knowledge work on the body and change it. It shows that the body is not just disciplined in Foucault's terms or commodified in the terms of Marx, but an object of endless reflexive processes that irrevocably change its nature (Giddens, 1991). While conventionally it addresses matters associated with genetic engineering, reproductive technologies, cloning, body sculpting, health, safety, diet and dying, it is equally apt that it address matters of worker health and safety, industry and the environment, technology and its implications for workers' bodies and the body politic at work and outworked.

Life politics is also interested in social reproduction and species reproduction and in how the first (how we live our lives) affects the second. It shows how the person is linked to the planet and how personal lives and planetary needs intersect; how the things we do as we *work and play* are linked through planetary systems and have unpredictable effects. The feminist axiom that the 'personal is political' is also an important aspect of life politics. It involves disputes and struggles about how we should work and how we should live. With regard to work, it asks questions about the relationships between unpaid and paid work – voluntary and involuntary (Goodnow and Bowes, 1994), between work, family and leisure (Deem, 1995), work and sexuality, job and life satisfaction (Probert and Mackey, 1996). It exposes the ethics (or lack thereof) that lie behind the whole linguistic repertoire of economic rationalism. In this respect, it is worth noting that people don't talk about firing workers any more, they talk about de-hiring, de-selecting, making people indefinitely idle, involuntarily separating, non-renewing, presenting a career change opportunity, selectively separating them, selecting out, vocationally relocating them. Institutions don't talk about firing people, they talk about downsizing, rightsizing, streamlining, de-staffing, rectifying a workforce imbalance, correcting a redundancy of human resources, implementing a skills mix adjustment, managing staff resources, engaging in reduction activities, and so on.

As some vocational educators have discovered, there is a potentially rich educational agenda associated with life politics. They are all too aware that many of their worker/learners, young and older, experience the unfortunate structures of feeling alluded to earlier. They feel alienated at work (for example, see Rogers, 1995) and have a generalised sense of anxiety, meaninglessness, emotional and moral disquiet, existential isolation and a separation off from the moral resources needed to live a full working life. They have trouble finding something to live for. As the work by Sweet (1996), Simon *et al.* (1991) and Kincheloe (1995) shows, attention to life politics in work education has some potential to turn this around. However, it is important not to lose sight of the connections between emancipatory and life politics, for the capacity to engage in the latter is influenced a great deal by the outcomes of the former. Further, it is not readily possible to live an ethical life and to subscribe to certain sets of greed and growth values.

The relationship between emancipatory and life politics

Emancipatory and life politics are linked in the sense that people are more likely to become involved in life politics after they have achieved the sorts of autonomy of action that are fought for through emancipatory politics. Such autonomy is basic to the pursuit of life politics. Those who do not have it are therefore unequal and are more likely to be exploited and oppressed by various contemporary forces. They will be marginalised and excluded from decisions around such matters. As Giddens indicates, reflexivity and globalisation may further inscribe and intensify previous systems of stratification. The disadvantaged may thus suffer double discrimination through the effects of material deprivation and through being disqualified from the reflexive order that allows them to participate in life politics (Giddens, 1994: 90–92).

Singer (1993) makes it clear that emancipatory and life politics are linked in other ways too. In making decisions about lifestyle we also make ethical choices about what values are to guide our lives. Free market economics has particularly negative implications for equity. To adopt it as an 'ethical' way of life is to adopt a lifestyle that is inherently oppressive.

Singer offers a most persuasive critique of the values associated with the free market, greed is good, 'what's in it for me?' sensibility. This sensibility dominates work, education and training; it contributes to various forms of exploitation, inequality, oppression, marginalisation and exclusion. Drawing upon economic data, cross-cultural, philosophical and historical studies, he demonstrates clearly the high consequence risks that arise from such a lifestyle. He refers to 'toxic chemical dumps, polluted streams, oil slicks on the oceans, and nuclear wastes that will be deadly for ten thousands of years' (Singer, 1993: 43) and also points to the general risks involved in thoughtlessly depleting our finite natural capital, including our atmosphere, in the pursuit of 'growth'. Speaking of both the so-called first and the third world, he says 'Our economy is simply not sustainable' (46).

Singer shows that these growth and greed values have not produced a thriving economy, a greater sense of well-being or happiness even for their most apparently successful advocates and practitioners. Also, as he shows, they have resulted in 'ecological and social disasters'. He argues against the equation of consumption with fulfilment. He claims that 'consumer society promotes acquisition as the standard of what is good'. But he then goes on to say that:

> Once we get rid of that dominant conception of the good life, we can again bring to the centre of the stage questions about the preservation of the planet's ecology and about global justice. Only then can we hope to see a renewal of the will to deal with the root causes of poverty, crime and the destruction of the planet's resources.
>
> (1993: 17–18)

Singer turns Adam Smith's arguments back on him. Smith's arguments are often used to promote corporate greed as a civic virtue with trickle-down benefits to us all. Singer points to the serious limits to such claims. He argues instead that there is a general interest in reconfiguring our priorities and our notions of self-interest.

For Singer, life politics contributes to emancipatory politics as it encourages us to take ourselves out of the spotlight, to identify with other and larger goals and longer-term views – to 'take the point of view of the universe' and adopt an ethical approach to life. This involves recognising the importance of 'doing something about the pain and suffering of others' (1993: 230–233) and taking a stance against 'avoidable pain' such as that caused by sectional privilege at the expense of others, various forms of violence and denials of human rights in workplaces, and the repressed moral concerns that I alluded to earlier. Life politics is about rebuilding damaged solidarities and active trust. It is about building social and political capital to enhance the political capital of workers to enable them to claim their rights and to accept their responsibilities.

A strong vocational education would help students to deal with the problems associated with the altered context of working life. It would help them to distinguish between productivity and productivism, individualism and an impulse towards personal development, to understand their sources of doubt, uncertainty and risk, and the effects of these processes on their bodies and psyches as workers. It would help them to deal with the existential and moral dilemmas of current workplaces. It would see its role as 'growing' social and political as well as human capital.

Conclusion

It is not good enough that vocational education is reduced to the barren lexicon of economics. This lexicon does not help educators or students much;

it is too thin. Education must move away from 'the false certainty of consensus' (Cox, 1995: 11–12) that such language both suggests and seeks to effect. Education only flourishes in an environment that stimulates 'new ideas, dissident views, debates and critics in the context of mutual respect and trust'. Further, in vocational education we require robust concepts that recognise our rich roles and responsibilities, treat our students as 'fully human', help us to enact and support socially just change and that enhance us as professionals. Australian education has quite a proud history in this regard but this history is at risk unless we mobilise a new policy discourse for change across VET policy and curriculum. My purpose in this article has been to offer a tentative and preliminary alternative framework that provides VET policy makes and curriculum developers with an ethical base rather than technical formulae for decision making. Clearly I am not saying that this is all there is to vocational education. Rather, I am suggesting that moral concerns must not be repressed from any vocational educational policy and practice. It is my view that VET qualifications frameworks are able to include emancipatory and life politics and that if they do so, they will be able to make a significant contribution to 'repairing damaged solidarities', to economic and social reconstruction and, overall, to the life of work and the work of life.

Notes

1   The Liberals have also developed a New Apprenticeship Scheme for entry-level training. I will not discuss this here.
2   I thank Sue Willis for her contribution to the text in this section of the chapter.
3   As we have indicated elsewhere (Kenway and Willis, 1995) there are many gender issues involved and interests at stake in competency-based education and training.

References

Adkins, L. (1997) Community and economy: the re-traditionalization of gender?, paper presented at the 'Transformations' Conference, Lancaster University, UK, 17–19 July.

Angwin, J. (1994) The reconstruction of women's work in adult education, in Deakin Centre for Education and Change (eds) Schooling What Future? (Geelong, Australia, Deakin Centre for Education and Change, Deakin University).

Australian National Training Authority (ANTA) (1997a) Assuring Quality and Choice in National Training (Canberra, ACT).

Australian National Training Authority (ANTA) (1997b) Australian Training: special edition (Canberra, ACT).

Australian National Training Authority (ANTA) (1997c) National Strategy for VET for 1998–2003 (Canberra, ACT).

Australian National Training Authority (ANTA) (n.d.) Australian Recognition Framework (Canberra, ACT).

Australian National Training Authority (ANTA) (n.d.) *Training Packages* (Geelong, Canberra, ACT).

Bagshaw, M. (1996) Access and equity strategies, in Australian National Training Authority *Second National Conference on Vocational Education and Training* (Adelaide, South Australia).

Beck, U. (1992) *Risk Society – towards a new modernity* (London, Sage).

Casey, C. (1995) *Work, Self and Society: after industrialism* (London, Routledge).

Castells, M. (1996) *The Rise of the Network Society* (Malden, MA., Blackwell).

Connell, B. (1995) Equity through education, *Australian Centre for Equity through Education*, p. 7.

Cox, E. (1995) *A Truly Civil Society*, 1995 Boyer Lectures (Sydney, ABC Books).

Curriculum Corporation (1996) *Australian Qualifications Framework, Introduction to the AQF* (Melbourne, Curriculum Corporation).

Deem, R. (1995) No time for a rest? An exploration of women's work, engendered leisure and holidays, *Invitational Address* to Faculty of Social Sciences, Cartmel College, Lancaster University, Lancaster.

Ecclestone, K. (1997) Energising or enervating: implications of National Vocational Qualifications in Professional Development, *Journal of Vocational Education and Training*, 49(1), 65–79.

Fitzclarence, L. and Kenway, J. (1993) Social justice in the post-modern age, in J. Knight, B. Lingard and P. Porter (eds) *Re/Forming Education in Hard Times: the Labor years in Australia and New Zealand* (London, Falmer Press).

Giddens, A. (1991) *Modernity and Self Identity: self and society in the late modern age* (Cambridge, Polity Press).

Giddens, A. (1994) *Beyond Left and Right: the future of radical politics* (Stanford, CA, Stanford University Press).

Goodnow, J. and Bowes, J. (eds) (1994) *Men, Women and Household Work* (Melbourne, Oxford University Press).

Jackson, N. (1997) Refraining the discourse of skill, in J. Kenway, K. Tregenza and P. Watkins (eds) *Vocational Education Today: some critical issues* (Geelong, Australia, Deakin Centre for Education and Change, Deakin University).

Jakupec, V. and McTaggart, R. (1996) *Commercialisation and Flexible Delivery: access in Vocational Education and Training* (Geelong, Australia, Deakin Centre for Education and Change, Deakin University).

Johnson, S. (1997) Leadership in an angry workplace, *Management*, p. 14.

Kenway, J. (ed.) (1994) *Economising Education: the post-Fordist directions* (Geelong, Australia, Deakin University Press, Deakin University).

Kenway, J. (1997) *Education in the age of uncertainty: an eagle's eye view*, working paper (Geelong, Australia, Deakin Centre for Education and Change, Deakin University).

Kenway, J. and Willis, S. (1995) *Critical Visions: policy and curriculum rewriting the future of education, gender and work* (Canberra, Australian Government Publishing Service).

Kincheloe, J. (1995) *Toil and Trouble: good work, smart workers, and the integration of academic and vocational education* (New York, Peter Lang Publishing).

Liff, S. and Wajcman, J. (1996) 'Sameness' and 'Difference' Revisited: which way forward for equal opportunity initiatives?, *Journal of Management Studies*, 33(1), 79–94.

Lim, L.L. (1996) *More and Better Jobs for Women: an action guide* (Geneva, International Labour Office).

Mckay, H. (1993) *Reinventing Australia: the mind and mood of Australia in the 90s* (Sydney, HarperCollins).

Probert, B. and Mackey, F. (1996) *The Work Generation: work and identity in the nineties* (Fitzroy, Brotherhood of St. Laurence).

Rogers, J. (1995) Just a temp: experience and structure of alienation in temporary clerical employment, *Work and Occupations*, 22(2), 137–166.

Schofield, K. and Dryen, R. (1997) *Equity Performance Measures for Women in VET* (Leabrook, NCVER).

Seddon, T. (1994) Reconstructing social democratic education in Australia: versions of vocationalism, *Journal of Curriculum Studies*, 26(1), 63–82.

Sedunary, E. (1995) Neither new nor alien to progressive thinking: interpreting the convergence of radical education and the new vocationalism in Australia, *Journal of Curriculum Studies*, 28(4), 369–396.

Simon, R., Dippo, D. and Schenke, A. (1991) *Learning Work: a critical pedagogy of work education* (Toronto, Ontario Institute for Studies in Education).

Singer, P. (1993) *How are we to Live? Ethics in the age of self-interest* (Melbourne, The Text Publishing Company).

Sobski, J. (1996) National Women's VET Strategy, in Australian National Training Authority (eds) *Second National Conference on Vocational Education and Training* (Adelaide, South Australia).

Sweet, R. (1996) School and beyond: a wider view, paper prepared for *Australian College of Education National Conference on General and Vocational Education*, Sydney, June 20–21.

Taylor, S. and Henry, M. (1994) Equity and the new post-compulsory education and training policies in Australia: a progressive or regressive agenda?, *Journal of Education Policy*, 9(2), 105–127.

Wallace, M. (1999) *Women and Workplace Training: an analysis of policy and practice*, Ph.D. Thesis (Geelong, Australia, Faculty of Education, Deakin University).

Chapter 9

Breaking the consensus
Lifelong learning as social control

Frank Coffield

Introduction

This chapter, like Roman Gaul, in three parts divided is. First, reasons will be advanced to reject the powerful consensus that has been developed over the last 30 years to the effect that lifelong learning is a wonder drug or magic bullet that, on its own, will solve a wide range of educational, social and political ills. It will be argued that this consensus is naive, limited and apparent as well as being deficient, dangerous and diversionary. This analysis prompts the question, if the thesis is so poor, why is it so popular? Second, alternative visions of the learning society and of lifelong learning will be presented and the relevance to policy of viewing lifelongs learning as social control will be stressed. Third, an attempt will be made to answer Lenin's great question, what is to be done? It is incumbent, I think, on researchers funded by the public purse to address policy, where appropriate.

Wherever possible, the findings from the Economic and Social Research Council's (ESRC) *Learning Society Programme* will be drawn on, but it is important to emphasise that neither the ESRC nor any of the 50-plus researchers in the 14 projects within the programme should be held responsible for what follows; they are guilty only by associating with the author in public.

I have one further introductory comment. The consensus is *not* a straw man, whose demolition may delight the reader but be of little significance beyond that; instead it constitutes a central plank in the policy of many Western governments in the field of education, training and employment. It is time, however, to move beyond this cosy consensus and develop more ambitious policies for creating economic prosperity and social justice.

The consensus criticised

The following critique has three objectives: to encapsulate the main features of the consensus in a few central tenets and to demonstrate its influence by

This is an edited version of an article published in *British Educational Research Journal*, 25, 4 (1999): 479–499.

means of a few representative quotations; then to list the pr[o]
and then to explain its popularity and resilience in the face [o]
the sake of variety, the consensus will also be called inter[
thesis, the orthodoxy, the regime or the settlement.[1]

Central tenets of the consensus

The prevailing orthodoxy within the UK contains the following elements:

- A nation's competitiveness in global markets ultimately depends on the skills of all its people.
- The new economic forces unleashed by globalisation and technology are as uncontrollable as natural disasters and so governments have no choice but to introduce policies to 'upskill' the workforce.
- Education must be modernised and become more responsive to the needs of employers. In some formulations, education becomes the mere instrument of the economy, e.g. 'Education is the best economic policy we have', as the Prime Minister expressed it (Blair, 1998: 9).
- The responsibility is passed to individuals to renew their skills regularly to ensure their employability.
- The model for educational institutions to follow is that of British business.

Each of these propositions is problematical and each deserves critical analysis. Here, there is space to deal only with the fifth commandment, namely, 'Thou Shalt Covet the Practices of Business'. Two objections suggest themselves immediately. First, a Treasury *Pre-Budget Report* recently argued that the UK has a productivity gap with the United States of around 40 per cent and around 20 per cent with France and Germany. 'In most sectors of the economy the UK is far short of the best in the world' (HM Treasury, 1998: 28). The Treasury report also produced evidence that showed that 'over the past decade the aggregate amount of R and D conducted by UK firms has continued to lag our international competitors' (32) and that 'The Government believes that at the root of much of the productivity problem in the UK lies a long history of underinvestment . . . For decades, the UK has invested less than our major contributors' (37).[2]

Given this evidence, the exhortation for education to emulate British business seems perverse, unless we in education are supposed to learn from comparative failure rather than from comparative success. Second, the Government has recognised the urgent need to modernise both business and education, but there the similarity ends. Legislation upon legislation and a punitive form of regulation are deemed necessary to modernise education, but the Prime Minister argues in his foreword to the Department of Trade and Industry's (DTI) White Paper on *Our Competitive Future* that in relation to business 'old-fashioned state intervention did not and cannot work' (1998a: 5). The voluntary framework for employers, inherited from the previous Conservative Government, is reconfirmed and strengthened in the DTI White Paper, where the only legislation proposed is to 'change the law to give businesses in difficulties more chance to turn things round' (1998a: 62). Perhaps the Government would care to explain why policies acknowledged to have failed when dealing with business are still thought appropriate for education. This issue will be picked up again in the final section but the consensus as a whole needs to be dealt with first.

The policy of upskilling the workforce is a simplified version of the theory of human capital, which came to dominate debates about the importance of education in promoting economic development after the publication of the ideas of Theodore Schultz (1961) and Gary Becker ([1964] 1975). In the subsequent 30 years the original reservations of the proponents have been forgotten and a degraded version has assumed the status of a conventional wisdom. It is this degraded version of human capital theory that is being criticised here. Gary Becker, for instance, emphasised that 'the attention paid to the economic effects of education and other human capital . . . is not in any way meant to imply that other effects are unimportant, or less important than the economic ones' (1975: 11). Unfortunately, those other factors have all but vanished from consideration and need to be reintroduced into the debate.

It would also be easy but tedious to show how this consensus enjoys the support of politicians of the left, centre and right (in most anglophone countries), of policy makers, industrialists and trade unionists, and of economists and educationists. Instead of quoting chapter and verse for all these groups, three representative quotations are given.

The first comes from an influential report[3] from the Confederation of British Industry (CBI) in 1989, *Towards a Skills Revolution*, which helped to persuade the Conservative Government of the time to establish National Targets for Education and Training:

> Individuals are now the only source of sustainable competitive advantage. Efforts must be focused on mobilising their commitment and encouraging self-development and lifetime learning.
>
> (CBI, 1989: 9)

This focus on individuals was repeated in each of the three reports on *Competitiveness* published by John Major's government in 1994, 1995 and 1996, and it resulted in the establishment of an Individual Commitment to Learning Division within the Department for Education and Employment.

The second quotation is taken from the first White Paper produced by the new Labour Government of 1997, *Excellence in Schools*, and shows an unbroken continuity in thinking between Conservative and Labour administrations. This is an example of that indolent cliché of modern politics 'joined up government':

> Investment in learning in the 21st Century is the equivalent of invest-
> ment in the machinery and technical innovation that was essential to
> the first great industrial revolution. Then it was physical capital; now it
> is human capital.
>
> (Department for Education and Employment
> (DfEE), 1997a: 15)

The idea that modern manufacture by Nissan or British Aerospace does not crucially depend on technological innovation and physical capital is, of course, ludicrous.

The final quotation comes from the Labour Government's first Minister for Lifelong Learning who, ironically, held the post for only one year:

> If we do *not* create a learning society – if we do *not* find the means of gen-
> erating the appropriate skills and craft and expertise, then we will fail to
> develop our most important resource – our people – and we will fail as an
> economy in this increasingly globalised market.
>
> (Howells, 1997, original emphasis)

The inflated claims in these quotations have become *the* conventional wisdoms at education and business conferences. They need to be cut down to size.

Problems with human capital theory

The orthodoxy has became a set of unquestioned articles of faith to, for instance, the Blair[4] and Clinton[5] administrations despite being subjected to continuous criticism. The reasons for its apparent invulnerability will be explored in the following section; here the main criticisms that have been levelled against it will be briefly rehearsed.

The thesis is diversionary   In 1997 Jerome Karabel and Chelly Halsey con-cluded at the end of an extended review that human capital theory did not 'provide an adequate framework for understanding the relationship between education and the economy' (1997: 15), as it was seriously flawed both the-oretically and empirically. Moreover, because the theory was used to explain that individuals, communities and whole nations were poor because their human capital had not been developed, it diverted attention away from struc-tural failures and injustices and blamed victims for their poverty.

In a similar manner, the two flagship initiatives of the Government's strategy for lifelong learning – the University for Industry and Individual

Learning Accounts – welcome as they are, both transfer responsibility for remaining 'employable' on to *individuals*, who do not have the power to remove the structural barriers that prevent them learning. The research projects in the ESRC's Learning Society Programme provide many examples of such structural barriers, but there is space here to describe only one. A study of the National Health Service by Jenny Hewison, Bobbie Millar and Therese Dowswell examined the shift towards regarding training as an individual responsibility to be completed in the employee's own time. The implications for staff with young children are serious, because not taking the opportunity to train is interpreted as evidence of lack of commitment: 'By these means, structural inequalities in access are turned into attributes of individuals' (Hewison *et al.*, 1998).

It overshadows social capital   Also, other forms of capital (e.g. cultural, material). The overconcentration on individual human capital leads to a corresponding neglect of social capital, by which is meant the social relationships and arrangements (e.g. strong social networks, shared values and high trust) needed to support learning. Again, within the Learning Society Programme, John Field and Tom Schuller have been studying the interaction between human and social capital in Northern Ireland and Scotland and one of their arguments is pertinent here: 'investment in human capital by an employer or by society requires the appropriate social context in order to be realised effectively' (Schuller and Burns, 1999).

The empirical basis of the theory is highly disputable   Henry Levin and Carolyn Kelley conducted another review of the research in the USA and found, just like Karabel and Halsey, that 'test scores have never shown a strong connection with either earnings or productivity' (Levin and Kelley, 1997: 241). The notion that the competitiveness of the USA can only be sustained by American students outperforming their counterparts abroad in scores on achievement tests is, according to Levin and Kelley, 'naïve and hardly supported by the overall empirical data' (243). Moreover, cross-sectional studies of earnings tend to overstate the longitudinal impact of education. And, thanks to Ivar Berg, we have known for 20 years that personal characteristics and job conditions are more important determinants of work performance than educational attainments (Berg, 1973).

The theory is seriously incomplete   Levin and Kelley (1997) also point out that, for education to be effective, it is crucially dependent on complementary inputs such as new investment, new methods of production and of organising work, new technologies, industrial relations based on trust, sufficient customers able to buy high-quality goods and services, and new managerial approaches. At its most obvious, highly educated and trained personnel need jobs commensurate with their abilities if they are to boost productivity.

It is dangerous   The danger lies in employers 'being reinforced in their beliefs that the main obstacle to their success is the poor education of the workforce' (Levin and Kelley, 1997: 245). The overconcentration on one factor – improving standards in education – distorts both industrial and educational policy in ways that are unlikely to improve competitiveness and delays the advent of more comprehensive strategies.

It ignores polarisation   Human capital theory has nothing to say about the sharpening polarisation in income and wealth both internationally (see Manuel Castells, 1998) and within the UK (see Joseph Rowntree Reports in 1995 and 1998). This polarisation is being exacerbated by performance indicators in education such as the school league tables. The pass rates at the General Certificate of Secondary Education (GCSE) examinations in 1998 revealed two trends: a rising number failing to obtain any passes; and a widening gap between this group at the bottom and those achieving average or high grades. Let us examine the data in more detail at both national and local level. Peter Robinson and Carey Oppenheim studied GCSE grades in England and Wales over the period 1991–6 and concluded (see Table 9.1) that the top 10 per cent of pupils had increased their average score by nearly nine points, while the bottom 10 per cent had shown hardly any improvement at all. The outcome of providing teachers with incentives to concentrate on those pupils capable of obtaining five or more higher-grade GCSE (A*–C) has been that those students with few or no qualifications have been correspondingly neglected. Robinson and Oppenheim (1998: 19) have provided hard evidence 'of how key indicators can distort incentives in a way which can have undesirable consequences'.

Table 9.1 Polarisation in GCSE scores, 1991–6 (average GCSE points score)

Decile group	1991	1996	Change
1	0.3	0.6	0.3
2	7.1	10.7	3.6
3	15.3	20.6	5.3
4	21.8	27.9	6.1
5	27.5	34.1	6.6
6	32.9	39.8	6.9
7	38.0	45.3	7.3
8	43.4	50.8	7.4
9	49.4	57.0	7.6
10	58.7	67.5	8.8
All	29.5	35.4	6.0

Note: GCSE points scores: A*–8; A–7; B–6; C–5; D–4; E–3; F–2; G–1.

Source: Robinson and Oppenheim (1998).

Table 9.2 School performance in Newcastle, 1988

Schools	% of 5 GCSEs A*–C	No. with SEN	Total no. of pupils
1	98	nil	906
2	97	31	501
3 =	96	4	440
	96	nil	1,056
...	...	...	...
16	25	243	810
17	14	17	1,198
18	10	164	561
19	6	300	1,396

Source: DfEE (1988) *Performance Tables* (London, DfEE).

To bring this argument home, the figures of the highest- and lowest-scoring schools at GCSE in Newcastle in 1998 have been extracted and are presented in Table 9.2. Such raw scores have been rightly criticised on a variety of counts by other commentators but the point to be made here is different. It does not take a detailed knowledge of social class in Newcastle to be able to identify the first four as schools from the private sector; and the bottom four as schools serving seriously deprived areas. No one is arguing for equality of outcome but such extreme *inequalities* of outcome, repeated year after year, are the mark of a society that is becoming dangerously polarised. These figures speak eloquently of an educational 'apartheid' in this and other cities throughout the country; the emotive phrase is used by George Walden (1996: 1) to describe the two segregated systems of education within this one country. The policy of publishing such tables, for all their unwelcome consequences, may still prove to be of value, *provided* it results in robust policies to tackle such unjustifiable, unacceptable but remediable inequality.

Manuel Castells has produced extensive evidence to show how new forms of capitalism are creating 'a sharp divide between valuable and non-valuable people and locales' (Castells, 1998: 161) and 'a fundamental split in societies all over the world: on the one hand, active, culturally self-defined elites . . . on the other hand, increasingly uncertain, insecure social groups, deprived of information, resources and power, digging their trenches of resistance' (340).

It ignores the sexual division of labour   Human capital theory treats skill as a measurable attribute of individuals, but Jill Blackmore (1997) argues that it is better viewed as a relational concept whose meaning shifts over time depending on, for example, the perceived status of particular tasks; the supply of and demand for skilled people; and the ability of the skilled to exclude others. In other words, skills are not neutral, technically defined

categories but are socially constructed by, for example, trade unions negotiating higher pay rates for their male members, or employers redefining skill
levels to reduce costs. For Blackmore, human capital theory has no sense of
history and has ignored 'the maintenance of particular gendered power relations in the workplace' (Blackmore, 1997: 233). To David Ashton and
Francis Green, 'the fundamental weakness of the theory ... is that in
regarding human capital as a "thing" to be acquired and utilised alongside
other factor inputs, it misses the social context of skill and of technology'
(Ashton and Green, 1996: 17).

It has created a new moral economy   Where some people are treated as
more 'desirable' than others (see Stephen Ball *et al.*, 1999 – another project
team within the Learning Society Programme). The Government's stated
aim is 'to rebuild the welfare state around work' (Department of Social
Security, 1998: 23) and paid employment is seen as the best means of
averting poverty and social exclusion. But if people are to be treated first
and foremost in relation to their potential contribution to the economy,
then a market value is attached to each individual according to that contribution. So people with learning difficulties may come to be seen as a
poor investment, more expensive to train, less flexible and less employable.
In such a moral climate, it becomes possible for an industrialist to question
whether public money should be wasted on research into adults with learning difficulties.[6] One project within the Learning Society Programme
makes it clear that, if learning is made the central organising principle of
society, those with learning difficulties may well be excluded (see Baron
et al., 1998).

In this way, the language of one research area within economics has
hijacked the public debate and the discourse of professionals so that education is no longer viewed as a means of individual and social emancipation,
but as either 'investment' or 'consumption', as having 'inputs' and 'outputs',
'stocks' that 'depreciate' as well as 'appreciate', and it is measured by 'rates
of return', an approach that produces offensive jargon such as 'overeducated
graduates' and 'monopoly producers'. The discourse that has been sidelined
as a result and that must now be brought centre stage is the discourse of
social justice and social cohesion.

Other options may be more appropriate   Ewart Keep and Ken Mayhew
(1998) have argued that, instead of upskilling their workforce, companies
have a range of competitive strategies to choose from, including seeking
protected markets, growing through takeover, shifting investment abroad,
developing monopoly power and cutting costs. Evidence for the cost-cutting
strategy can be seen in the proliferation of retail outlets in the high streets
of the UK with names like Aldi, Poundstretcher and Superdrug, where
competitive advantage is based on low prices and bulk purchases. As Keep

and Mayhew contend, 'many employers are pursuing perfectly rational training policies because their competitive strategies do not necessarily require them to upskill their entire workforce' (1998: 8).

Upskilling creates credential inflation   The upskilling debate is conducted as though all skills and qualifications are equally valued in the labour market. But the value of educational credentials begins to fall as a higher percentage of each generation achieves graduate status when there is no corresponding expansion of elite jobs. Moreover, the new graduates from the expanded higher education system expect the same benefits from their university qualifications as those qualifications brought to their predecessors from the much smaller elite system. In such an inflationary spiral, selection is intensified and the class of degree (first vs. lower second), the subject (physics vs. media studies), the level (undergraduate vs. postgraduate) and the awarding institution (Oxbridge vs. ex-polytechnic) form the basis of a more steeply graded hierarchy of prestige.[7] Ralph Fevre, studying patterns of participation in education in South Wales as part of the Learning Society Programme, predicts that, as a result of policies designed to increase our investment in human capital, we run the serious risk that 'the UK will veer towards the US model of higher participation rates but with much education and training being of dubious value', because students will increase their credentials rather than their understanding (Fevre, 1997: 15).

If the thesis is so poor, why is it so popular?

The list of weaknesses could be extended (e.g. input–output models ignore the processes of education) but sufficient damage has been inflicted to add force to the question, if the thesis is so poor, why is it so popular? Each of the criticisms on its own makes a substantial dent in the theory of human capital; taken together, they damage its credibility beyond repair as the sole justification for policy. And yet the consensus continues to be referred to reverentially on public platforms as though it contained articles of unquestionable faith. Four main reasons are advanced to explain this invulnerability to criticism.

It legitimates increased expenditure on education   According to Karabel and Halsey, human capital theory flourished in the USA because it offered 'quantitative justification for vast public expenditure on education' (1997: 13). It continues to be used by Secretaries of State for Education as a means of prising open the coffers of the Treasury in favour of increased spending on education; this is a considerable argument in its favour, but if the policy fails, there may well be a backlash.

It provides politicians with the pretext for action   'Politicians', argued Tony Edwards, 'exalt educational reform because they believe they see in it unusual opportunities for acting both decisively and nationally. They then tend to greatly over-estimate the problems which more effective schooling would alleviate or solve' (1998: 144). It will prove difficult to wean politicians off an idea that is so readily translatable into the kind of short-term initiatives on which their careers depend.

It deflects attention from the need for economic and social reform Legislation to change the behaviour of individuals and educational institutions diverts attention away from more fundamental causes of low productivity, such as the short-termism of British financial institutions, which denies manufacture the long-term investment it depends upon. Another attraction of the theory for politicians is that it converts deep-seated economic problems into short-lived educational projects.

It offers the comforting illusion that for every complex problem there is one simple solution   To many politicians and policy makers, 'the seductive appeal' of this approach at a time of economic uncertainty 'offers the illusion of control and of managerial solutions' (Hodkinson *et al.*, 1996: 138).

To sum up, we shall not create a learning society in the UK by investing all our hopes in a single policy of expanding human capital. The Treasury's *Pre-Budget Report*, for instance, lists four historic weaknesses in the UK's economy; improving the skills base is the fourth and last. The three factors considered more important causes of the UK's relative economic decline are: the absence of a culture celebrating innovation and enterprise; the failure of capital markets to provide sufficient investment; and the need for more competition in business to tackle vested interests and 'to expose management to international best practice' (HM Treasury, 1998: 42). These are challenges to which education has a distinctive contribution to make, but the main onus of change falls squarely on British business. In a logical world, there would now be an end to treating education as *the* whipping boy for the country's economic ills, which has been the sport of politicians from all parties since James Callaghan's Ruskin College speech in 1976.

Alternative visions of a learning society and of lifelong learning

The full title of the ESRC research programme is '*The Learning Society: knowledge and skills for employment*', which might suggest that researchers were being invited to study lifelong learning in the service of the national consensus, which has been so severely criticised above. In practice, the project directors and the director of the programme have, from the very beginning, sought to examine changes in the labour market in the context of broad notions of citizenship, social justice and the quality of life. One of our objectives was to explore critically the concept of the learning society and the various versions of it proposed so far, as a necessary prelude to addressing that vital question: what is to be done?

For example, two researchers within the Learning Society Programme, Teresa Rees and Will Bartlett (1999), have suggested that the term can be viewed in three contrasting ways, which help to make sense of the myriad uses to which the phrase is put. The first version is the human capital thesis, which they call *the skill growth model*. They too consider the assumed link between upskilling and economic prosperity to be dangerously oversimplified and deterministic and therefore introduce a second approach – *the personal development model*, which argues for 'an increase in capacities to achieve individual self-fulfilment in all spheres of life, not just in economic activities' (Rees and Bartlett, 1999: 21). Again, those critics who think it unlikely that a learning *society* will ever be established by developing *individuals*, offer a third mode – *social learning* – which celebrates social as well as human capital and which emphasises 'the role of institutions of trust and co-operation in promoting economic growth on an equitable basis' (Rees and Bartlett, 1999: 22). These three models are convenient devices for making sense of the research and policies on lifelong learning. Other projects within the Learning Society Programme have, however, developed different models of a learning society (e.g. Michael Young, Ken Spours, Cathy Howieson and David Raffe, 1997[8]) and it has also been suggested that, instead of treating the learning society as a future destination that the UK may or may not reach, it may be preferable to use the concept reflexively to enable this society to learn about itself and to evaluate progress (Coffield, 1997).

In similar fashion, lifelong learning appears in the literature and in political discourse in a bewildering number of different guises. For instance, it is an instrument *for* change (in individuals, organisations and society) and as a buffer *against* change (see Isabelle Darmon *et al.*, 1999); it is a means of increasing economic competitiveness and of personal development; it is a social policy to combat social exclusion and to ease the re-entry of the unemployed into the labour market; it is a way of promoting the professional and social development of employees and of acquiring new knowledge through the labour process; and it is a strategy to develop the participation of citizens in social, cultural and political affairs. But there is also a sceptical version of lifelong learning that has received little attention in this country, namely, that it has become a form of social control and has the potential to become so ever more powerfully (see Tight, 1998). We are clearly not dealing with an unambiguous, neutral or static concept, but one that is currently being fought over by numerous interest groups, all struggling for their definition.

The insight that lifelong learning has become a moral obligation and a social constraint came from projects within the ESRC programme with a strong comparative dimension and from contacts with researchers like Walter Heinz at Bremen University (1999). To our European counterparts it is obvious that both the state and employers throughout Europe are using the rhetoric of lifelong learning first and foremost to make workers more flexible and more employable. In the words of the Tavistock research team within the Learning Society Programme:

> This new discourse on flexibility and employability legitimates the already well-advanced shift of the burden of responsibility for education, training and employment on to the *individual*, and implicitly denies any notion of objective structural problems such as lack of jobs, and the increasing proportion of poorly paid, untrained, routine and insecure jobs.
>
> (Darmon *et al.*, 1999, original emphasis)

The Tavistock team describes in detail the settlements that France and Spain are formulating in response to the challenges of the global market and technological innovation, compared with which the British consensus is seriously out of kilter. The French social compromise, for instance, seeks to *limit* flexibility by, *inter alia*, issuing regulations to make firms more socially responsible (e.g. the same working conditions for part-time, fixed contract and full-time staff). Meanwhile, in Spain, in 1992, the social partners agreed to a new training tax on employers and employees that devotes 50 per cent of all the funds to the training of the unemployed in accordance with the principle of solidarity. What all three countries (France, Spain and the UK) have in common is that trade unionists are reluctantly accepting increased flexibility in return for training to improve employability. But the researchers consider such deals not 'so much a trade-off as a trap' (Darmon *et al.*, 1999), particularly in view of the estimate of more than 25 per cent redundancies over the next ten years. The term 'employability' also disguises the tension between training workers to meet the short-term needs of employers and the preparation for frequent changes of job for which high-level general education may be more useful.

In short, in the rest of the European Union, lifelong learning is not a self-evident good but contested terrain between employers, unions and the state. Lifelong learning is being used to socialise workers to the escalating demands of employers, who use: 'empowerment' to disguise an intensification of workloads via increased delegation; 'employability' to make the historic retreat from the policy of full payment and periodic unemployment between jobs more acceptable; and 'flexibility' to cover a variety of strategies to reduce costs that increase job insecurity. Such a critical approach exposes both 'the fiction that workers and management are on the same team', and the 'new structures of power and control' introduced by flexibility, such as 'the discontinuous reinvention of institutions' (see Sennett, 1998: 47).

From an employer's perspective, the ideal 'portfolio' workers of the future are those who quickly internalise the need for employability, who willingly pay for their own continuous learning and who flexibly offer genuine commitment to each job, no matter how short its duration or how depressing its quality. There is more chance of Scotland winning the World Cup. A more likely and more rational response from employees would be to show loyalty in future only to their own careers. But the rhetoric of that myth-ical beast the learning organisation requires total commitment from all workers, who in return are likely to be treated as totally expendable by foot-loose employers such as Siemens and Fujitsu. The equation does not add up and this conflict at the heart of the concept of the learning organisation helps to explain why so few, if any, organisations are worthy of the title.

Such views may be dismissed as the morbid anxieties of German sociolo-gists from the unreconstructed Left. Consider, in that case, the recently expressed views of Alan Tuckett, Director of the National Institute for Adult Continuing Education and vice-chair of the Government's National Advis-ory Group for Continuing Education and Lifelong Learning:

> I find to my surprise that I have been thinking about compulsory adult learning . . . In the information industries continuing learning is a neces-sary precondition to keeping a job, and your capacity to keep on learning may affect the job security of others. Learning is becoming compulsory. And if it is true for people in some sectors of industry, why not for people who might want to rejoin the labour force later?
>
> (Tuckett, 1998)

It is not too difficult to detect in this quotation not only the voice of moral authoritarianism, which Walter Heinz (1999) believes to be the hidden agenda behind the rhetoric, but also mounting frustration among liberal educators who, after 20 years in the political wilderness, have now become policy advisers, and are confronted with the same seemingly intractable statistics on low levels of participation in lifelong learning by certain groups. Within a short time, however, genuine social concern to widen the social base of participation appears to be turning opportunities to learn into impositions to be obeyed. Ivan Illich and Etienne Verne predicted such an outcome when they argued that lifelong learning would become 'not the symbol of our unfinished development, but a guarantee of our perma-nent inadequacy' and would constantly reassign learners to their place in a meritocracy (Illich and Verne, 1976: 13). Compulsory emancipation via life-long learning is a contradiction in terms.

Please also take into consideration the British Government's policy frame-work on competitiveness, which is set out for the next ten years in the DTI's White Paper on *Our Competitive Future* (1998a). This document is so one-sided it could have been written by the Institute of Directors; for example, it claims that the 'DTI will . . . champion business needs in government' (1998a: 61). Surely it is the role of government to champion the public good and the national interest, which is frequently in conflict with the short-run needs of business. Moreover, the White Paper contains no discussion of the fundamental changes in the labour market *as they affect workers*, such as the move to core and peripheral workforces, i.e. the simultaneous growth of longer working hours for some and of many more casual, part-time, temporary and insecure jobs for others. In higher education, for example, the proportion of staff on fixed-term contracts is increasing (41.1 per cent of the total in 1996–7), while the proportion on permanent contracts is declining. No measures are included in the White Paper to protect workers from galloping flexibility, but it does list no less than 75 commitments, many of which are *designed 'to reduce the burdens of unnecessary regulation'* on business (DTI, 1998a: 21).

Seventy-five proposals for government action suggest that 'old-fashioned state intervention' is still popular with politicians. And the introduction of a national minimum wage, the signing of the Social Chapter and the implementation of the Working Time Directive (a limit of 48 hours of work a week) are welcome examples of positive action by this Government, which are detailed in the White Paper *Fairness at Work* (DTI, 1998b). The Prime Minister explains, however, in his Foreword to the White Paper that these proposals 'put a very minimum infrastructure of decency and fairness around people in the workplace' (DTI, 1998b). But if redundancies, contracting out, delayering, casualisation, mergers and shifting investment overseas intensify, workers, their families and communities will need more protection than that provided by 'a very minimum infrastructure'. Moreover, *Fairness at Work* takes an uncritical and complacent view of what are called the two 'keys to securing efficiency and fairness . . . employability and flexibility', with the latter being talked up as follows: 'By enabling business success flexibility promotes employment and prosperity' (DTI, 1998b: 14).

According to Peter Mandelson, the former Secretary of State for Trade and Industry, in an article introducing *Our Competitive Future*, 'the starting point for the Government's analysis is that knowledge and its profitable exploitation by business is the key to competitiveness' (Mandelson, 1998). So knowledge that is created by universities with public funds is to be transferred to British firms who will then 'exploit' it for private profit. No hint appears in the White Paper that this proposal creates moral, financial and logistical problems. Socrates taught me that knowledge would set me free; Peter Mandelson tells me that its modern function is to make employers rich. It is time to turn from the pleasures of criticism to the pain of creation.

So what is to be done?

What follows are some reflections on possible ways forward, reflections that have been shaped by five years of working for the ESRC's Learning Society Programme[9] and by the findings produced so far by the 14 projects. The earlier disclaimer needs to be repeated – no one but the author should be held responsible for these recommendations for action, which are offered as a constructive contribution to the public debate.

A more detailed plan of action will come later, and will tackle such issues as the changes that need to be made to the curriculum. The intention here is to present parts of a skeleton, to use feedback to produce some solid flesh, and then, given a favourable wind, to breathe life into what is admittedly only an idiosyncratic selection of four disconnected bones.

A historical caveat is appropriate here. In 1972, Edgar Faure, the former French prime minister, as chairman of an international commission established by UNESCO, published a report, *Learning To Be*, which proposed 'lifelong education as the master concept for educational policies in the years to come' (Faure, 1972: 182). It has not happened; instead, flexibility has become the master concept in Western societies and Faure's enlightened and democratic vision of lifelong learning has been largely and unfairly forgotten (see Boshier, 1997). *Education permanente* proved to be a rather transient phenomenon and the same fate may befall lifelong learning.

Although the consensus remains the dominant discourse, alternative visions of the learning society are beginning to be articulated, especially by the ESRC programme. Such creative dissent is healthy in a democracy, but we have in the UK no forum where the positive qualities of all these possible futures begin to coalesce into one policy. Let us be clear about the importance of the issue. In discussing various versions of the learning society, we are talking about the present and future shape of British society and how our systems of education, training and employment can help us to realise the type of society we want to create. It is also worth considering why the ESRC decided to commission research into the learning society rather than, say, 'the socially just society' or 'the competitive society'. What is being developed in the UK is best described as a *flexible society*, fit for the global market. And the most appropriate slogan for the National Campaign for Learning should, in my opinion, be 'Lifelong learning: your flexible friend for your flexible future'. The education system is to be modernised, but some of the worst features of modernity (e.g. the dark side of the market principle, polarisation, and 'the concentration of power without centralization of power' (Sennett, 1998: 55)) are being built into it.

Whatever vision is finally decided upon, it will have to deal directly with capitalism, which is now the only show in town. In Anthony Giddens' words 'No one any longer has any alternatives to capitalism – the arguments that remain concern how far, and in what ways, capitalism should be governed and regulated' (Giddens, 1998: 43–44). But Richard Sennett argues powerfully that the aim of curbing the destructive aspects of the new capitalism should have a rationale beyond restraint: 'it must ask what value is the corporation to the community, how does it serve civic interests rather than just its own ledger of profit and loss?' (1998: 137). Armed with this insight, let us examine the Training and Enterprise Council (TEC) National

Council's call for 'a competitive society which succeeds in achieving a dynamic equilibrium between wealth creation and social cohesion, between competitiveness and social inclusion' (1997). This appears to be an astute compromise, but the Government has inherited a serious disequilibrium and the UK needs more than social cohesion; it also needs a renewal of democracy, citizenship and social justice.

Preference is, therefore, accorded to the stance of Martin Carnoy and Henry Levin, who argued that 'the relationship between education and work is dialectical – composed of a perpetual tension between two dynamics, the imperatives of capital and those of democracy in all its forms' (1985: 4). For over 20 years the economic imperative has dominated the democratic imperative and it will take a long, hard and concerted struggle to redress the imbalance. What is needed is a new consensus but, as Isabelle Darmon and her colleagues have shown, 'the nature and workability of these compromises very much depend on the relative strength of the institutional actors' (Darmon *et al.*, 1999: 40). New 'terms of engagement' between the main players also need to be introduced and that issue is addressed now.

A new social contract between the state, business, the trade unions and education

The present framework for developing policy and the current consensus, shot through as it is with economic values, have failed this country. As argued earlier, our productivity gap with our major trading competitors is substantial and it is not closing, and the deprived continue to receive a deprived education, which is both socially unjust and economically inefficient. The most important lesson we could learn from Europe is that this divided society could begin the process of healing by developing jointly agreed plans for our future through *the social partners*. What is needed is nothing less than a new social contract (please, *not* a *'strategic partnership'*[10]) between the state, business, the trade unions and education, each of which should be treated as equal and respected partners.

The Government is right to insist that a fundamental change in culture is needed in both education and in business, but the Government must take the lead by showing itself capable of such change. There is little prospect of developing a culture of lifelong learning in the UK if the Government itself does not become a model of learning. Similarly, we need a government that routinely uses research (including disconcerting findings) in the formation of policy, a government that welcomes constructive criticism, a government that is not only prepared to tolerate dissent but one that recognises and uses the innovative potential of dissenting voices. In a knowledge-driven economy, the Government must take the lead by showing how it incorporates the latest knowledge, namely research findings, into its thinking and policies.

The consultations in which the DfEE engaged over the goals and priorities of the Department (DfEE, 1997b) are evidence of a welcome change in style from the *dirigiste* approach of the previous administration. But a major change of heart has still to take place right across government: can departments, for instance, desist from claiming that their latest initiatives are instant successes before any independent evaluation has even begun? Such ministerial claims of instant success are as satisfying as instant coffee.

Education also needs to improve upon its usual negotiating stance (that of the pre-emptive cringe) and make demands of its partners in the new social contract. Just as industrialists have realised that education is too important to be left to teachers, so we in education must argue that British business is too important to be left to employers and politicians. For example, if the Shell Oil Company can be pushed into establishing a Social Responsibility Committee (in response to the vigorous protests of consumers to the Brent Spar incident), then all major firms could be positively encouraged to act likewise. Learning at work has also become so significant in the creation and management of knowledge (see Coffield, 1998) that a statutory framework is needed to prompt employers:

- to establish learning committees with representatives from management and workers;
- to develop in conjunction with unions learning agreements that lay out the rights and responsibilities of both parties; and
- to account for their investment in the learning of all their staff (full-time, fixed-term and part-time) in annual reports. (See Trade Union Congress (TUC), 1998 for detailed proposals for the union card to become an access card to learning.)

Furthermore, British financial markets should be exhorted to invest in new businesses (see Holtham, 1998) not in Malaysia, Morocco or Manitoba but in Middlesbrough, Manchester and Motherwell. The ownership and location of major industrial enterprises *does* matter and, for all that the arrival of Nissan has been beneficial to the North-east, the profits of the work of over 4,000 North-easterners are still transmitted to Japan; and the North-east remains a branch plant economy, with the key decisions about its future being taken in Japan, the USA and London. It will, however, take determined action by a supranational power (e.g. the European Union) to protect the rights of workers and their communities in dealings with multinationals whose main loyalty is to the maximisation of profits.

The Faure report rightly predicted that industry and commerce would develop extensive educational functions and that education would need 'to work hand in hand with industry' (1972: 199). Education should develop further the many types of productive relationships that have been formed over the intervening years with business, provided it remembers that 'the primary concern of the schools should not be with the living that [the students] will earn with but the life they will lead' (Halsey *et al.*, 1961, foreword). The tensions come from the multifaceted role of education, which seeks to develop participating citizens, wise parents and discriminating consumers, sceptical thinkers and decent human beings and lovers, as well as creative workers. But an unofficial hierarchy of types of learning is being created with 'learning for earning' at its apex. What must be resisted are the great moral purposes of education being reduced to serving the needs and demands of business. To quote the DTI White Paper yet again, 'The Government wants to help businesses get the skills they want and to get the best out of education and training providers' (1998a: 31). With friends like that in high places, education should publicly reaffirm its broader mission. It also needs to be surer of the professional contribution it brings to the new social contract; that issue is dealt with next.

Put a new theory of learning into the learning society and Into lifelong learning

There is a large hole in the heart of the Government's policies for lifelong learning and the same fatal weakness can be detected in the rhetoric about the learning society: plans are afoot to create a new culture of lifelong learning without either any theory of learning or a recognition that a new *social* theory of learning is required. Briefly, a *social* theory of learning argues that learning is located in social participation and dialogue as well as in the heads of individuals; and it shifts the focus from a concentration on individual cognitive processes to the social relationships and arrangements that shape, for instance, positive and negative 'learner identities' that may differ over time and from place to place (see Lave and Wenger, 1991; Rees *et al.*, 1997). Such a social theory also criticises the fashionable eulogising of learning and the denigration of teaching by treating teaching and learning not as two distinct activities, but as elements of a single, reciprocal process. Moreover, this social theory is transforming the study of the transfer of knowledge (see Engestrom, 1998).

To ask a politician, a civil servant or a professional specialising in education what their theory of learning is and how it helps them improve their practice tends to produce the same kind of embarrassed mumblings that result from a direct question about their sexual orientation. Teaching and learning remain, even for many experts in education, unproblematical processes of transmission and assimilation, but no learning society can be built on such atheoretical foundations.

Within the Learning Society Programme, the theoretical advances made by Michael Eraut *et al.* (1998) on non-formal learning, implicit learning and tacit knowledge; the research by Gareth Rees *et al.* (1997) into the central significance (still largely unrecognised) of informal learning and of the widening contexts for learning; and the project by Pat Davies and John Bynner, describing the spectacular success in London of the credit system of learning in attracting non-traditional adults (e.g. ethnic minorities and unemployed adults) into learning are just three examples of the many contributions being made to put the learning into the learning society.[11]

Informal learning was not the central focus of any of the 14 projects within the Learning Society Programme but it quickly became clear to a number of project directors that it represents a largely neglected aspect of lifelong learning. Both policy and academic discourse on access to, provision of, and achievement in lifelong learning concentrate heavily on *formal* education and training. And yet the latter constitutes only a small part of work-based learning, which was:

> non-formal, neither clearly specific nor planned. It arose naturally out of the demands and challenges of work – solving problems, improving quality and/or productivity, or coping with change – and out of social interactions in the workplace with colleagues, customers or clients.
>
> (Eraut *et al.*, 1998: 1)

This finding, which was replicated by other projects, requires us to reassess our conventional understanding of lifelong learning as exclusively concerned with target-setting, formal courses and qualifications. The policy implications of this finding are also significant: the need to appoint and educate managers who know how to develop their staff by creating a climate that promotes informal learning.

The concept of lifelong learning also needs to be rescued from all those pressure groups who have adopted this wide-ranging term to pursue their sectional interests in a particular phase within education. For example, there are adult educators who argue in a self-interested way that no further resources should be spent on initial education because it would 'puff up a front-loaded system to new dimensions rather than fostering a system of lifelong learning' (Schuller, 1996: 2). It makes more sense, however, to prevent thousands of young people leaving school unprepared to compete for jobs in a knowledge-driven economy than to build extensions to the system to cope with failure. What is also required is a new cadre of professionals who owe their loyalty to lifelong learning and not to a particular phase.

Use an appropriate model of change

The same task of creating a change in culture confronts the three sectors under discussion – government, business and education – but the model of change thought appropriate for education now varies to an extreme degree from those employed in the other two areas. Since 1988 a powerful hold on education has been taken by the state via legislation (e.g. a national curriculum backed by national testing; the market principle to encourage competition among parents, students and institutions; and a quality control system to enforce compliance), but in stark contrast 'the Government believes that it is for business itself to consider how . . . it can achieve the best results' (DTI, 1998a: 48).

Increased powers for ministers are proposed in the most recent White Paper from the DfEE to restructure the teaching profession (e.g. 'a contractual duty for all teachers to keep their skills up-to-date' and 'a national Code of Practice for training providers and a new inspection programme' (DfEE, 1998c: 8)). Paul Black's strictures on the debacle over the introduction of the National Curriculum and assessment should be remembered: 'in the management of educational change, our national approach has been clumsy to the point of incompetence' (Black, 1995: 8). Yet little appears to have been learned from these failures. The Labour government is attempting to transform the teaching profession on which it depends to implement its reforms, but it has already squandered much of the goodwill of the profession, despite devoting an additional £19 billion to education and introducing a whole raft of welcome new measures. The crass tactic of 'naming, blaming and shaming' schools thought by the Office for Standards in Education (OFSTED) to be failing has been dropped, but the profession has been given no reason to believe that the Prime Minister does not still think that teachers are part of the problem rather than part of the solution. The Government urgently needs a new model of change to release the creativity and commitment of teachers, but the more teachers' professional practice is hollowed out by top-down change, the less the likelihood of developing independent-minded and enterprising young people who know how to learn throughout their lives.

How many of us believe, for example, that, if a clear majority of the teaching profession reject the proposals for performance-related pay, they will not be implemented? If the proposals are to be introduced irrespective of the reasoned objections of the profession, then the consultation exercise is a dishonest sham. Teachers' leaders should not only be consulted (receiving information and submitting their own ideas), but should be involved in the decision-making process (forming the policy and influencing the final decision). Twenty-five years ago, the Faure report described governmental attempts at reforming education:

> The aim appears to be to act *on* teachers – for them, possibly, but rarely *with* them. This technocratic paternalism is based on distrust and evokes distrust in return. Teachers, on the whole, are not against reforms as much as they are offended at the way they are presented to them, not to mention imposed on them.
>
> (Faure, 1972: 181, original emphasis)

Hence the importance of governments showing they can learn from past mistakes by involving teachers from the beginning in their plans for reform as well as encouraging teachers' ideas for reshaping the system to bubble up from below.

Tackle inequalities and structural barriers

The findings of projects within the Learning Society Programme confirm a long-standing, brutal and awkward truth: the roots of educational disadvantage lie beyond education in our social structure and so beyond the remit of the DfEE (see, for example, Gorard et al., 1998 and Ball et al., 1999). Concerted action by the Government as a whole will be needed, for example, to respond to the 9 million adults in Britain living in poverty (below 50 per cent of average income after housing costs) or the 2.2 million children in families receiving income support (see the Acheson report, 1998: 34). Contrary to the Government's beliefs, structure is separable from standards, but education is not the best economic policy we could have. Educational policy needs to be integrated with an industrial strategy and with a well-resourced, community-focused, anti-poverty campaign.

Revealingly, the Government is publishing the 'Competitiveness Index – to track British performance and guide policy development' (DTI, 1998a: 8), but it has been slower to respond to the demands for an annual poverty and social exclusion report (see Howarth et al., 1998, who have produced a model of what such a report should cover). And Tom Schuller and Caroline Bamford (1998) have called for the 'annual publication of a state of the nation report on lifelong learning', part of which could be devoted to an account of the action taken to combat unjustifiable inequalities and structural barriers in education.

There remains, of course, a powerful but secondary role for education to play. Having reviewed the mounting evidence on educational polarisation of the kind referred to in Newcastle earlier, the Acheson report comments 'Logic and equity argue that children most in need should receive increased resources for their education' (Acheson, 1998). It specifically recommends that 'the Revenue Support Grant formula and other funding mechanisms should be more strongly weighted to reflect need and socio-economic disadvantage' (39). But instead of continually pleading for extra help to be extended to the casualties of the system, it would be preferable to mainstream equality, that is 'integrate equal opportunities into all structures and systems, and into all policies, programmes and projects' (39). (See Rees (1998) for further explanation.)

It is also not difficult to find examples of structural barriers that militate against the interests of a lifelong learning culture and that need to be swept away: the 16-hour rule, which controls the amount of time the unemployed can devote to study; the indefensible differential in the funding of part-time and full-time students; output-related funding, which encourages 'cream skimming' (i.e. the concentration on those most likely to obtain a qualification); and the remorseless drive in all sectors of education and training to demand more for less.

The scale of the task facing policy makers can be gauged from one of the conclusions of the project within the Learning Society Programme, directed by Gareth Rees et al. in South Wales. They argue that removing barriers to participation, such as costs, time and lack of childcare, will have only limited impact because:

> those who failed at school often come to see post-school learning of all kinds as irrelevant to their needs and capabilities. Hence, not only is participation in further, higher and continuing education not perceived to be a realistic possibility, but also work-based learning is viewed as unnecessary.
>
> (Rees et al., 1997: 11)

Moreover, the Secretary of State for Education and Employment should seize the historic opportunity, missed by Sir Ron Dearing, to replace the divisive binary line between further and higher education with a *tertiary* system that celebrates diversity. Students would not only move from further to higher education, but, as happens in the Community Colleges in the USA, from higher to further education for postgraduate vocational training. Running prestigious, high-level courses of continuing professional development for British scientists and engineers (e.g. master's degrees while at work) would help to raise the status of further education colleges and of the University for Industry, which runs the risk of becoming associated primarily with basic skills courses for the unemployed – important though these courses are. The learning society needs to be underpinned by multiple learning opportunities at every age, at every stage and at every level of achievement.

All of these inherited problems could be rectified, but there would still remain significant obstacles such as the lack of high-quality jobs in the labour market. This point reinforces the general argument that there are strict limits to an *educational* solution to creating a learning society. And addressing both the inequalities and the barriers means, of course, redistributing income and wealth via increased progressive taxation.

Coda

This chapter ends on a personal and optimistic note. Someone who has studied different versions of the learning society and of lifelong learning for the past five years can reasonably be asked what skills will be required for success in the next century. The official list of skills culled from the ubiquitous rhetoric

– information technology, communication skills and teamwork etc. – will not serve this country well. Instead the following are recommended: love, work, music, humour, friends, doubt and good red wine.[12]

Notes

1 Avis *et al.* prefer the term 'settlement' because it 'extends beyond that of consensus in providing for the possibility of inconsistencies and contradictions. Settlements are based upon superficial consensus and, though prone to rupture and disintegration, are marked by their capacity to hold diverse interests together within an unstable equilibrium which has to be continually reworked and remade' (1996: 5). On the other hand, Richard Sennett plumps for 'regime' because 'it suggests the terms of power on which markets and production are allowed to operate' (1998: 55).

2 The charts on the productivity gap, the R and D gap and on underinvestment in the UK are to be found in the Treasury's *Pre-Budget Report* (1998), on pages 29, 33 and 37 respectively.

3 Alison Wolf describes how successful the CBI has been as a lobbying organisa-tion for the large corporations: 'Thanks to its activist policies – the promotion of NVQs, the development of training targets – it has seen off the threat of compulsory levies' (Wolf, 1998: 13).

4 The first report of the National Skills Task Force explains its vision in the following terms: 'To compete effectively on the world stage, employers need access to the best educated and best trained workforce; to compete effectively in a dynamic labour market, individuals must acquire the skills needed; while education and training providers and Government must be responsive to those requirements' (DfEE 1998b: 11).

5 In a major speech on education in 1992, Bill Clinton argued that 'In the 1990s and beyond, the universal spread of education, computers and high-speed communications means that what we earn will depend on what we can learn and how well we can apply what we learn to the workplaces of America' (quoted by A.H. Halsey *et al.*, 1997: 8).

6 At a conference for researchers within the Learning Society Programme, an industrialist, who deserves to remain nameless, was invited to comment on the shape and objectives of the programme as a whole. The inclusion of a project on 'The Meaning of the Learning Society for adults with Learning Difficulties' was, he thought, an inappropriate use of scarce research resources.

7 See the research of Geoff Whitty, Sally Power and Tony Edwards (1998) for data on the very close connection between the status of the university attended and the type of job (and size of salary) obtained. Graduate unemployment varies considerably across pre- and post-1992 universities according to data from the Higher Education Management Statistics group.

8 These researchers distinguish four models: the *schooling* model that aims at high levels of participation; the *credentialist* model that prioritises qualifications; a model that stresses improving *access*; and a *reflexive* model that 'prioritises learning as a major feature of all social relationships' (1997: 534)

9 I should like to thank the ESRC publicly for the opportunity to carry out the most exciting and the most demanding job I have ever had and the researchers in the 14 projects for teaching me so much.

10 As I have written elsewhere (Coffield, 1990), 'strategic partnerships' are the kind of weasel words used by bureaucrats when they wish to disguise a major shift in

power or resources; for example, the DfEE currently recommends a 'strategic partnership' because it wishes to transfer part of the cost for lifelong learning to employers and individuals.

11 The phrase is Michael Eraut's (1999) and it deserves to be repeated and spread abroad.

12 I wish to thank two people particularly – Geoff Whitty, Chair of the Steering Committee of the Programme, who is that rare creature, a good manager, and Tony Edwards, who not only commented most usefully on an earlier version of this chapter, but has also shown me by example what it is to be a Professor of Education.

References

Acheson, Sir D. (1998) Independent Inquiry into Inequalities in Health (London, Stationery Office).

Ashton, D. and Green, F. (1996) Education, Training and the Global Economy (Cheltenham, Edward Elgar).

Avis, J., Bloomer, M., Esland, G., Gleeson, D. and Hodkinson, P. (1996) Knowledge and Nationhood: education, politics and work (London, Cassell).

Ball, S.J., Macrae, S. and Maguire, M. (1999) Young lives at risk in the 'futures' market: some policy concerns from on-going research, in: F. Coffield (ed.) Speaking Truth to Power: research and policy on lifelong learning, 30–45 (Bristol, Policy Press).

Baron, S., Stalker, K., Wilkinson, H. and Riddell, S. (1998) The learning society: the highest stage of human capitalism? in: F. Coffield (ed.) Learning at Work, 49–59 (Bristol, Policy Press).

Becker, G.S. (1975) Human Capital: a theoretical and empirical analysis, with special reference to education (Chicago, IL, University of Chicago Press) (First edition 1964).

Berg, I. (1973) Education and Jobs: the great training robbery (Harmondsworth, Penguin).

Black, P. (1995) Ideology, evidence and the raising of standards, Second Education Lecture, King's College, London, 11 July.

Blackmore, J. (1997) The gendering of skill and vocationalism in twentieth-century Australian education, in: A.H. Halsey, H. Lauder, P. Brown and A.S. Wells (eds) Education: culture, economy and society, 224–239 (Oxford, Oxford University Press).

Blair, Rt Hon. T. (1998) quoted in Department for Education and Employment The Learning Age: a renaissance for a new Britain (London, Stationery Office, Cmnd 3790, 9).

Boshier, R. (1997) Edgar Faure after 25 years: down but not out, Conference paper, 'Lifelong learning: reality, rhetoric and public policy', University of Surrey, Department of Educational Studies, 4–6 July.

Carnoy, M. and Levin, H.M. (1985) Schooling and Work in the Democratic State (Stanford, Stanford University Press).

Castells, M. (1998) End of Millennium, Vol. III (Oxford, Blackwell).

Coffield, F. (1990) From the decade of the enterprise culture to the decade of the TECs, British Journal of Education and Work, 4(1), 59–78.

Coffield, F. (1997) The concept of the learning society explored, Journal of Education Policy, 12(6), 449–558.

Coffield, F. (ed.) (1998) *Learning at Work* (Bristol, Policy Press).

Confederation of British Industry (1989) *Towards a Skills Revolution* (London, CBI).

Darmon, I., Frade, C. and Hadjivassiliou, K. (1999) The comparative dimension in continuous vocational training: a preliminary framework, in: F. Coffield (ed.) *Why's the Beer Always Stronger Up North? Studies of Lifelong Learning in Europe*, 31–42 (Bristol, Policy Press).

Davies, P., Bynner, J., Cappizzi, E. and Carter, J. (1999) *The impact of credit-based systems of learning on learning cultures* (London, City University, Department of Continuing Education, Research Report).

Department for Education and Employment (1997a) *Excellence in Schools* (London, Stationery Office, Cm 3681).

Department for Education and Employment (1997b) *Living and Working Together for the Future* (Sudbury, DfEE Publications).

Department for Education and Employment (1998a) *The Learning Age: a renaissance for a new Britain* (London, Stationery Office, Cm 3790).

Department for Education and Employment (1998b) *Towards a National Skills Agenda*, First Report of the National Skills Task Force (London, DfEE).

Department for Education and Employment (1998c) *Teachers: meeting the challenge of change* (London, Stationery Office, Cm 4164).

Department of Social Security (1998) *A New Contract for Welfare: new ambitions for our country* (London, Stationery Office, Cm 3805).

Department of Trade and Industry (1998a) *Our Competitive Future: building the knowledge driven economy* (London, Stationery Office, Cm 4176).

Department of Trade and Industry (1998b) *Fairness at Work* (London, Stationery Office, Cm 3968).

Edwards, T. (1998) A Daunting Enterprise? Sociological enquiry into education in a changing world, *British Journal of the Sociology of Education*, 19(1), 143–147.

Engestrom, Y. (1998) Transfer of knowledge, Conference Paper at COST *A11 Conference* at the University of Newcastle, 28 November.

Eraut, M. (1999) Non-formal learning, implicit learning and tacit knowledge, in: F. Coffield (ed.) *The Necessity of Informal Learning* (Bristol, Policy Press).

Eraut, M., Alderton, J., Cole, G. and Senker, P. (1998) *Development of Knowledge and Skills in Employment* (Brighton, University of Sussex, Institute of Education, Research Report No. 5).

Faure, E. (ed.) (1972) *Learning To Be: the world of education today and tomorrow* (Paris, UNESCO).

Fevre, R. (1997) Some sociological alternatives to human capital theory and their implications for research on post-compulsory education and training (Cardiff, University of Cardiff, School of Education, Working Paper 3).

Giddens, A. (1998) *The Third Way: the renewal of social democracy* (Cambridge, Polity Press).

Gorard, S., Rees, G., Renold, E. and Fevre, R. (1998) Family influences on participation in lifelong learning (Cardiff, University of Cardiff, School of Education, Working Paper 15).

Halsey, A.H. *et al.* (1961) *Education, Economy and Society* (New York, Free Press).

Halsey, A.H., Lauder, H., Brown, P. and Wells, A.S. (1997) *Education: culture, economy and society* (Oxford, Oxford University Press).

Heinz, W. (1999) Lifelong learning – learning for life? Some cross-national observations, in: F. Coffield (ed.) *Why's the Beer Always Stronger Up North? Studies of Lifelong Learning in Europe*, 13–20 (Bristol, Policy Press).

Hewison, J., Millar, B. and Dowswell, T. (1998) *Changing Patterns of Training Provision: implications for access and equity*, Swindon, Economic and Social Research Council, end of award report.

HM Treasury (1998) *Pre-Budget Report: steering a stable course for lasting prosperity* (London, Stationery Office, Cm 4076).

Hodkinson, P., Sparkes, A.C. and Hodkinson, H. (1996) *Triumphs and Tears: young people, markets, and the transition from school to work* (London, David Fulton).

Holtham, G. (1998) Lie back, think of South Korea, *The Guardian*, 3 August.

Howarth, C., Kenway, P., Palmer, G. and Street, C. (1998) *Monitoring Poverty and Social Exclusion: Labour's inheritance* (York, New Policy Institute and Joseph Rowntree Foundation).

Howells, K. (1997) Howells welcomes Kennedy Report to the further education debate, *Department for Education and Employment Press Release*, 1 July.

Illich, I. and Verne, E. (1976) *Imprisoned in the Global Classroom* (London, Writers and Readers Publishing Cooperative).

Joseph Rowntree Foundation (1995) *Inquiry into Income and Wealth* (York, Joseph Rowntree Foundation).

Joseph Rowntree Foundation (1998) *Income and Wealth: the latest evidence*, edited by John Hills (York, Joseph Rowntree Foundation).

Karabel, J. and Halsey, A.H. (1997) *Power and Ideology in Education* (New York, Oxford University Press).

Keep, E. and Mayhew, K. (1998) *Was Ratner Right? Product Market and Competitive Strategies and their Links with Skills and Knowledge* (London, Employment Policy Institute).

Lave, J. and Wenger, E. (1991) *Situated Learning: legitimate peripheral participation* (New York, Cambridge University Press).

Levin, H.M. and Kelley, C. (1997) Can education do it alone? in: A.H. Halsey, H. Lauder, P. Brown and A.S. Wells (eds) *Education: culture, economy and society* (Oxford, Oxford University Press).

Mandelson, P. (1998) We are all capitalists now, *The Daily Telegraph*, 17 December.

Rees, G., Fevre, R., Furlong, J. and Gorard, S. (1997) Notes towards a social theory of lifetime learning: history, place and the learning society (Cardiff, University of Cardiff, School of Education, Working Paper 6).

Rees, T. (1998) Mainstreaming equality, Inaugural Lecture, University of Bristol, School for Policy Studies, 15 October.

Rees, T. and Bartlett, W. (1999) Models of guidance services in the learning society: the case of the Netherlands, in: F. Coffield (ed.) *Why's the Beer Always Stronger Up North? Studies of Lifelong Learning in Europe* (Bristol, Policy Press).

Robinson, P. and Oppenheim, C. (1998) *Social Exclusion Indicators* (London, Institute for Public Policy Research).

Schuller, T. (1996) Building social capital: steps towards a learning society, Inaugural Lecture, Centre for Continuing Education, University of Edinburgh.

Schuller, T. and Bamford, C. (1998) *Initial and Continuing Education in Scotland: divergence, convergence and learning relationships* (Edinburgh, Centre for Continuing Education, Edinburgh University).

Schuller, T. and Burns, A. (1999) Using social capital to compare performance in continuing education, in: F. Coffield (ed.) *Why's the Beer Always Stronger Up North? Studies of Lifelong Learning in Europe* (Bristol, Policy Press).

Schultz, T.W. (1961) Investment in human capital, *American Economic Review*, March (51), 1–1.7.

Sennett, R. (1998) *The Corrosion of Character: the personal consequences of work in the new capitalism* (New York, W.W. Norton).

TEC National Council (1997) *Developing a Learning Society: a lifetime of learning, a lifetime of work* (London, TEC National Council).

Tight, M. (1998) Lifelong learning: opportunity or compulsion? *British Journal of Educational Studies*, 46(3), 251–263.

Trades Union Congress (1998) *Union Gateways to Learning: TUC learning services report* (London, Trades Union Congress).

Tuckett, A. (1998) Recruits conscripted for the active age, *Times Educational Supplement*, 22 May.

Walden, G. (1996) *We Should Know Better: solving the education crisis* (London, Fourth Estate).

Whitty, G., Power, S. and Edwards, T. (1998) Education and the formation of middle class identities, paper given at *ECER Conference*, Ljubljana, Slovenia, 19 September.

Wolf, A. (1998) The training illusion, *Prospect*, August/September, 12–13.

Young, M., Spours, K., Howieson, C. and Raffe, D. (1997) Unifying academic and vocational learning and the idea of a learning society, *Journal of Education Policy*, 12(6), 527–537.

Chapter 10

Governing the ungovernable

Why lifelong learning policies promise so much yet deliver so little

John Field

Introduction

Over the past decade, lifelong learning has enjoyed a remarkable rise up the policy agenda. Particularly in the Western world, one government after another has placed lifelong learning at the core of policy, and this priority has been repeatedly endorsed by the main intergovernmental actors. Yet the development of concrete measures, and their actual implementation, have lagged substantially behind the language and ambition of the policy community. Why? And does it make a difference, particularly to those who manage and deliver learning programmes?

Of course, a degree of distance between policy rhetoric and policy achievement is inevitable. Between conception and delivery lies a series of mediating institutions and actors, and lifelong learning has been no exception to this general rule. It is also true that no government is likely to tax its voters in order to provide the resources required to match the level of problems identified by the very same government. To take one recent example, the UK government's National Skills Task Force has recommended an entitlement of a qualification at Level 2 or above for all adults who do not hold one, estimating that the initial cost would add up to over £400 million over the first three years (DfEE, 2000: 49). Even this marks a retreat from an earlier proposal by the Kennedy Committee, which suggested an entitlement of a qualification at Level 3 (Kennedy, 1997). Externally, policy makers are unlikely to identify lifelong learning as the next Big Idea in delivering electoral success. The teaching workforce in post-initial education and training is typically dispersed, often part-time and poorly organized into lobbying bodies. Representative national associations frequently depend on government largesse for their existence, and are easily co-opted. So at one level, the absence of progress might be easy to explain, were it not for one rather obvious problem. Despite these weaknesses, governments internationally persist in placing lifelong learning at the core of their agenda for

This is an edited version of an article published in *Educational Management and Administration*, 28, 3 (2000): 249–261. Sage Publications Ltd © British Educational Management and Administration Society (BEMAS) 2000.

education and training. Why, then, has so little of consequence happened as a result?

This article offers an alternative explanation, couched in terms of the type of policy challenge that lifelong learning represents. Unlike most policy goals that were characteristic of welfarism, lifelong learning is typical of the new policy objectives in requiring action by civil society rather than by agencies of the state. Developing in response to the perceived problems of globalization and technological change, as well as the accompanying social changes of the past three or four decades, these new policy objectives often deal with 'soft', intangible and complex issues – notably learning rather than education, for example. Further, they involve a broad and diverse range of actors, including large numbers of individual citizens and a variety of policy agencies rather than a single department. What makes matters even more uncertain is that the nature of government itself is changing, partly in response to electorates who are increasingly affluent, individualistic and sceptical of authority (Giddens, 1991). In these circumstances, I argue, it is not surprising that governments face difficulties in identifying and promoting concrete policies for lifelong learning, and that their preferred solutions involve active attempts to mobilize civil society – including education and training providers. However, this in turn poses remarkably difficult challenges to those who manage and lead the institutions of provision.

The impact of lifelong learning: 'HRD in drag'?

Lifelong learning has emerged on to the policy scene with the suddenness of a new fashion. In a slightly different formulation (lifelong education), the idea was widely touted in the early 1970s, and it briefly won a degree of political favour. Although the debate over lifelong education had some influence on government behaviour, particularly in Sweden, its main power base lay in the relatively innocuous world of intergovernmental think-tanks such as UNESCO and the Organization for Economic Co-operation and Development (OECD) (Knoll, 1998). It then re-emerged in the labyrinthine policy corridors of the European Commission, where it formed one of the cornerstones of Jacques Delors's White Paper on competitiveness and economic growth (European Commission, 1994). When the Commission subsequently declared 1996 to be the European Year of Lifelong Learning, the idea rapidly re-entered the mainstream political vocabulary.

Britain offers an instructive example of the speed with which this process occurred. In 1997, the incoming Labour government appointed Dr Kim Howells as the country's first Minister of Lifelong Learning. Advisory committees on further and higher education, appointed by agreement between government and opposition before 1997, published reports calling for reform to enable their respective sectors to contribute fully to the learning society

(Dearing, 1997; Kennedy, 1997). In the following year, separate Green Papers outlined proposals for Wales, Scotland and England, followed by a White Paper (*Learning to Succeed*) for post-16 education and training in England. An Advisory Group for Continuing Education and Lifelong Learning, created in early 1998, produced two wide-ranging reports on future policy developments (Fryer, 1998, 1999). But Britain is hardly alone in this development. In Germany, the federal education ministry published a series of reports on lifelong learning by Günther Dohmen, one of which appeared simultaneously in English translation – presumably in an attempt to shape opinion more widely in western and central Europe rather than in Britain or the USA (Dohmen, 1996, 1998). Lifelong learning policy papers have also appeared from the Dutch, Norwegian, Finnish and Irish governments (Department of Education and Science, 1998; Ministry of Culture, Education and Science, 1998). As a phrase, it might be said that lifelong learning, or the learning society, has in several European nations become a convenient political shorthand for the modernizing of education and training systems.

How did this happen? A number of writers have traced the genesis of the concept back to the intellectual ferment of the late 1960s, which perhaps influenced educational thinking more than any other area of public policy (Boshier, 1998; Knoll, 1998). Like many 1960s ideas, it drew both on the radical thinking of the student movement and on the post-industrial rhetoric of future-gazers like Alvin Toffler, whose apocalyptic warnings of 'mass disorientation' posed a direct challenge to educational planners. No doubt the early slowing down of post-war economic growth rates also had something to do with the rethinking of educational priorities and institutions. Following the prolonged recession of the later 1970s and for much of the 1980s, the international and intergovernmental bodies found relatively little to say on the topic. Tackling unemployment replaced earlier preoccupations as the central task for adult education and training. However, they returned to it in the 1990s with renewed vigour, with key policy texts appearing from the European Commission (1996), OECD (1996), UNESCO (Delors, 1996) and the Group of Eight industrial nations (1999).

The European Commission's diagnosis followed what has now become a familiar pattern. Western Europe was faced by the threats and opportunities of globalization, information technology and the application of science. If they were to stand up to Japan and the USA, the EU's member states had to pool some of their sovereignty and resources in education and training as in other policy areas; this would also help develop a sense of European citizenship and foster social inclusion. The central role of lifelong learning had already been flagged in the Commission's 1994 White Paper on competitiveness:

> Preparation for life in tomorrow's world cannot be satisfied by a once-and-for-all acquisition of knowledge and know-how ... All measures must

therefore necessarily be based on the concept of developing, generalising and systematising lifelong learning and continuing training.

(European Commission, 1994: 16, 136)

The education and training White Paper stressed the same message (European Commission, 1996), as did the OECD's report, *Lifelong Learning for All* (1996) and the G8's charter for lifelong learning (1999). Prepared during the build-up for its 1997 world conference on education, UNESCO's report was drafted by an international commission chaired by Jacques Delors, the recently retired president of the European Commission. More radical in tone than papers from the other intergovernmental agencies, the UNESCO report was also the least likely to result in concrete measures, thanks to its provenance from a rather discredited body with a vague remit and a large and diffuse membership.

At the level of general commitment, policy endorsement of lifelong learning is virtually universal. When we turn to policy development and implementation, the picture is much patchier. In this field, a favourable policy climate has paradoxically failed to generate much that is new or innovative in terms of specific policy measures (Green *et al.*, 1999; Rubenson, 1999). Moreover, in so far as policy developments have evolved into deliverable measures, these have almost universally focused on one of two areas: interventions designed to improve the skills and flexibility of the workforce; and the extension and partial reform of initial education.

It is a common complaint that lifelong learning is little but 'human resource development (HRD) in drag' (Boshier, 1998: 4). And certainly it is true that the debate has been largely driven by economic preoccupations. Significantly, some of the leading proponents of lifelong learning have come in recent years from such temples of human capital thinking as the OECD and the European Commission, where lifelong learning is regarded primarily as a source of competitive advantage. Marred by its narrow vocationalism, this dominant definition of lifelong learning has rightly been criticized by those who seek a more humanistic approach. Yet it is too easy to dismiss this aspect of the policy agenda as more evidence that social democracy remains firmly locked into the trajectory of permanent capitalist growth – what Ralf Dahrendorf calls, dismissively, 'globalisation plus' (1999). For governments are also busily extending the duration of initial education, with proposals for further increases in staying-on rates for the 16–19 age group, and further widening of participation in full-time initial higher education. Reform of vocational education and training, and the extension of initial education, remain legitimate areas for traditional types of policy intervention. Lifelong learning, though, is a much more amorphous policy goal, delivery of which lies largely beyond government's capacities.

Seeking a new balance between public and private spheres

The lack of immediate policy direction is indeed striking. A team of specialists from the OECD concluded in one of a number of national surveys of education policy conducted in the late 1980s and early 1990s that:

> There has been much reference to the ideal of lifelong learning and the importance of second-chance education . . . but, as in nearly all other countries, there is no evidence of any concerted effort to render it a reality.
>
> (OECD, 1991: 33)

It is almost as though governments have noticed that they face a considerable policy challenge, but are reduced to rebranding and posturing when it comes to developing specific measures. In a survey of international policy for UNESCO, Ursula Giere and Mishe Piet (1997: 3–4) concluded that:

> Everywhere in the world statements identify adult education as a key to the survival of humankind in the 21st century, attributing adult education with the magic to contribute positively to education for all . . . and yet, almost everywhere in the world, adult education is a widely neglected and feeble part of the official educational scene.

Surveying the OECD nations, Kjell Rubenson has reached similar conclusions (Rubenson, 1999). In the wider context of aid policy, Josef Müller has commented on the gap between a powerful policy emphasis upon human resource development and a relatively narrow focus – and overall decline – in educational aid budgets (1997: 37).

Others have noted that, even where there has been action, it has tended to concentrate almost exclusively upon work-related education and training. By and large, policy makers have tended to concentrate on microprocessors rather than lifeworlds, at least in their approach to public policy. The director of the UNESCO Institute for Education, for instance, has warned of the imbalance between 'the many areas of activity where there is a need for a more active, informed and competent citizenry', on the one hand, and the 'economy element' that dominates current continuing education policy initiatives on the other (Bélanger, 1999: 187). While much has been promised in the public domain, most of the action has taken place within the private domain, by individual actors and firms. What achievements there have been in public policy have mainly fallen within the vocational domain. Was this simply a result of political bad faith or lack of political will, as so many claim? (Examples include Baptiste, 1999: 95; Boshier, 1998: 9; Collins, 1998: 45; West, 1998: 555.)

One school of thought argues that this policy sterility is inherent in the concept. Bernt Gustavsson, for example, suggests that while the term itself is 'used as a vision', it tends to be 'rather empty of content', with no clue as to how it may be 'transformed into practice' (Gustavsson, 1995: 92). And, indeed, one difficulty lies in the nature of the issue itself. It is not governments that will produce more learning among more people, but citizens. This is an issue that requires citizens to act (Beck and Sopp, 1997). For governments, this presents obvious difficulties. Rather than government doing things directly, it is required to persuade citizens to change their ways. Lifelong learning is far from being the only such issue; others driven by civil society include public health, environmental action, racial tolerance and tackling crime. And in the process of shifting away from service delivery or legislation to offering guidance and trying to steer citizens' behaviour, government has had to change its own ways of working.

Lifelong learning is one of several policy areas where there is a new balance of responsibilities between individuals, employers and state. Of course, unlike schooling or conventional higher education, it has never been the case that adult learning was solely a public responsibility. Apart from anything else, many of the most important providers have always been non-governmental bodies. Indeed, much of the modern adult education system is inherited from nineteenth-century social movements that were created partly to challenge the state of their time, like the Swedish temperance movement or the British trade unions. Similarly, many of the costs have been paid by individuals or employers; the public contribution has always been relatively small. But even if adult education and training were widely seen as Cinderella services, by the 1950s they were acknowledged as part of the family of public provision that had been established through the social settlements of the late nineteenth and mid-twentieth centuries. And although there has not been a single, dramatic blow to the adult learning Cinderella – despite occasional attempts to axe spending levels – there has been a steady, incremental change in their status. Adult learning now has so many suitors that she has – to pursue the metaphor – perhaps become rather promiscuous.

Training is now a major industry in its own right. In the USA, it is estimated that in the year 2000 the training market was worth $60 billion a year. Part of this growth has taken place with little reference to the public sector of provision; many of the corporate players are powerful actors in their own right. Motorola, for example, has its own 'university', operating at a range of levels as deemed appropriate for the company's employees. Motorola University was said in 1998 to have some 1,000 academic staff, with centres in 49 countries and classes in 24 languages. William Wiggenhorn, president of the Motorola University, estimated that around 10 per cent of his staff came from existing universities, but that generally lecturers from this sector were 'too boring' to hold an audience and wanted to 'do their own thing' rather than what the company required (*EUCEN News*, June 1999: 9). But this explosion has also driven through changes in the public sector.

In more conventional universities, the demand for MBA (Masters in Business Administration) courses has continued rising inexorably since the 1950s, despite the hefty premium charged by universities to students or their employers. Moreover, despite constant warnings that the market is saturated, this demand-led growth has taken place among both individuals and employers. On a smaller scale, we have seen similar growth in the demand for other forms of adult learning from individuals; as was frequently pointed out in the UK when government was considering the introduction of tuition fees for undergraduates, the adult students of the Open University had always paid privately for their studies. By 1999, when the private fee system was well established, the Labour Minister for Higher Education was urging universities to treat their students as 'customers' (*Times Higher Education Supplement*, 1 October 1999). Peter Scott (2000) has argued that these developments, taken together with the considerable expansion in access to third-level education, represent the early stages of a new paradigm of life-long learning, rooted more in emerging patterns of private consumption than the traditional context of public, state-provided education (see also Field, 1994). What role is available for government to play in this emerging system, with its new and potentially unstable balance between what had previously been regarding as the private and the public spheres?

The new governance

If learning is a business, government itself is in flux. In a reflexive world, the idea of an all-powerful, providing state is attractive neither to politicians and bureaucrats nor to citizens. It is not simply that the modern state machinery has become too expensive, although this is frequently a charge levelled by fiscal conservatives. Robert Reich, Secretary of Labor for the first four years of the Clinton administration, has attributed the failure of policy in this area to a combination of Treasury caution and business lobbying. Instead of approving Reich's proposals for human capital tax credits and job training programmes for unemployed youngsters, his Cabinet colleagues earned his scorn by opting for public deficit reduction, combined with subsidies to corporate America (Reich, 1997). Yet this insider view, though it offers highly significant insights into the power and influence of the Treasury and the Federal Reserve in determining macroeconomic policy, only tells part of the story. A high level of public spending is a relatively small problem in the post-scarcity societies of the Western world, and it is notable that those governments that most vigorously advocated the principle of fiscal conservatism ended up, like the Reagan and Thatcher administrations, spending just as much as ever (Castells, 1989: 28).

The principle of state provision has in recent years run up against two broad trends. First, there are increasing numbers who can either supplement or opt out of state-provided benefits. In areas such as housing, pensions, health and even education, citizens who have provided for their own needs (or think they have, which is not always the same thing) are not often happy when it comes to spending their taxes on citizens who have chosen (as they see it) to spend their own money elsewhere. Second, universal and direct state provision can serve as an unintended bureaucratic block on society's capacity for learning and innovation. In the field of welfare provision and labour market regulation, for example, this has encouraged a widespread search for 'active measures' that place responsibility on citizens to plan and develop their biographies, in place of 'passive measures' that enable individuals to cope with their present predicament (Rosanvallon, 1995). The trick, as Castells has put it, is 'to be able to steer a complex society without suffocating it' (1989: 18).

During the 1980s, a number of Western governments experimented with new forms of governance. Seeking to introduce private sector management, governments explored privatization, market testing, purchaser–provider splits, disaggregation of separate activities, and closeness to the customer. At the same time, new methods of public management were developed for those services that remained within the public sector: hands-on professional management, decentralized authority, service-level standards and target-related funding. Third, efforts were made not simply to provide services, but to engage with the private and voluntary sectors through catalytic partnerships. Finally, and most recently, there has been a new preoccupation with bringing together the different arms of government (and corporate decision-making) at a number of different levels, including the transnational, to function as a coherent network – the so-called 'joined-up government' approach (Benington, 1998).

Taken together, this transformation of the public sector has been described as involving '"less government" (or less rowing) but "more governance" (or more steering)' (Rhodes, 1996: 655). And although this process took different shapes in different countries and at different times (in Britain there was more emphasis on privatization in the 1980s, for instance, and a stronger interest in social partnerships after the 1997 change of government), the general thrust has been broadly similar in a broad range of countries.

The new public management is not without its problems, however. With the move towards a contract culture, voluntary organizations are being confronted with a series of control mechanisms as government seeks to ensure accountability for public spending. There is a greater emphasis upon the identification of 'approved providers' and the specification of government-approved quality standards; there has been a shift towards steering by output-related funding. By adopting the language of partnership, policy makers clearly hope to make this change more palatable. Yet the discourse of partnership frequently cloaks a profound inequality between the so-called partners, with the voluntary sector coming a poor third after government and business (Geddes, 1997). Voluntary organizations find themselves competing against one another (and against the private sector) for contracts, and this can destabilize relations within the voluntary sector and unsettle previously harmonious relationships between voluntary bodies and local government (Commission on the Future of the Voluntary Sector, 1996: 53). The language of markets and competition is, moreover, in tension with the trust, interdependence and stability required for effective network building, as is shown by the failure of Training and Enterprise Councils in Britain to steer the training system in ways that overcame existing deficits (Rhodes, 1996: 664).

Further, many of the new approaches have been found to generate widespread negative unintended consequences. Thus output-related funding, rather than improving performance of service-delivery agencies such as colleges, has often distorted their behaviour. Rather than pursuing the aims originally envisaged by those who drew up the approved list of eligible outputs, organizational managers often seek to improve their share of resources by focusing on reported achievement against the key indicators, or reclassifying existing activities in order to meet new funding criteria, and downplaying other (unmeasured or less generously rewarded) core activities. Finally, the entire approach risks rejection by public opinion. Thus the respected social scientist and Liberal Democrat thinker Ralf Dahrendorf has ridiculed 'Third Way' social democracy for its belief that government should 'no longer pay for things, but tell people what to do' (1999: 27). This has a ready resonance, not just with those who manage public services that are effectively privately financed, but also with those service users who pay an increasingly large share of the bill.

In addition, the new policy challenges cut across existing departmental boundaries. Conventional service delivery models of government usually fit well with government departments organized along classical Weberian lines. Schools policy, for example, belongs in most countries to the Ministry of Education or its equivalent body, as does higher education policy. Lifelong learning, though, crosses these boundaries and involves a wide range of government departments and agencies. In Learning to Succeed, it is noted that the new national system of local Learning and Skills Councils for post-16 training and education will need to relate systematically to the Department of Trade and Industry's structures for small firms development, the Regional Development Agencies of the Department of Transport, Environment and the Regions, and the benefits offices of the Department of Social Security, as well as to local government (DfEE, 1999). Developing co-ordinated measures that cross departmental boundaries is an ambitious project, given the extent to which civil service careers and cultures tend to follow well-established, vertical tramlines. Pursuing policy objectives that transcend boundaries is therefore likely to provoke turf wars, to the point of intensifying interministerial rivalries at the highest levels.

For all its shortcomings, the new public management holds particular relevance for lifelong learning. Lifelong learning is precisely the sort of problem that persuaded governments that the old ways of working were not enough. As in a number of other policy areas, such as public health or environmental protection or enterprise promotion, government alone can deliver very little. Participation in a more open, learning-network society requires, according to one German policy adviser, that

> learners themselves will have to choose and combine learning processes and strike the right balance between available routes of learning in a way that meets their specific needs. In other words, they will be largely responsible for directing their learning themselves.
>
> (Dohmen, 1996: 35)

Individual behaviour and attitudes are at the heart of the new approach – and this at a time when values of autonomy and independence are deeply embedded in our culture. Insofar as lifelong learning is consistent with these values, we can expect individuals to respond positively; equally, where lifelong learning is perceived as a dissonant experience, we can expect individuals to respond with a radical scepticism.

One example of this is the problem of 'soft' objectives. Governments have to win people over by articulating a vision and seeking to change people's culture and values, and unlike income levels or types of qualification these are not easily measured. In its White Paper on post-16 education and training, the British government proclaimed that 'Our vision of the Learning Age is to build a new culture of learning and aspiration' (DfEE, 1999: 13). Cultural change was also central to the recommendations of the Fryer Committee (Fryer, 1998, 1999). But building a 'new culture' is at best a rather fuzzy political objective, and it is unlikely to be one where ministers or civil servants will feel confident in their capacity to develop clear criteria for judging success (or failure).

An illustration of the difficulties emerged when the government revised the National Targets for Education and Training, which then became the National Learning Targets (DfEE, 1999). They now included a target for 'reducing non-participation' among adults; while utterly admirable in itself, the difficulties in reaching an agreed definition of 'non-participation' are likely to prove formidable, as are the prospects of deciding who is responsible if this target is not achieved (Tight, 1998). Similar complexity characterizes the question of informal learning, yet increasingly economic policy as well as education policy focuses on the role of networks and trust in facilitating the informal transmission of skills and knowledge (OECD, 1999).

As many governments have pointed out, responsibility for participation in adult learning is usually shared. Yet if it is for citizens rather than governments to act, what measures are then legitimate if citizens fail in their duty? Two and a half years into office, the New Labour government in Britain noted the problem of 'insufficient demand' as central, and identified as a key goal that of 'driving up demand' (DfEE, 1999: 55–56). It designed a number of reforms with this aim in mind, including tax incentives for vocational training, the creation of a national system of individual learning accounts, the launch of a national helpline (Learning Direct) and the inclusion of a major promotional function in the early plans for the University for Industry (UfI). All of these are designed primarily to stimulate demand from individuals rather than to change the culture of society. By contrast, initiatives such as the Adult and Community Learning Fund (ACLF) were allocated relatively minor sums, partly because of the difficulties faced by government of establishing whether the results offered value for money.

Cultural change is, by its nature, not readily amenable to quantitative measurement, so that it is impossible for finance ministries to determine whether or not this is an efficient investment of government funds. More broadly, intangible factors invariably present policy makers with measurement problems, as was recently acknowledged during an OECD seminar on knowledge management:

> In particular, knowledge is extremely heterogeneous in nature, and its value is not intrinsic but depends on its relationship to the user, so it cannot be quantified in the same terms as physical objects such as land or industrial capital.
>
> (OECD, 1999)

Of course, lack of measurability does not make an objective any the less worthwhile, but it does present problems of political management that may make for a degree of volatility and exposure to criticism. In the absence of agreed and standardized outcome measures, though, the only alternative to high-trust governance appears to be restrictive and heavy-handed regulation, stifling the very process of change that policies have been designed to foster.

Pursuing soft objectives through partnerships with non-governmental actors also lays government open to the charge of throwing money away. Unpleasant it may be to say so, but partnership-based initiatives occasionally show a tendency to fall victim to fraud and abuse. Examples include not only some of the more questionable activities of Training and Enterprises Councils in England, or further and higher education institutions' sometimes relaxed approaches to franchising, but also strategies for community development (for example, see FEFC, 1999; NI Audit Office, 1995, 1996). In recent years, such abuses have in turn attracted the attention of government watchdogs, including the House of Commons Public Accounts Committee, and of an ever less deferential educational press. Professionals responsible for learning programmes therefore find their actions increasingly exposed to public scrutiny, while at the same time being encouraged to be entrepreneurial and to take risks.

Conclusions

Lifelong learning is, then, inherently a difficult area for government. Perhaps these intrinsic obstacles help explain why it is that general policy so rarely leads to innovative measures. It may also explain why it is that, when governments do act, they restrict themselves to the area of vocational training. First, it has considerable legitimacy, and is therefore 'safe' in political terms. Particularly in respect of training for unemployed people, this is a long-established area of direct intervention; it is associated with wealth-creation and living standards; and state training subsidies are usually welcomed by employers. Second, it represents a relatively easy field for non-regulatory types of intervention. Much responsibility for implementation and delivery will rest with relatively low status and local actors (FE colleges, employment offices and so on); partners can be won over through incentive funding; and the prospect exists of hard short-term targets (such as jobs found, qualifications gained or people trained). Third, finance ministries are usually favourable to this type of public spending (this is an extremely important quality for policy makers). As a glance at the World Bank's website will confirm, finance ministries the world over share a faith in the human capital approach to human resource planning (www.world-bank.org). Investments and returns are priced in a way that seems largely impossible for such new, intangible areas as social capital, cultural change or citizenship. Vocational training is, then, one area where governments feel impelled to act: and even here they choose relatively familiar and uncontroversial measures.

The general policy banner of lifelong learning also cloaks a second arena for action where governments appear to feel comfortable: initial education. In Britain, for example, the new Labour government's Green Paper on lifelong learning was used to launch a substantial expansion in initial higher education, aimed at drawing in new types of younger student following two-year vocational programmes (DfEE, 1998). In the Netherlands, the supposedly 'new' public spending on lifelong learning was largely allocated to such measures as lowering the age of starting compulsory education to four, the provision of guidance and counselling to secondary school dropouts, and the in-service training of teachers (Ministry of Culture, Education and Science, 1998). Otherwise, lifelong learning suffers not so much from policy neglect as bafflement and uncertainty in the face of complexity, immeasurability and risk.

Does all this matter? It could be argued that the general expansion of participation in adult learning, undertaken largely at the behest of individuals and employers, is already driving progress towards a learning society. If so, perhaps it is best that government's role is uncertain and faltering. The financial costs of tackling the very problems that have caused governments to become interested in this area are considerable, yet electoral support for increasing public spending on supporting adult learning is likely to be limited. Interdepartmental boundaries and rivalries mean that many of the most serious weaknesses can only be tackled in a piecemeal manner. Many of the desirable characteristics of a learning society turn out to be fuzzy, and unsusceptible to ready measurement. There are, then, sizeable barriers to sustained and coherent policy intervention to promote lifelong learning.

The prospect of continued faltering of policy intervention, though, also has its costs. Many of these will fall upon those who manage and deliver public programmes of learning opportunities. Ironically, the renewed focus of attention upon the learner has meant that the vicissitudes and predicaments of institutions are frequently neglected. There is remarkably little research, for example, on the impact upon teachers in further and higher education of sharp changes in the organization of the curriculum, and the nature of teaching and learning, arising from the influx of adult returners into institutions that were designed for young initial entrants. Policies in relation to this phenomenon appear to consist largely of an increased emphasis on quality enhancement and performance measurement, both understood in somewhat narrow, managerialist terms. Continued policy neglect and inconsistency also increase the likelihood that unintended consequences will exact a substantial price. One obvious example is the way that a general push towards lifelong learning is likely to impact upon social inequality and marginalization.

A vigorous and far-reaching debate over policy is therefore long overdue. Promoting lifelong learning does not simply require new government measures, but rather a new approach to government. This requires the development of a broad range of new capabilities not only on the part of the wider population 'out there', but also of policy makers and providers. It also requires a new concept of government that is rooted in a recognition of interdependence and interrelationships between state (and its different arms), market and civil society, where values are made explicit and contested openly and widely through democratic processes across an expanded public space.

References

Baptiste, I. (1999) 'Beyond Lifelong Learning: A Call to Civically Responsible Change', International Journal of Lifelong Education 18(2): 94–102.

Beck, U. and Sopp, P. (1997) 'Individualisierung und Integration – eine Problemskizze', in U. Beck and P. Sopp (eds) Individualisierung und Integration: Neue Konfliktlinien und neuer Integrationsmodus, 9–19. Opladen: Leske and Budrich.

Bélanger, P. (1999) 'The Threat and the Promise of a "Reflexive" Society: The New Policy Environment of Adult Learning', *Adult Education and Development* 52: 179–195.

Benington, J. (1998) 'Risk, Reciprocity and Civil Society', in A. Coulson (ed.) *Trust and Contracts*. Bristol: Policy Press.

Boshier, R. (1998) 'Edgar Faure after 25 Years: Down but Not Out', in J. Holford, P. Jarvis and C. Griffin (eds) *International Perspectives on Lifelong Learning*, 3–20. London: Kogan Page.

Castells, M. (1989) *The Informational City: Information Technology, Economic Restructuring and the Urban–Regional Process*. Oxford: Blackwell.

Collins, M. (1998) 'Critical Perspectives and New Beginnings: Reforming the Discourse on Lifelong Learning', in J. Holford, P. Jarvis and C. Griffin (eds) *International Perspectives on Lifelong Learning*, 44–55. London: Kogan Page.

Commission on the Future of the Voluntary Sector (1996) *Meeting the Challenge of Change: Voluntary Action into the Twenty-first Century*. London: National Council for Voluntary Organisations.

Dahrendorf, R. (1999) 'Whatever Happened to Liberty?', *New Statesman* (6 Sept.): 25–27.

Dearing, R. (1997) *Higher Education in the Learning Society*, Report of the National Committee of Inquiry into Higher Education. London: DfEE.

Delors, J. (1996) *The Treasure Within*, Report to UNESCO of the International Commission on Education for the Twenty-first Century. Paris: UNESCO.

Department for Education and Employment (1998) *The Learning Age: A Renaissance for a New Britain*, Sheffield, DfEE.

Department for Education and Employment (1999) *Learning to Succeed: A New Framework for Post-16 Learning*. London: Stationery Office.

Department for Education and Employment (2000) *Tackling the Adult Skills Gap: Upskilling Adults and the Role of Workplace Training*, Third Report of the National Skills Task Force. Sheffield: DfEE.

Department of Education and Science (1998) *Adult Education in an Era of Lifelong Learning*. Dublin: Stationery Office.

Dohmen, G. (1996) *Lifelong Learning: Guidelines for a Modern Education Policy*. Bonn: Bundesministerium für Bildung, Wissenschaft und Forschung. (English version of the original, *Das lebenslange Lernen: Leitlinien einer modernen Bildungpolitik*, which appeared simultaneously.)

Dohmen, G. (1998) *Zur Zukunft der Weiterbildung in Europa: Lebenslanges Lernen für Alle in veränderten Lernumwelten*. Bonn: Bundesministerium für Bildung, Wissenschaft und Forschung.

European Commission (1994) *Growth, Competitiveness, Employment*. Luxembourg: Office for Official Publications.

European Commission (1996) *Teaching and Learning: Towards the Learning Society*. Luxembourg: Office for Official Publications.

Field, J. (1994) 'Open Learning and Consumer Culture', *Open Learning* 9(2): 3–11.

Fryer, R.H. (1998) *Learning for the Twenty-first Century*, First Report of the National Advisory Group for Continuing Education and Lifelong Learning. Sheffield: DfEE.

Fryer, R.H. (1999) *Creating Learning Cultures: Next Steps in Achieving the Learning Age*, Second Report of the National Advisory Group for Continuing Education and Lifelong Learning. Sheffield: DfEE.

Further Education Funding Council (1999) *Bilston Community College Inspection Report*. Coventry: FEFC.

Geddes, M. (1997) *Partnership Against Poverty and Exclusion? Local Regeneration Strategies and Excluded Communities in the UK*. Bristol: Policy Press.

Giddens, A. (1991) *Modernity and Self-Identity*. Cambridge: Polity.

Giere, U. and Piet, M. (1997) *Adult Learning in a World at Risk: Emerging Policies and Strategies*. Hamburg: UNESCO Institute for Education.

Green, A., Wolf, A. and Leney, T. (1999) *Convergence and Divergence in European Education and Training Systems*. London: Institute of Education.

Group of Eight (1999) *Köln Charter: Aims and Ambitions for Lifelong Learning*, 18 June 1999. Cologne: G8.

Gustavsson, B. (1995) 'Lifelong Learning Reconsidered', in M. Klasson, J. Manninen, S. Tøsse and B. Wahlgren (eds) *Social Change and Adult Education Research*, 89–100. Linköping: Linköping University.

Kennedy, H. (1997) *Learning Works: Widening Participation in Further Education*. Coventry: FEFC.

Knoll, J. (1998) ' "Lebenslanges Lernen" und internationale Bildungspolitik: Zur Genese eines Begriffs und dessen nationale Operationalisierungen', in R. Brödel (ed.) *Lebenslanges Lernen: Lebensbegleitende Bildung*, 35–50. Neuwied: Luchterhand.

Ministry of Culture, Education and Science (1998) *'Life-long Learning': The National Action Programme of the Netherlands*. Zoetermeer: Ministry of Culture, Education and Science.

Müller, Josef (1997) 'Literacy and Non-Formal (Basic) Education: Still a Donors' Priority?', *Adult Education and Development* 47: 37–60.

Northern Ireland Audit Office (1995) *Community Economic Regeneration Scheme and Community Regeneration and Improvement Special Scheme*. Belfast: Stationery Office.

Northern Ireland Audit Office (1996) *Department of the Environment: Control of Belfast Action Teams' Expenditure*. Belfast: Stationery Office.

OECD (1991) *Reviews of National Policies for Education: Ireland*. Paris: Organisation for Economic Co-operation and Development.

OECD (1996) *Lifelong Learning for All*, Meeting of the Educational Committee at Ministerial Level, 16/17 January 1996. Paris: Organisation for Economic Co-operation and Development.

OECD (1999) *Measuring Knowledge in Learning Economies and Societies*, Report on Washington Forum on 17–18 May 1999 organised jointly by the National Science Foundation and the Centre for Educational Research and Innovation. Paris: Organisation for Economic Co-operation and Development.

Reich, R.B. (1997) *Locked in the Cabinet*. New York: Random House.

Rhodes, R.A.W. (1996) 'The New Governance: Governing Without Government', *Political Studies* 44(4): 652–667.

Rosanvallon, P. (1995) *La Nouvelle Question Sociale: Repenser l'État-providence*. Paris: Éditions du Seuil.

Rubenson, K. (1999) 'Adult Education and Training: The Poor Cousin. An Analysis of OECD Reviews of National Policies for Education', *Scottish Journal of Adult Continuing Education* 5(2): 5–32.

Scott, P. (2000) 'The Death of Mass Higher Education and the Birth of Lifelong Learning', in J. Field and M. Leicester (eds) *Lifelong Learning: Education across the Lifespan*. London: Falmer.

Tight, M. (1998) 'Bridging the "Learning Divide": The Nature and Politics of Participation', *Studies in the Education of Adults* 30(2): 110–119.

West, L. (1998) 'Intimate Cultures of Lifelong Learning: On Gender and Managing Change', in P. Alheit and E. Kammler (eds) *Lifelong Learning and its Impact on Social and Regional Development*, 555–583. Bremen: Donat Verlag.

Index